Ottawa Cooks

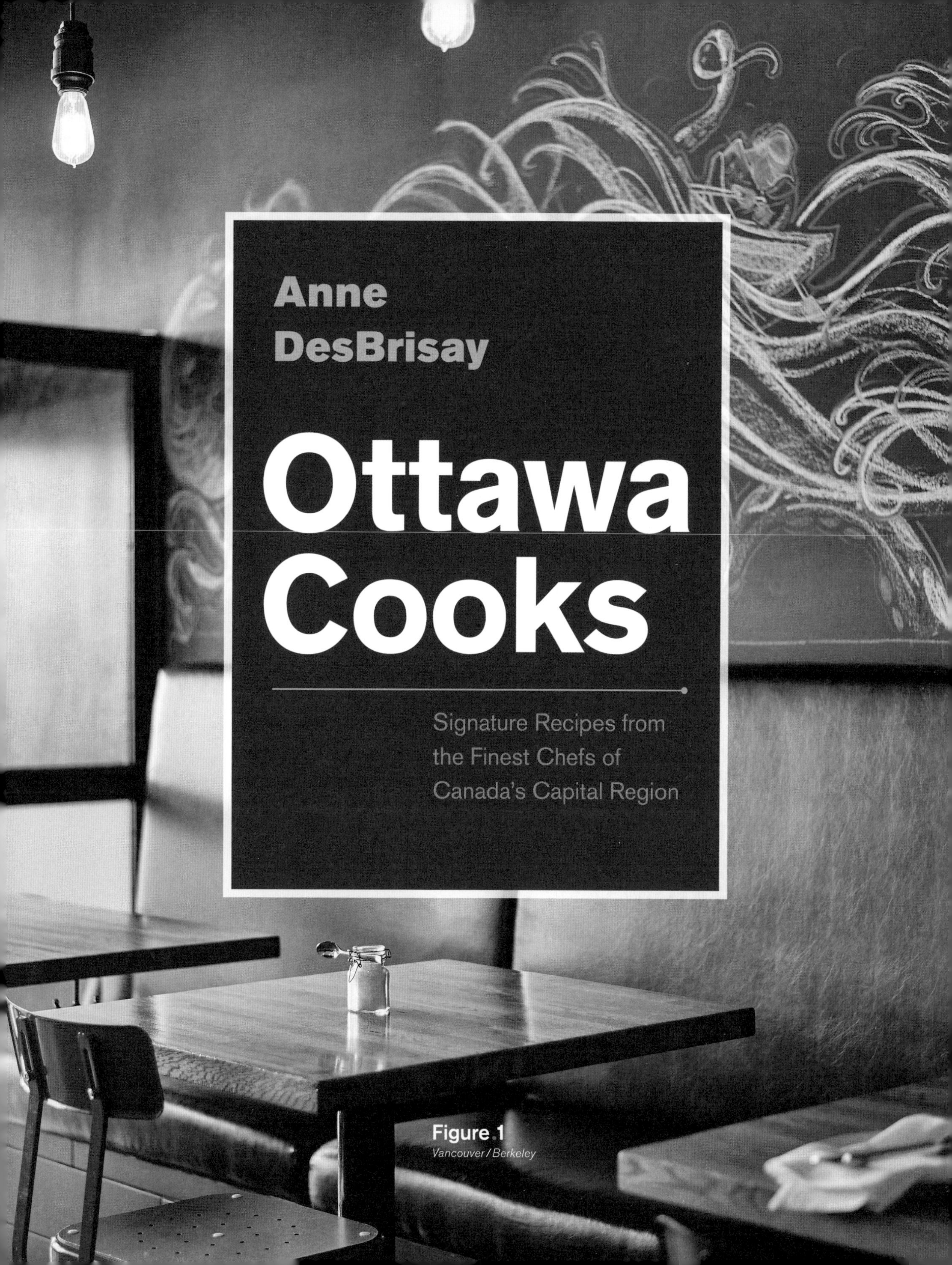

Anne DesBrisay

Ottawa Cooks

Signature Recipes from
the Finest Chefs of
Canada's Capital Region

Figure 1
Vancouver / Berkeley

Cataloguing data available from Library and Archives Canada
ISBN 978-1-927958-53-7 (hbk.)

Photography © Christian Lalonde,
Photoluxstudio.com/commercial, All Rights Reserved
Food styling by Noah Witenoff, nustyling.com
Prop styling by Irene Garavelli
Design by Jessica Sullivan

Editing by Lucy Kenward
Copy editing by Tracy Bordian
Proofreading by Renate Preuss
Indexing by Iva Cheung

Printed and bound in China by C&C Offset Printing Co., Ltd.
Distributed in the U.S. by Publishers Group West

Figure 1 Publishing Inc.
Vancouver BC Canada
www.figure1pub.com

To Ottawa cooks in every kitchen, the inspiring and the inspired.

Contents

Introduction

A GREAT DEAL has happened in the twenty-five years I've been writing about the restaurant landscape in this city. Let's just say it tastes so very much better than it used to—thanks, in large measure, to the "cooks" in these pages.

So who are they? Well, they come from across Canada's Capital Region and they are all, in my books, chefs at the top of their game, cooking their hearts out, contributing to our region's flourishing food scene. Some are in charge of the city's most glamorous restaurants. Others run a diner, a brewery kitchen, a doughnut shack. One drives a truck. Another works in the converted barn of a duck farm. They are chefs from established restaurants that have been raising the bar—splendidly—for decades. And they are chefs from places still in their infancy, but ones that have excited our senses and filled our bellies in immensely satisfying ways. It's been my great pleasure and privilege to gather them all in one big, delicious book.

And what of their recipes? You may recognize some as the signature dishes of the kitchens they run. But many aren't from any menu at all. They are the dishes made for staff meals and family picnics, or whipped up for a child's birthday, or even passed down from a grandmother. All of them, however, give us a peek into who these chefs are, these men and women who feed us so well. What culinary languages they speak, what global adventures they bring to their plates, what regional ingredients they turn to and what tricks of modern—or sometimes ancient—cooking they favour.

Some of these recipes are pretty no-nonsense. Others may tax you. That's part of the fun of any cookbook, the effort of duplicating in your kitchen what the pros do in theirs. Who knows, maybe you'll find them a snap. Maybe you'll even improve on the originals! Anything is possible because cookbooks are like that. They are travel guides, the adventure laid out for you to follow precisely or to simply trace the broad strokes, then look in your own larder and go from there.

If any of the recipes sends you screaming out of the kitchen, let it be as far as the phone. Go ahead, call the restaurant. But not for advice. Book a table, and see how it's done. They'll be happy to show you.

Cocktails, Appetizers, Sides and Small Plates

Desserts, Breads and Sweets

Preserves and Vinegars

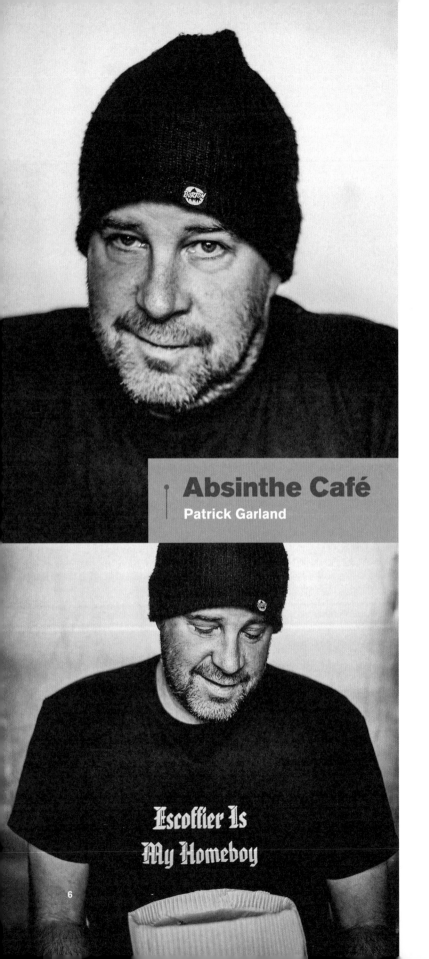

Absinthe Café
Patrick Garland

I'VE KNOWN Absinthe Café for the dozen years it's called West Wellington home. The country got to know Absinthe Café when Patrick Garland posed for his 2015 Canadian Culinary Championship portrait stubbly faced with chef's knife in mouth and toque on fire. The other national Gold Medal Plates competitors wore white and smiled for the camera. Garland brings that same playfulness to his plates, tempered with a rock-solid understanding of bistro cuisine. He presents the classics, yes, but nothing at Absinthe tastes old hat. With a polished duck and bison terrine he pairs a maple pork pogo of formidable flavour. He candies jalapeños to give a yellowfin tuna ceviche some startling sweet-hot rev. And who else would bother to fashion a fennel bavarois for a chilled asparagus velouté?

Absinthe's home is also Garland's. He was born in this neighbourhood, went to school here. The people of Hinton-burg are his people. Wander into the tall, moody room and you feel tucked in. Belly up to the bar for an Absinthe cocktail and the Benevolent Burger (with a wild garlic aioli, and a donation of a buck-a-burger to Cornerstone Housing for Women), or settle in for the full-on table d'hôte matched with some star wines.

1208 WELLINGTON STREET WEST, 613-761-1130

facing: **Chocolate Moelleux with Crème Anglaise and Raspberry Coulis**

6

Chef says: This moelleux has been on the Absinthe menu since Day One. It was a cake I made for my final practical exam at cooking school. The chef instructor dubbed it a chocolate "moelleux," but this was pre-master chef Jean-Georges Vongerichten (who created the molten chocolate cake), and though this cake is very moist, its centre doesn't ooze out. In the summer we serve this at room temperature; in the winter we warm it up a bit in the oven. Chocolate, raspberries and custard pair brilliantly well together; just be sure to source the finest chocolate you can afford. For convenience we use Valrhona callets, little chocolate coins that melt quickly and evenly, and a fairly bitter chocolate. Somewhere around 75% cocoa works best, but you can use semi-sweet chocolate if you prefer.

Serves 14 (Makes one 9-inch round cake)

Chocolate Moelleux with Crème Anglaise and Raspberry Coulis

Chocolate moelleux Preheat the oven to 325°F. Prepare a 9-inch round cake pan by chilling it, then rubbing it thoroughly with butter and dusting it with cocoa powder, tapping out the excess powder.

In a medium bowl set over a pot of lightly simmering water, melt chocolate. In the bowl of a stand mixer on medium-high speed, or by hand, whisk eggs and sugar until thick, 3 to 4 minutes. In a separate bowl, sift together flour and ¼ cup of the cocoa powder. Whisk 1 cup of the butter into the warm chocolate, then add the egg-sugar mixture. Fold in the dry ingredients until the batter is smooth and well combined.

Fill a kettle with water and bring to a boil. Pour the batter into the prepared pan and rap the bottom on the counter to get rid of any air pockets. Set the cake pan inside a roasting pan and carefully pour the boiling water into the roasting pan until it comes halfway up the sides of the cake pan. Bake for at least 30 minutes. The cake is done when it is set three-quarters of the way to the centre but still a little jiggly in the middle. Remove the roasting pan from the oven and let the cake pan cool in the water. Once the cake has cooled, unmould it onto a plate. Set aside while you prepare the sauces. (The cake can be wrapped in plastic and refrigerated for up to 5 days.)

Crème anglaise In a medium pot over medium-high heat, combine milk, half of the sugar and the vanilla bean and heat until bubbles appear around the inside of the pan. Remove from the heat and let infuse for about 20 minutes. Using a spoon, remove the vanilla bean, rinse it and save for a future use.

Have ready a bowl of ice. In the bowl of a stand mixer (or by hand using a whisk), cream yolks, remaining sugar and salt. Slowly pour the scalded infused milk over the yolk mixture, whisking constantly, then pour the mixture back into the pot and return to medium-high heat. With a rubber spatula, stir the custard continuously, getting into all the corners and cooking

Chocolate moelleux

1 cup unsalted butter, at room temperature + more for greasing pan

¼ cup Dutch process cocoa powder + more for dusting pan

½ lb good-quality dark chocolate callets (or roughly chopped bar)

4 eggs

1 cup white sugar

3 Tbsp all-purpose flour

Crème anglaise

1 cup whole milk

3 Tbsp white sugar, divided

1 vanilla bean, split lengthwise and seeds scraped

3 egg yolks

Pinch of salt

Raspberry coulis

1 Tbsp water

2 cups fresh or frozen raspberries (reserve a few fresh berries for garnish)

2 Tbsp white sugar

1 tsp freshly squeezed lemon juice

until it reaches roughly 175 to 180°F (the consistency should be *nappé*—when you run the spatula through the hot sauce it leaves a clear and distinct line where it passed).

Set a fine-mesh sieve over a clean bowl and pour the custard through it; discard solids. Place the bowl in the ice to cool.

Raspberry coulis In a medium pot, bring the water to a simmer, add raspberries and sugar and cook until berries are soft, 5 to 10 minutes. Press berries through a fine-mesh sieve into a small saucepan; discard solids. Add lemon juice.

Carefully test the consistency of the sauce by running your finger through it. It should leave a clear and distinct line where your finger passed. If the sauce is too thick, add a little water; if too thin, reduce it slightly over high heat. (The sauce will thicken a little as it cools.) Add more lemon juice if it is too sweet; if not sweet enough, add a little sugar.

To serve Serve thin slices of cake with crème anglaise and raspberry coulis in either a pretty design (draw a toothpick through the coulis to make hearts in the custard) or "go all Jackson Pollock on it" (says Garland, which is what he would do). Garnish with small, ripe raspberries.

Chef says: I like tarts. They can be made ahead, which is always wise when you have company and you want to be with your guests. And the pastry recipe will yield a bit more than you need for this tart, so freeze the leftovers (like money in the bank!) and use them for another application (sweet or savoury). Just toss the salad at the end, and you're good to go. This tart can be served for breakfast, brunch or lunch.

Serves 8 for a light lunch or 12 as an appetizer

Smoked Trout and Leek Tart with Arugula Pear Salad

Tart dough Sift flour and salt into a stainless steel bowl. With a pastry cutter, two knives or your fingers, cut butter into flour until the mixture resembles coarse meal. Add 1 egg yolk and ice water and gently mix by hand until it just comes together.

Turn the dough out onto a lightly floured work surface and, using the heel of your hand, gently but firmly knead until the dough is almost homogeneous (you should still see small flecks of butter). Divide the dough into 3 equal discs, wrap in plastic wrap and refrigerate for at least 30 minutes.

Remove 2 discs of dough from the fridge and, if very cold, allow them to come to slightly cooler than room temperature. Reserve remaining disc for a future application. (Wrapped tightly in plastic wrap, dough will keep refrigerated for up to 5 days or frozen for up to 3 months.)

Have ready two 6-inch tart rings. Lightly dust a work surface, the 2 discs of dough and a rolling pin with flour. Working with one disc of dough at a time, roll out dough into a circle about 8 inches in diameter and ¼ inch thick. Gently roll the flattened dough around the rolling pin and then unroll it overtop the tart ring. Using your thumb, gently push the pastry into the grooves, allowing any excess dough to hang over the rim (this helps prevent the pastry from shrinking; you will shave off any extra dough after baking). Prick the dough all over with a fork to prevent it from puffing. Line the dough with plastic wrap and fill with dried beans, peas or rice to help prevent the dough from rising. Refrigerate the tarts for an hour or so.

Preheat the oven to 400°F. Remove the tarts from the fridge and bake (with the weights in place; no, the plastic wrap will not melt) until golden brown, about 20 minutes. Remove the plastic wrap and weights. The bottom of the tarts will still be a little undercooked, so return the tarts to the oven for about 3 minutes to dry them out.

In the meantime, in a small bowl, make an egg wash by whisking remaining egg yolk with 2 tsp of water. Lightly brush the tarts all over with the egg wash and return them to the oven for a further 3 minutes (this step seals the prick holes, which prevents the filling from draining out and making

Tart dough

1½ cups unbleached all-purpose flour
Pinch of salt
1 cup cold unsalted butter, cut in small dice
2 egg yolks, divided
2 Tbsp ice water

Smoked trout filling

2 Tbsp butter
1 cup chopped leeks (cut into ¼-inch slices)
2 eggs
½ cup crème fraîche, sour cream or ricotta cheese
1 lb boneless, skinless smoked trout (or smoked sturgeon, salmon or sablefish), chopped
¼ cup minced fresh chives
¼ cup minced fresh dill
Salt and freshly ground black pepper

Sherry walnut vinaigrette

Pinch of salt
3 Tbsp sherry vinegar
2 tsp Dijon mustard
¼ cup walnut oil
¼ cup vegetable oil
Freshly ground black pepper

Arugula, pear, walnut salad

4 generous handfuls of arugula
¼ cup walnuts, toasted
¼ cup minced fresh thyme
¼ cup minced fresh flat-leaf (Italian) parsley
1 ripe pear, cored and diced
3 Tbsp Romano or Parmesan cheese
Salt and freshly ground black pepper

the pastry soggy). Remove the pastry from the oven and, using a sharp knife, carefully shave off and discard any dough hanging over the rim of the tart shells. Set aside.

Smoked trout filling Melt butter in a medium saucepan. Add leeks and cook until soft but not coloured, about 5 minutes. Spread cooked leeks over a tray to cool.

In a large bowl, beat eggs. Add remaining ingredients along with the cooled leeks and gently stir together. Season with salt and pepper to taste.

Finish tart Preheat the oven to 400°F. Divide the filling mixture evenly between each blind-baked tart shell and bake for about 20 minutes, until the filling is set around the edges but still slightly wobbly in the middle. Remove from the oven and set aside to rest while you make the salad.

Sherry walnut vinaigrette In a small bowl, combine salt and vinegar and whisk to dissolve. Whisk in mustard, and slowly pour in walnut and vegetable oils, whisking to emulsify. Season with pepper to taste. Taste with a piece of arugula and adjust the acidity or seasoning, if necessary.

Arugula, pear, walnut salad Just before serving, so the greens stay bouncy and the nuts crunchy, place arugula in a salad bowl and dress with the sherry vinaigrette to taste. Add remaining ingredients and toss gently to combine.

To serve Serve tarts warm or at room temperature, with a side of arugula salad.

Ace Mercado
Trisha Donaldson

IT WAS THE second sip that did it. A few minutes at the Ace bar with a Black Magic Woman (tequila base, chocolate and mole bitters, a black salt rim) and the day-old knot between my shoulder blades was history. First bites of the scallop ceviche (with juicy bursts of passion fruit seeds and the crunch of hibiscus salt) and I'm hooked, ready to mine more of the modern Mexican-inspired food and drinks list. Ace Mercado deals out more than good looks and an edgy energy to a primo corner of the ByWard Market; it also brings serious intent to a menu of small plates with titanic flavours: roasted eggplant with Mexican kimchee and apricots; tuna tostada with onion sofrito; and homier dishes like the cast-iron arepas, buttery rich with a cap of fresh mozzarella, scattered with spiced-up peanuts. Ace's menu was created by executive chef (and *Top Chef Canada* winner) René Rodriguez. It's delivered by chef de cuisine Trisha Donaldson. I've followed Donaldson's career for many years and with great pleasure, popping in wherever she's settled down, sure of an excellent meal. Ace is home now, and to these plates she brings her own distinct style, experimenting with fruit, citrus and teas, injecting a fresh elegance into muscular Mexican dishes.

121 CLARENCE STREET, 613-627-2353

**Simple syrup
(makes ¾ cup)**
½ cup water
1 cup white sugar

Cocktail
⅛ cup unpeeled seeded
 diced cucumber
1 oz Hendrick's gin
½ oz St-Germain elderflower
 liqueur
1 oz freshly squeezed lime
 juice (about 1 lime)
1 egg white
¾ oz Simple Syrup (see here)
½ cup ice
3 dashes lavender bitters
1 long thin cucumber slice,
 for garnish

Makes one 4-oz drink

Cucumber Sour

Chef says: The origins of sour cocktails date back 150 years. Ace's opening bar chef Troy Gilchrist crafted this one. It starts with small-batch Hendrick's Gin, which is infused with rose and cucumber, herbs, fruits, seeds and spices. To this the bar adds sweet, aromatic St-Germain elderflower liqueur, with its hints of pear and lychee. The egg white gives the drink a lovely foam cap, a silky body and rich mouth feel. The lavender bitters just brings all the floral notes into balance.

Simple syrup In a small pot over high heat, bring water and sugar to a boil, stirring until sugar is dissolved. Remove from the heat and set aside to cool completely. (Refrigerate leftover syrup in an airtight container for the next cocktail, or use it to flavour coffee or tea.)

Cocktail Refrigerate a coupe glass until well chilled and have ready a 4-inch clear skewer. Muddle cucumber in a cocktail shaker until well crushed. Add gin, elderflower liqueur, lime juice, egg white and simple syrup and dry-shake for 15 seconds to emulsify all the ingredients. Add ice and shake again for 10 to 15 seconds. Double-strain the mixture into the chilled coupe glass and finish with 3 drops of lavender bitters.

Roll the ribbon of cucumber around the clear skewer, overlapping it as you move down the skewer so it looks like an extended telescope. Place over the cocktail and serve.

Lime crema (makes 1 cup)

1 cup full-fat (14%) sour cream

1 tsp white sugar

¾ tsp kosher salt

1 tsp freshly ground coriander seeds

½ tsp green Tabasco sauce

Juice of 1 lime

Heirloom salsa (makes 3 cups)

2 cups diced heirloom tomatoes

½ jalapeño pepper, seeded and finely minced

¼ cup finely minced white onions, rinsed well, then drained

¼ cup coarsely chopped artichoke hearts, drained

1 clove garlic, minced

1 Tbsp minced pitted green olives

2 Tbsp olive oil

1 Tbsp chopped fresh flat-leaf (Italian) parsley leaves

1 Tbsp chopped fresh cilantro leaves

½ tsp dried Mexican oregano

1 tsp Maldon sea salt

½ tsp freshly ground white peppercorns (or black peppercorns)

Eggplant filling

1 large eggplant, unpeeled and trimmed

2 Tbsp sea salt, divided

Canola oil, for frying

2 tsp Tajín Clásico seasoning (or 1 tsp each of chili powder, salt and lime juice)

3 cups cooked and mashed peeled purple potatoes (or other non-waxy potato; about 3 large potatoes)

1 cup finely grated Manchego cheese

2 Tbsp thinly sliced dried apricots

1 tsp cumin seeds, toasted and ground

Pinch of chili powder

¼ cup roughly chopped fresh flat-leaf (Italian) parsley leaves

2 Tbsp minced fresh chives

Zest of 1 lemon

1 Tbsp fresh lemon juice

Serves 6

Chiles Rellenos

Chef says: This is my take on a northern Mexican dish that originated in the city of Puebla. The poblano chili pepper is mild with a bit of tingle and a lovely sweet-bitter quality when roasted. The tortilla soup is a traditional Central Mexican soup. We add dried ancho chilies, which are slightly spicy and fleshy with a prune-like sweetness. Good tomatoes and authentic tostadas are paramount. There are lots of moving parts to this recipe, but each can be made for separate occasions and served on its own or prepared a day ahead and assembled just before serving. Many of these ingredients can be found at a Latin grocery store, and others at natural food stores.

Lime crema In a medium bowl, whisk sour cream with sugar, salt, coriander seeds and Tabasco until well combined. Whisk in lime juice.

Heirloom salsa Set a fine-mesh sieve over a large bowl. Place tomatoes in the sieve and let drain for 10 minutes.

In a large bowl, combine drained tomatoes, jalapeño peppers, onions, artichokes, garlic, olives, olive oil, parsley, cilantro, oregano, salt and pepper and stir to combine. Cover and refrigerate for at least 2 hours or up to 1 day.

Eggplant filling Cut eggplant lengthwise into 8 equal wedges. Sprinkle 1 Tbsp of the salt over the eggplant flesh and let rest for about 1 hour to release any bitterness and excess water. Rinse eggplant under cold water and pat dry with paper towels.

Line a plate with paper towels. Preheat a deep fryer or fill a heavy-bottomed skillet with about ¼ inch of canola oil and set over high heat. When the oil reaches 350°F (use a deep-fry thermometer to test the temperature of the oil), add eggplant and fry until golden, 2 to 4 minutes. Using a slotted spoon, transfer eggplant to the lined plate. While eggplant is still warm, season with Tajín. Once it is cool to the touch, chop eggplant into 1-inch pieces and place in a large bowl. Add mashed potatoes, cheese, apricots, cumin, chili powder, parsley, chives, remaining 1 Tbsp of salt, and lemon zest and juice and stir gently until combined. Set aside. (Can be refrigerated for up to 1 day.) *continued*

Sopa de tortilla

2 ancho chili peppers
2 Tbsp canola oil
3 whole Roma tomatoes
1 corn tostada (5 inches in diameter), broken into pieces
¼ bunch fresh cilantro, leaves picked and stems finely diced
1 tsp epazote leaves
½ Spanish onion, chopped
1 tsp salt
1 clove garlic, roasted
1 can (28 oz/796 mL) whole peeled tomatoes, with juice

Onion sofrito

2 Tbsp olive oil, divided
2 Spanish onions, thinly sliced
2 poblano peppers, seeded and thinly sliced
1 jalapeño pepper, seeded and thinly sliced
1 tsp kosher salt, divided
½ tsp ground bay leaves, divided
2 tsp coriander seeds, toasted then ground
1 tsp black peppercorns, toasted then ground

Stuffed poblano peppers

6 poblano peppers (each about 6 inches long)
1 recipe Eggplant Filling (see here)
1 Tbsp canola oil (or melted butter)
½ tsp sea salt
½ tsp coriander seeds, toasted and coarsely crushed

Sopa de tortilla Place chili peppers in a dry skillet and toast over medium-low heat for 5 minutes, until blistered. Transfer to a container with a tight-fitting lid. Cover with 2 cups of hot water, seal and set aside at room temperature for 45 minutes to rehydrate. With a spoon, remove the chilies from the water; reserve water. With a sharp knife, gently open chilies and cut out and discard stems and seeds. Set aside.

Set a 6-quart heavy-bottomed pot over medium-high heat. Add canola oil and tomatoes and *without* turning frequently, blacken heavily on all sides, 12 to 15 minutes. Turn down the heat to medium and add tostadas, diced cilantro stems, epazote leaves, onions and salt. Cover and cook for 5 to 7 minutes. Add roasted garlic, canned tomatoes and their juice, and simmer, uncovered, for 20 minutes. Remove from the heat and let cool for 15 minutes.

With an immersion blender, purée the soup until all major lumps are broken down (it will look thicker and more rustic than a regular tomato soup because of the tostadas). Stir in cilantro leaves, and more salt if necessary. Let cool completely.

Onion sofrito Heat 1 Tbsp of olive oil in each of two separate cast-iron pans over medium-low heat. Add onions to one pan and both poblano and jalapeño peppers to the other. Add ½ tsp of salt and ¼ tsp ground bay leaves to each pan. The peppers will cook and caramelize within 30 minutes; turn off the heat. The onions may take twice as long: be patient, stirring from time to time until all the liquid has evaporated from the pan and the onions are a nice rich caramel colour. Stir the onions into the roasted peppers, add the coriander and black pepper, and set aside to cool. Cover and refrigerate until ready to use.

Stuffed poblano peppers Line a plate with paper towels. Bring an 8-quart stockpot of water to a boil. Add peppers, place a bowl on top to weigh them down and boil for 2 minutes. Remove the bowl and, with a slotted spoon, carefully transfer the peppers to the lined plate to cool.

Assembly

2 Tbsp canola oil (or melted butter)
6 tostadas (each 5 inches)
Maldon sea salt
¾ cup Lime Crema (see here)
12 sweet potato chips
Microgreens, for garnish

Set the peppers on their sides. With a serrated knife, carefully slice a small portion off the top of the pepper, leaving ⅝ of the body of the pepper for stuffing; reserve this top portion. Gently remove the seeds and membrane from inside the peppers and discard.

Forty minutes before serving, stuff the 6 peppers evenly with the eggplant filling. Place their tops back on and rub the peppers gently with canola oil (or melted butter). Sprinkle with salt and coriander, gently wrap in plastic wrap and refrigerate for 40 minutes so they become less fragile.

To assemble Remove stuffed peppers from the fridge and allow them to come to room temperature. Preheat the oven to 400°F. In a small pot on medium-low, warm the sopa de tortilla.

Heat a large cast-iron skillet or an ovenproof sauté pan large enough to comfortably hold all the peppers over medium-high heat. Add 2 Tbsp of canola oil (or butter) to the hot pan. Place stuffed peppers, bottoms down, in the pan and sear for

2 minutes without moving them. Transfer pan to the oven and bake until peppers begin to blister, 10 to 12 minutes. Remove from the oven and let peppers rest in the pan while you assemble the plates.

In each bowl, arrange 2 Tbsp of sofrito down the centre. Place a tostada over the sofrito. Ladle about ½ cup of the soup over each tostada and gently place a stuffed pepper in the centre of the soup. Add 3 heaping spoonfuls of the salsa on top of each pepper. Garnish with Maldon salt, lime crema, sweet potato chips and microgreens.

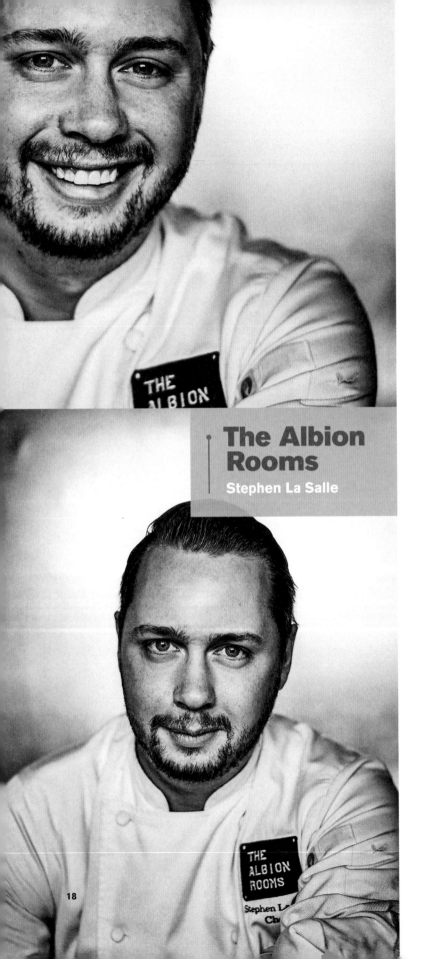

The Albion Rooms
Stephen La Salle

"IF I WERE to overthink it, I guess I'd call it Commonwealth Cuisine." We're at the über-Canadiana bar of The Albion Rooms eating Scotch eggs dressed in Valley pork. Ottawa boy and executive chef Stephen La Salle is struggling to define the kind of food he offers in these rooms. "We have our own Canadian constitution here: 'Food, Drink and Good Company.'" The menu makes the charter clear. It doesn't get more "Commonwealth" than to take Quebec foie gras, poach it in traditional English meade and plate it with torched honey from the bees of the Rosewood Estates Winery in Beamsville, Ontario. Charcuterie—some house made, some from the excellent Seed to Sausage butchers—is piled high and plated pretty. Lake Erie pickerel in a Beau's Lug-Tread batter with fat chippies thrice-cooked makes for a natural go-to. Same for the fat and juicy elk burger. But don't overlook the vegetables on this menu: a kale salad with trumped-up Caesar flavours, or the Brussels sprouts that are so very not-your-granny's. Even the humble cauliflower hits home runs. Democratic seating at The Albion Rooms creates many options—a flop-into-it lobby lounge, by-the-window high tops, a band of swivelling bar stools and two dining rooms: one dark and romantic, the other more like an elegant English tavern in an Ottawa heritage space.

33 NICHOLAS STREET, 613-760-4771

facing: **Roasted Cauliflower, Two Ways**

Chef says: Originally created for The Albion Rooms launch menu, this vegetable-forward appetizer soon cemented itself on the menu. Even other chefs have told me not to take it off, so a rendition of roasted cauliflower has been a constant. It makes for a pretty easy way to tell your guests to eat their vegetables! Feel free to change up your ingredients for the seasons and mood. We like to keep it with the same soul of roasted cauliflower, but play with the sauce, roasted nuts, dried fruit, strong herbs and bread or grains. Here are two Albion Rooms variations: one with saffron aioli, the other with romesco sauce.

Serves 4

Roasted Cauliflower, Two Ways

Saffron aioli In a small bowl, stir together vinegar and lemon juice with saffron. Cover and let sit overnight, at room temperature or in fridge, to maximize the colour.

Place the saffron mixture, garlic and mayonnaise in a food processor fitted with the metal blade (not a blender) and process until well combined and saffron is incorporated. If the aioli is pale yellow, add a pinch of turmeric to brighten the colour.

Roasted cauliflower Preheat the oven to 350°F. To make croutons, cut baguette into ½-inch cubes and place in a medium bowl. Add olive oil and garlic and toss to coat well. Arrange in a single layer on a baking sheet and toast for 20 minutes or until golden brown and crunchy. Remove from the oven and set aside to cool.

Reduce the oven temperature to 325°F. Line a baking sheet with parchment paper. Place cauliflower florets in a large bowl. Add melted butter and salt and pepper to taste, and toss until well coated. Arrange in a single layer on the baking sheet and roast until lightly browned and tender, about 30 minutes.

To serve In a large bowl, toss warm roasted cauliflower with about ¼ cup of the saffron aioli, croutons and raisins. Place a large dollop of remaining saffron aioli on a serving platter and pull the spoon across the platter to create a large smear. Arrange roasted cauliflower mixture on top. Sprinkle with pine nuts and garnish with parsley and/or lovage. Serve warm.

Variation: Romesco sauce Preheat the broiler. Place bell peppers on a baking sheet and broil for 25 minutes, turning every 5 minutes, until very tender.

Remove from the oven, place in a bowl, cover and let rest for about 5 minutes. Peel off the charred skins, then cut out and discard the seeds. Set aside to cool.

Saffron aioli

1 Tbsp white wine vinegar
1 Tbsp freshly squeezed lemon juice
¼ tsp saffron threads
1 tsp finely chopped garlic
2 cups mayonnaise
Pinch of ground turmeric (optional)

Roasted cauliflower

1 French baguette
⅓ cup olive oil
1 Tbsp rasp-shaved garlic
3 medium heads cauliflower (use a mix of colourful varieties if you can source them), cut into medium florets
2 Tbsp butter, melted
Salt and freshly ground black pepper
2 Tbsp sultana raisins
¼ cup pine nuts, toasted to golden brown
½ bunch fresh flat-leaf (Italian) parsley or fresh lovage, leaves picked, for garnish

***Variation:* Romesco sauce**

4 red bell peppers
2 large tomatoes, cut in half
½ cup + ⅔ cup olive oil
Salt and freshly ground black pepper
2 heads garlic
1¼ cups hazelnuts, toasted, divided
2 Tbsp red wine vinegar
2 Tbsp liquid honey
1 Tbsp hot smoked paprika
½ bunch fresh flat-leaf (Italian) parsley or fresh lovage, leaves picked, for garnish

Reduce the oven temperature to 400°F. Place tomatoes in a shallow roasting pan, cut sides up, drizzle with ¼ cup of the olive oil and sprinkle liberally with salt and pepper. Set garlic on a sheet of aluminum foil, cover with ¼ cup of the olive oil, wrap completely in foil and add to the pan with the tomatoes. Roast until tomatoes are well coloured and garlic is soft, about 1 hour. Remove from the oven and set aside to cool. Once cool, squeeze roasted garlic from its skin (discard skins) and place in a small bowl.

In a food processor fitted with the metal blade, blitz 1 cup of the toasted hazelnuts until ground to the consistency of flour (reserve the rest of the hazelnuts for garnish). Add bell peppers, tomatoes, garlic, vinegar, honey, paprika and ⅔ cup olive oil and process until smooth. Season with salt and pepper to taste.

To serve In a large bowl, toss warm roasted cauliflower with ¼ cup of the romesco sauce, croutons and raisins. Place a large dollop of romesco sauce on a serving platter and pull the spoon across the platter to create a large smear. Arrange roasted cauliflower mixture on top. Sprinkle with pine nuts and reserved toasted hazelnuts and garnish with parsley leaves and/or lovage. Serve warm.

We couldn't have a lounge and bar called The Albion Rooms without giving a nod to England and great British gastropubs. The Scotch egg is quintessential English picnic food, almost like a handheld pie. Our version is served hot, always with a runny yolk. The Sugar Shack Scotch Egg is one of our favourites, perfect for that early spring maple season. Any type of sausage can be used—simply remove the meat from the casing and follow the steps to assemble with your 6-minute eggs.

Making your own sausage is another option that's worth the effort. Pork shoulder has a good ratio of meat to fat, perfect for a sausage filling. Since an average pork shoulder is around 9 pounds, ask your butcher for half a shoulder if you don't want extra meat. To give the pork extra flavour, you may quick-cure it overnight. If you don't have a meat grinder or prefer to skip this step, just ask your butcher to grind the pork shoulder twice for a smoother texture.

Serves 6

Sugar Shack Scotch Eggs

Sausage meat If curing the pork, combine brown sugar, salt, sage and allspice in a bowl. Add entire pork shoulder and coat evenly with the mixture. Drizzle maple syrup over the pork. Cover and refrigerate overnight. The next day, drain off any extra liquid from the cured meat.

Have ready a large bowl filled with ice. Set a second bowl on top of the ice. If grinding the pork at home, cut marinated pork into 5-inch strips, each about 1 inch wide, so the grinder can catch on to the meat and pull it in. If you did not cure the pork, place pork in a bowl, add sage and maple syrup and stir well. Using a meat grinder or a stand mixer fitted with the grinder attachment and a medium die, grind the meat into the empty bowl, passing it through the grinder twice and making sure to keep it cold at all times by setting the bowl over the ice.

To test for seasoning, heat a small cast-iron pan over medium heat until hot. Add a small piece of the sausage and cook for about 4 minutes or until fully cooked. Taste, and season with more salt if desired. Cover and refrigerate the uncooked pork until needed.

Maple-mustard sauce In a medium bowl, stir together all of the ingredients until well combined.

Scotch eggs Fill a medium bowl with ice water. Thirty minutes before cooking, let 8 to 12 eggs come to room temperature (reserve 4 in the fridge). Fill a medium saucepan with water and bring to a boil. Carefully lower in eggs and simmer for 6 minutes. With a slotted spoon, transfer eggs to the bowl of ice water to stop the cooking. Once cool, carefully peel eggs and discard the shells. Set aside 8 cooked eggs. Refrigerate any extra cooked eggs for topping salads.

To assemble the Scotch eggs, cut 2 sheets of plastic wrap, each 12 inches square. Place the first sheet on a clean work surface, place half the sausage meat on top and cover with the second

Sausage meat (makes extra)
1¼ cups packed brown sugar
1½ cups kosher salt
1 bunch fresh sage, chopped
1 tsp ground allspice
½ boneless pork shoulder (4½ lb)
½ cup pure maple syrup

Maple-mustard sauce
2 Tbsp grainy mustard
2 Tbsp Dijon mustard
2 Tbsp prepared yellow mustard
6 Tbsp pure maple syrup
¼ bunch fresh flat-leaf (Italian)
    parsley, leaves picked and chopped

Scotch eggs
12 to 16 eggs (they are very delicate,
    so cook more than you need)
2 cups all-purpose flour
2 cups unseasoned panko bread
    crumbs
2 Tbsp water
½ lb Sausage Meat (see here)
Canola oil, for frying
Fresh sage leaves, for garnish

sheet of plastic wrap. With a rolling pin, roll the meat to a thickness of about ½ inch. Remove and discard the top layer of plastic, set a salad plate on top and, using a sharp knife, cut around the plate to create a circle of sausage meat. Repeat with remaining sausage meat. You should have 8 circles.

Line a 12-cup muffin pan with paper liners. Place flour in one shallow bowl and panko crumbs in another shallow bowl. In a third bowl, whisk the 4 reserved (uncooked) eggs with water to create an egg wash.

Roll a boiled egg in the flour to coat completely and place in the centre of a circle of sausage meat. In the palm of one hand, cup the cooked egg in the sausage and carefully wrap the egg in the meat, pinching to seal. Trim and set aside any excess meat to use for the next egg. Dip the sausage-wrapped egg in the flour, coating it well. With a clean hand, dip the floured egg into the egg wash, coating it well (the egg will adhere to the

flour). Then transfer the egg to the panko and coat well. Dip the breaded egg in the egg wash, coating completely, and then in the panko, so the egg is now double-breaded. Place in the lined muffin cup. Repeat with remaining eggs, sausage and breading and refrigerate until ready to cook.

Preheat a deep fryer or fill a deep-sided saucepan with canola oil and heat over medium heat until it reaches 350°F. Line a plate with paper towels. With a slotted spoon, carefully drop the Scotch eggs into the oil (one at a time if you are using a saucepan) and fry for 5 to 6 minutes. Transfer Scotch eggs to the lined plate, patting eggs dry.

To serve On each plate, spread a generous amount of maple-mustard sauce. With a serrated knife, carefully slice open an egg, ensuring the yolk doesn't ooze out. Place the two halves over the mustard and garnish with fresh sage.

allium
Arup Jana

CHEF-OWNER Arup Jana brings to his food only that which he knows best. Call it honesty, or integrity, he simply believes he should cook what he understands at a gut level. Fortunately, he is a man of deep and broad understanding. Jana has a razor-keen eye for quality and, as a Prairie-born child of a globe-trotting professor, has travelled extensively through India, lived in Turkey for a year, and journeyed throughout the Middle East and Southeast Asia. Years before the small plates craze took over this town, Jana launched a Mondays-only, tapas-only menu at allium, where he indulged an anything-goes smorgasbord of treats. The neighbourhood fell hard for them, and the affection shows no sign of abating. (There's many a Monday when my husband and I will look at each other and say one word: "allium?" And if we're lucky enough to get a table, off we go to feast on his flavour bombs.) Crab cakes with pickled jalapeño and a summer pea purée; beef tartare with a sharp cheddar aioli and a gentle celery salad; curried shrimp with pickled raisins. Other nights we show up for the Blind Main. Surprise us, we say, and find us a wine to match from allium's top-notch list. Leaving the decisions in the hands of ones who understand food at a gut level: our kind of dinner. 87 HOLLAND AVENUE, 613-792-1313

facing: **Shrimp Pancakes with Carrot Aioli and Sweet Pea Relish**

Chef says: I like this dish because everything can be prepared ahead of time and assembled quickly before serving—terrific for a cocktail party! In this recipe, we use sidestripe or wild pink shrimp because of their sweetness and delicate texture, but you can substitute any crustacean you like. Nova Scotia lobster, chopped raw in the pancake batter, and sliced and sautéed for the top, works really well. Try making larger pancakes and serving them either folded as a sandwich or flat for a nice, easy lunch dish.

For a quicker version of the carrot aioli in this recipe, boil and purée the carrot, mince a small clove of garlic and add these to 2 tablespoons of store-bought mayonnaise. Season with lemon juice and salt to taste.

Serves 12 as a starter/appetizer (Makes twelve 2-inch pancakes)

Shrimp Pancakes with Carrot Aioli and Sweet Pea Relish

Sweet pea relish With a sharp knife, finely mince peas (see Note, below). Place peas, shallots, cilantro, chives, mint, honey, lemon juice and canola oil in a small bowl and stir until well combined. Season with salt and pepper to taste. Add Sriracha sauce if you like spice!

Note: If you have a mezzaluna (a double-handled knife with one or two curved blades), use it to finely mince the peas; otherwise, cut each pea in half, then roughly chop using a chef's knife.

Carrot aioli Bring a small pot of salted water to a boil. Add carrot and cook until soft, about 12 minutes. Remove from the heat and let cool.

In a blender, purée cooked carrot at medium-high speed until very smooth. Add mustard, garlic, egg yolks and lemon juice. With the motor running at medium speed, slowly pour in canola oil at a steady stream. Once emulsified, add salt and a bit more lemon juice to taste.

Shrimp pancakes Reserve 12 whole shrimp in a small bowl in the fridge. Roughly chop remaining shrimp and set aside.

In a large bowl, combine flour, baking powder, salt and lemon zest. In a separate bowl, combine lemon juice, milk, egg, cilantro, chili peppers, minced green onions, melted butter, carrot and chopped shrimp. Add the dry ingredients to the shrimp mixture and stir until you have a batter the consistency of a thin milkshake. Let rest on the counter for 10 minutes. Stir again, quickly.

Lightly grease a cast-iron skillet with canola oil, removing any excess with a paper towel, and set over medium heat. Spoon about 1 heaping Tbsp of the batter into the hot pan to form a 2-inch-wide circle. Cook until the pancake bubbles completely across the top, about 2 minutes, then flip and cook for a further 2 minutes on the other side. Transfer to a plate. Repeat with remaining batter (you should have 12 pancakes).

Sweet pea relish

1 cup podded fresh peas

1 shallot, minced

2 Tbsp minced fresh cilantro, leaves and stems

1 Tbsp chopped fresh chives

1 Tbsp minced fresh mint leaves

1 tsp local liquid honey

1 tsp freshly squeezed lemon juice

1 Tbsp canola oil

Salt and pepper

Sriracha sauce (optional)

Carrot aioli

½ medium carrot

1 Tbsp Dijon mustard

1 small clove garlic

2 egg yolks

1 Tbsp freshly squeezed lemon juice

2 cups canola oil

1 tsp salt, or to taste

Shrimp pancakes

1 lb shrimp (21–25), peeled and deveined

1½ cups pastry flour

1 Tbsp baking powder

2 tsp salt

Zest and juice of 1 lemon

1 cup milk

1 egg

¼ cup chopped fresh cilantro, leaves and stems + extra leaves for garnish

1 green chili pepper (or 2 to 3 if you like spice), minced

½ bunch whole green onions, split and minced + 2 green onions, green parts only, sliced, for garnish

2 Tbsp melted butter

½ medium carrot, grated

2 Tbsp canola oil, for greasing skillet

2 Tbsp butter, room temperature

While you make the last of the pancakes, sauté remaining shrimp. In a large skillet over medium-high heat, heat the room temperature butter to sizzling, add shrimp (being careful not to crowd them; you may need to cook them in batches), season lightly with salt and cook for about 2 minutes on each side.

To serve Place one or two pancakes on each serving plate. Top each pancake with a sautéed shrimp, a good dollop of carrot aioli and a teaspoon of relish. Garnish with fresh cilantro leaves and sliced green onions.

Apple and beer soup

1 Tbsp canola oil
4 white onions, thinly sliced
1 large Yukon Gold potato,
  peeled and sliced
8 Cortland apples (or Galas or
  Honeycrisps), peeled, cored
  and sliced
2 cups Beyond the Pale Rye Guy
  IPA (or other slightly fruity IPA)
4 cups vegetable stock or reduced-
  sodium chicken stock
1 cup heavy (18 to 35%) cream
Salt

Chanterelles

1 Tbsp butter
1 medium shallot, minced
2 cups local chanterelle
  mushrooms, torn into strips
Salt and freshly ground black
  pepper
1 heaping Tbsp chopped
  fresh tarragon (about 3 sprigs)

Garnish

¼ cup Back Forty Bonnechere
  cheese, shaved with a vegetable
  peeler
3 Tbsp fresh flat-leaf (Italian) parsley
  leaves
2 Tbsp local liquid honey

Serves 8 for lunch

Fall Apple and Beer Soup with Chanterelles and Bonnechere

Chef says: We use a local artisan cheese called Bonnechere with this soup because of the nice smokiness it imparts and the way it melts, but any medium-firm sheep's milk cheese will work. We like Cortland apples best, but feel free to use any variety that is neither too sweet, too mealy nor too tart. The flavour of the soup will change depending on the apple you choose. It will also change with the beer! If you can't source Beyond the Pale, any other quality IPA with a slight fruitiness, and preferably a bit of citrus fruit, will do fine.

Apple and beer soup In a large sauté pan, heat canola oil over medium heat. Add onions and cook until soft and translucent but not brown. Stir in potatoes and apples and cook until apples just start to break down on the outside. Add beer, increase the heat to medium-high and cook, stirring often, until the beer is totally absorbed and evaporated from the onions and apples. Pour in stock and cook until the liquid has reduced by half. Add cream and boil for 6 minutes. Remove from the heat and let cool to lukewarm. Transfer to a blender and purée at low speed, gradually increasing to high speed, until very smooth. Season with salt to taste.

Chanterelles In a large sauté pan over medium-high heat, melt butter and cook until it begins to brown. Add shallots and mushrooms and cook until the liquid from the mushrooms is released and evaporates. Remove from the heat, season with salt and pepper to taste, and stir in tarragon.

To serve Return the soup to the pot and warm slowly over medium heat. Ladle hot soup into serving bowls and divide sautéed chanterelles over each serving. Sprinkle cheese and parsley around the soup and drizzle with a little honey.

atelier
Marc Lepine

ALONG WITH AN edible garden, there's a 230-litre tank of liquid nitrogen behind atelier, the highly acclaimed modernist restaurant run by the unassuming super-star chef Marc Lepine. "So Marc," say I, discussing this book. "The recipes should be ones the home cook can manage." The two-time Canadian Culinary Champion goes wide-eyed for a moment. "But that's our whole thing here: food that people can't do at home." Lepine had his culinary epiphany during a post–cooking school *stage* at Grant Achatz's Alinea in Chicago. After six years at The Courtyard Restaurant—where he was given tools and freedom to play—Lepine opened atelier in a purposefully modest-looking house on Rochester Street in 2008. His twelve-course tasting menu begins with irreproachable product. And there begins the fun. With precise technique and creative intuition, he re-imagines the raw materials, creating dishes of extraordinary quality. Dishes that also toy with the senses, that seem one thing but eat like another. Wobbly rust-coloured bobbles that burst into liquid gazpacho; black dirt in a shot glass that becomes a gin and tonic on the deck; a star-hunk of sous-vide bison with a dozen clever dribs and dabs and pretties, all dazzlingly delicious. Creative, yes, disciplined, yes, but never earnest—it's this playfulness, along with star sommelier Steve Robinson's delicious pours, that makes the atelier experience one-of-a-kind. And yes, you can master these recipes. Just remember to breathe.

540 ROCHESTER STREET, 613-321-3537

facing: **Pomelo Anderson**

Chef says: This dish makes a great first course to a meal. It has big punchy flavours that will quickly wake up the palate. If you have no smoker available, it's perfectly fine to serve this dish with unsmoked avocado purée. At atelier, we also add a piece of raw sea urchin to really put this dish over the top.

Serves 4 as an appetizer (add more tuna and other ingredients to make it a main course)

Pomelo Anderson

Pickled jalapeños Bring 3 cups of water to a boil in a medium pot and add sliced jalapeños. Let boil for 1 minute, then drain.

In a separate pot, combine 1 cup of water, vinegar, salt, sugar and garlic and bring to a boil over medium heat. Let simmer for 10 minutes, then strain through a fine-mesh sieve over the jalapeños; discard solids. Let chili peppers cool completely, then transfer them in their liquid to an airtight container and refrigerate until needed, up to 1 week.

Yuzu pudding In a small pot, combine all of the ingredients and boil for 15 seconds. Transfer the mixture to a bowl and refrigerate for 30 to 40 minutes, until set.

Pour the mixture into a high-speed blender (or use an immersion blender) and blend at high speed for about 1 minute, until a smooth fluid gel is achieved. Strain the mixture through a fine-mesh sieve into a bowl and then transfer to a squeeze bottle. Refrigerate until needed.

Sake-soy gel sheets Have ready a large plastic tray (a cafeteria-style tray will work best, but anything with raised edges is fine). In a small pot, stir together all of the ingredients and bring to a boil. Let boil for 15 seconds to activate the agar agar, then turn off the heat.

While the mixture is still quite hot, ladle just enough of the liquid onto the bottom of the tray to cover it in a thin layer. Working quickly, tilt the tray from side to side to ensure the bottom of the tray is evenly coated. Immediately place the tray on a flat, level table where it can set (it will set within a couple minutes). If you are making the gel a day ahead, cover the tray with plastic wrap and refrigerate until needed. If not, after 5 minutes cut the gel into 10-inch × 1-inch rectangles or any other shape you want (use cookie cutters to ensure an even presentation on all plates).

Pomelo supremes Using a rasp, remove all of the zest from the outside of the pomelo. Reserve for tuna recipe (see below).

Pickled jalapeños
4 cups water, divided
3 jalapeño peppers, sliced
1 cup rice vinegar
2 Tbsp salt
1 Tbsp white sugar
2 cloves garlic

Yuzu pudding
½ cup freshly squeezed lemon juice
2 Tbsp yuzu juice (or lime juice)
¼ cup white sugar
1 tsp agar agar
Three-finger pinch of salt

Sake-soy gel sheets
½ cup sake
½ cup soy sauce
½ cup mirin
1 Tbsp white sugar
1 tsp agar agar

Pomelo supremes
1 pomelo

Scallion curls
2 green onions, green parts only

Smoked avocado purée
1 avocado
1 Tbsp vegetable oil
1 Tbsp liquid honey
1 tsp freshly squeezed lemon juice

Pomelo-seared tuna
10 oz skinless yellowfin tuna fillet
Three-finger pinch of salt
Reserved pomelo zest (see here)
1 Tbsp vegetable oil
8 French marigolds or other citrus-
  flavoured edible flowers, for garnish
  (if available)
1 sliced Lebanese cucumber, for garnish

With a sharp knife, slice a small portion from the top and bottom of the pomelo to create flat surfaces and expose the flesh. Carefully cut away the peel, ensuring that no white pith remains. Cut pomelo into individual segments, separating the flesh from the pithy membrane (discard membrane). Place the flesh in a small bowl and refrigerate until needed.

Scallion curls Have ready a large bowl of ice water. With a sharp knife, julienne green onions (cut into small matchsticks) and place in the ice water. Soak for 15 minutes, then drain; discard water. Refrigerate until needed.

Smoked avocado purée Have ready a cold smoker or a handheld smoking device. Peel and pit the avocado, then set the avocado halves on a wire rack or grill, place in the smoker and smoke for 15 minutes. (If you are using a handheld smoking device, place the avocado halves in a bowl and cover with plastic wrap, leaving just enough of an opening at one edge to insert the hose. Thread the hose through the opening and

smoke for 5 minutes. Leave avocado covered for another 5 minutes before continuing.)

Transfer the smoked avocado to a blender along with remaining ingredients and blend at high speed until smooth, about 1 minute. Pour the mixture into a squeeze bottle and refrigerate until needed.

Pomelo-seared tuna Place tuna on a clean plate. In a medium bowl, stir together equal parts salt and pomelo zest and sprinkle generously over the tuna.

Heat vegetable oil in a steel pan over high heat, add tuna and sear for 8 seconds per side. Remove from the heat and cut seared tuna into ½-inch slices.

To serve Place a strip of the soy-sake gel sheet on each plate. Using the gel sheet as a frame, arrange the other ingredients on top: set the tuna slightly off centre and squeeze dots of avocado purée and yuzu pudding in a random pattern. Arrange pomelo supremes and edible flowers on either side, using the cucumber, scallions and jalapeños to fill in the empty spots.

Chef says: Aside from the visual fun of this dish, it's also a warm, fragrant mélange of buttery potatoes, herbs and garlic, with the punchy flavours of black olive and black radish. It does require some planning ahead, as some of the steps must be started a day in advance. You can pick your own spruce tips off the ends of spruce trees in Ottawa in mid- to late May. Look for the tender green ends popping out. If you're making this dish at another time of year, you can substitute asparagus, cucumber, mushrooms, etc. Serve this as a side dish, or even just as a stand-alone appetizer course.

Serves 4 as an appetizer or a side dish

Dirty Potatoes

Black olive "dirt" Have ready a food dehydrator and at least one drying tray. Drain olives of any brine or marinade, blotting them on paper towels if necessary. Slice each olive into 3 or 4 pieces (this will make mincing them later easier), arrange them in a single layer on the drying tray and dehydrate at 150°F for 10 to 15 hours. (If you don't have a dehydrator, arrange the olives on a baking sheet lined with parchment paper and dry in a 150°F oven for 10 to 15 hours.)

Turn dried olives out onto a cutting board and mince (the olives should feel and look like coffee grinds; if they get at all pasty, you've gone too far). Store olive dirt in an airtight container at room temperature for up to 3 weeks.

Garlic chips Have ready a food dehydrator and at least one drying tray. Using a very sharp knife, slice garlic almost paper-thin but not quite. Place 1 cup of milk in a small pot, add garlic and bring to a boil over medium heat. Turn down the heat and simmer for 30 seconds. Drain.

To the pot of garlic, add 1 cup of milk and repeat the boiling, simmering and draining process. Repeat a third time with remaining cup of milk. Set the garlic slices on a drying tray (or baking sheet lined with parchment paper) and sprinkle with salt. Dehydrate in the food dehydrator or in the oven at 150°F for 6 to 8 hours. Store garlic chips in an airtight container at room temperature until ready to use.

Pickled spruce tips Combine vinegar, water, sugar, salt and chili flakes in a medium pot and bring to a boil.

In the meantime, heat a dry cast-iron skillet over medium-high heat, add cumin, fennel and coriander seeds and toast until fragrant, about 45 seconds. Pour seeds into the vinegar mixture and simmer for 3 minutes. Remove from the heat and let stand for 10 minutes.

Place the spruce tips in a heatproof bowl and strain the hot liquid through a fine-mesh sieve over top of them. Let cool, then transfer spruce tips in their liquid to an airtight container and refrigerate until ready to use.

Black olive "dirt"

1 cup pitted black olives (choose ones with the darkest skins)

Garlic chips

2 cloves elephant garlic (or other large garlic)

3 cups 1% milk, divided

Salt

Pickled spruce tips

1 cup champagne vinegar

1 cup water

¼ cup white sugar

1 tsp salt

¼ tsp red chili flakes

1 tsp cumin seeds

1 tsp fennel seeds

1 tsp coriander seeds

½ cup spruce tips (or sliced asparagus, cucumber or mushrooms)

Classic aioli

1 egg yolk

1 Tbsp Dijon mustard

Juice of 1 lemon

3 cloves garlic

Three-finger pinch of salt

2 cups vegetable oil

Butter-poached potatoes

2 cups salted butter

½ cup water

8 "marble" or "mini" purple potatoes (unpeeled), halved

4 fingerling potatoes, halved

½ bunch fresh thyme

6 cloves garlic

Black radish and dill

1 black radish (unpeeled)

½ bunch fresh dill

Classic aioli In a blender, combine egg yolk, mustard, lemon juice, garlic and salt and blend at high speed for 30 seconds. Reduce the speed to low and with the motor running, pour in vegetable oil in a very slow, steady stream. You should have a very thick emulsion. If your mixture "splits" and is almost water-thin after blending, begin the process again using the same ingredients. When it comes time to add the oil, use the broken mixture instead (so that you don't have to throw it away).

Butter-poached potatoes Line a plate with paper towels. In a wide pot, combine butter and water and heat gently until butter is melted. Add potatoes, thyme and garlic, and simmer until potatoes just become tender, about 20 minutes. With a slotted spoon, transfer potatoes to lined plate to drain.

Place a fine-mesh sieve over a small clean pot and strain the butter mixture through it; discard solids. Keep warm over low heat. (Use this to reheat the potatoes just prior to serving.)

Black radish and dill Cut radish into julienne (small matchsticks) and place in a small bowl. Cover with cold water and refrigerate until ready to use.

Place dill in a small bowl, cover with very cold water and soak until ready to use. Transfer to a small salad spinner and spin dry or blot dry with paper towels. Divide dill into smallish sprigs.

To serve Gently warm potatoes in reserved garlic and thyme butter over medium-low heat. Spoon a tablespoonful of aioli into the bottom of each bowl. Lay two fingerling potato halves and four purple potato halves over the aioli and spoon a bit of the butter mixture from the pot over the potatoes. Sprinkle some black olive dirt over the potatoes. Garnish each bowl with four or five garlic chips, five or six pieces of black radish, four or five pickled spruce tips and eight or nine sprigs of dill. Serve immediately.

Beau's All Natural Brewing

Bruce Wood
Steve Beauchesne

BEAU'S BREWERY is a Beauchesne family business that just clinked steins this past Canada Day in celebration of ten terrific years. It started out with a group of seven family members and friends, led by (Chief Cheerleading Officer) Steve Beauchesne and his dad, Tim, and three goals: to be a leader in sustainability, to be as community-minded as possible and to have more fun than any other craft brewery. Today, Beau's has 140 full-time staff and brews 4 million litres of beer a year. (The amount Beau's sold in its first year would now fit into the largest of its thirty-six fermenting tanks.) To say the business has been a craft beer success story doesn't begin to tell the tale. And if you've been to the Beau's-hosted Oktoberfest in Vankleek Hill (Beau's HQ and family homestead), you know all about the fun bit. As for sustain-ability, the brewery has used certified organic ingredients from the get-go; spent grains are diverted to feed livestock; and more and more hops are being grown locally, exclusively for Beau's. They grow on the seasonal patio, too. That's where Brewery chef Bruce Wood serves beer-friendly food. Local sausages and pulled pork on house-made bread. Smoked fish cakes. A lovely plate of charcuterie and cheeses. A duck magret rubbed with Marmite and beer. Beer pairings are written for every dish. And on any given day, there are about eight Beau's beers to inspire Bruce's brewery kitchen. 10 TERRY FOX DRIVE, VANKLEEK HILL, 866-585-2337

facing: **Beau's Beer-Braised Brisket with Seasonal Vegetables**

Chef says: Warming comfort food, this brisket recipe is incredibly versatile. Brined, rubbed and braised with one of Beau's spice-infused gruit ales, it can be the star of many special meals. Try it as part of a boiled dinner with steamed winter vegetables, sides of hot mustard and horseradish, and—if you are ambitious—it is glorious with dumplings! Sliced thinly, it can be built into an open-faced Reuben with braised red cabbage and Beau's beer-washed cheese from Gunn's Hill. Note that if you have a smoker, you can cold-smoke the rubbed brisket for two hours to give it additional flavour and then proceed with the braising. You'll need to start this recipe at least a week before you plan to serve it, so the beef has time to brine.

Serves 8 with leftovers

Beau's Beer-Braised Brisket with Seasonal Vegetables

Beef rub In a small bowl, combine all of the ingredients. (Will keep in an airtight container at room temperature for up to 3 months.)

Beef brine Combine all of the brine ingredients in a large pot and bring to a boil. Remove from the heat, let cool completely and refrigerate for at least 12 hours.

Braised beef Place beef in a plastic container large enough to hold it flat. Pour in brine, cover with enough plates to keep the beef submerged and refrigerate for 48 hours. Remove the plates, turn the brisket, replace the plates to ensure beef is submerged and refrigerate for another 48 hours. Repeat twice more, until the beef has brined for 7 days.

Preheat the oven to 300°F. Remove brisket from the brine (discard brine) and rinse well under cold running water. Pat dry with paper towels and place on a clean baking sheet. Using your hands, rub the entire brisket with sunflower oil, then with the beef rub.

Place onions, carrots, celery and garlic in a roasting pan large enough to hold the brisket flat and pour in ale. Add seasoned brisket and cover with parchment paper. Cut a piece of aluminum foil bigger than the roasting pan and set over the parchment paper, snugging the edges of the foil around the edges of the pan. Braise in the oven for 4 hours.

Let brisket cool in the braising liquid, then remove beef from the pan, wrap well and refrigerate until needed. Place a fine-mesh sieve over a clean bowl and strain braising vegetables, reserving liquid and discarding braising vegetables. Cover liquid and refrigerate until needed.

Beef rub

1 Tbsp freshly ground
   black pepper
1 tsp dried culinary lavender
1 Tbsp kosher salt
1 Tbsp dried rosemary
1 Tbsp dried thyme

Beef brine

8 cups water
8 cups Beau's gruit ale (or a
   craft-brewed wheat beer)
½ cup kosher salt
1 tsp bog myrtle (also known
   as sweet gale; if possible)
2 Tbsp dried oregano
2 tsp dried culinary lavender
2 Tbsp black peppercorns
2 Tbsp yellow mustard seeds
2 Tbsp dried juniper berries
1 Tbsp dried marjoram (or oregano)
6 sprigs fresh thyme
6 sprigs fresh rosemary
1 head garlic, split in half widthwise
2 tsp curing salt (or pink curing
   salt, if available)

Braised beef

1 beef brisket, 6 to 8 lb
1 recipe Beef Brine (see here), cold
¼ cup cold-pressed sunflower oil
1 recipe Beef Rub (see here)
1 onion, cut into 1-inch pieces
1 carrot, cut into 1-inch pieces
3 celery stalks, cut into 1-inch
   pieces
1 head garlic, split widthwise
1 bottle (600 mL) Beau's gruit ale
   (or craft-brewed wheat beer)
10 cups mixed seasonal vegetables
   (turnips, small new potatoes,
   garlic cloves, parsnips, kale),
   cut into 2-inch cubes

Garnish

Sea salt
½ cup grainy mustard
½ cup prepared horseradish

To assemble Using a spoon, skim and discard the fat from the top of the braising liquid. In a medium saucepan over medium-high heat, simmer liquid until reduced by one-third. Add seasonal vegetables and cook until tender, 8 to 12 minutes. Remove brisket from the fridge and slice into ½-inch-thick pieces.

To serve Divide cooked vegetables evenly among serving bowls and top with some of the reduced braising liquid. Finish with a sprinkle of good-quality sea salt and serve with grainy mustard and horseradish.

Serves 4 to 6 as appetizer (Makes twelve 8-inch crepes)

Quinoa Crepes Stuffed with Beau's Lug-Tread Ricotta and Smoked Chicken

Quinoa crepes Place eggs, thyme, 1 cup of cooked quinoa, salt and pepper in a food processor fitted with the metal blade. Add ½ cup of the flour and half the milk and process until well blended. Add remaining flour and milk and melted butter and process until batter is smooth. Transfer to a large bowl and fold in remaining ½ cup of cooked quinoa. Let batter rest on the counter for 20 minutes before using.

Preheat an 8-inch non-stick skillet over medium heat. When the skillet is hot, brush with melted butter. Pour about ¼ cup of batter into the centre of the skillet, tilting the pan until the batter evenly covers the bottom of the skillet. When the edges begin to peel back and the crepe begins to brown, 1 to 2 minutes, use a spatula to flip it over and cook for about 10 seconds more. Transfer to a clean plate. Repeat until you have used all the crepe batter (you should have 12 crepes). Cover the cooked crepes with a clean tea towel to keep them from drying out.

Ricotta and smoked chicken filling Heat the milk and 1 cup of cream in a large saucepan to just below the boiling point. Turn down the heat slightly and simmer, stirring occasionally, for 5 minutes. Add 1 tsp of salt and lemon juice and stir very gently. Remove from the heat and let sit for 10 minutes.

Line a fine-mesh sieve with a layer of cheesecloth and place it over a bowl. Using a slotted spoon, scoop curds into the sieve and let drain for 30 minutes. Reserve solids to make crepe stuffing. (Pour liquid whey into an airtight container and freeze for making bread. Will keep for up to 3 months, frozen.)

Place 2 cups of the ricotta, 3 Tbsp of the cream and beer in a food processor fitted with the metal blade and pulse just to combine. Season with salt and pepper to taste and transfer to a clean bowl.

Quinoa crepes

4 large eggs

2 tsp fresh thyme leaves, chopped

1½ cups cooked quinoa, divided

¼ tsp sea salt

¼ tsp freshly ground black pepper

1 cup all-purpose flour, divided

1¾ cups whole milk, divided

3 Tbsp melted butter + extra for the crepe pan

Ricotta and smoked chicken filling

8 cups whole milk

1 cup + 3 Tbsp whipping (35%) cream

1 tsp sea salt + more to taste

¼ cup freshly squeezed lemon juice

3 Tbsp Beau's Lug-Tread beer (or other lager-style beer)

Salt and freshly ground black pepper

2 cups good-quality shredded smoked chicken

1 cup rhubarb (or other tart fruit) chutney, for serving on side

To assemble Preheat the oven to 350°F. Line a baking sheet with parchment paper. Place a crepe on a clean work surface, spread with a thin layer of the ricotta mixture and top with smoked chicken. Lay a second crepe over the chicken, spread with a thin layer of ricotta and some chicken and top with a third crepe. Set the layered crepe on the baking sheet. Repeat with remaining crepes, ricotta and chicken until you have 4 layered crepes. Bake for 5 minutes to warm through, then remove from the oven and slice each crepe in four.

To serve Arrange four quarters on each serving plate and serve with chutney on the side.

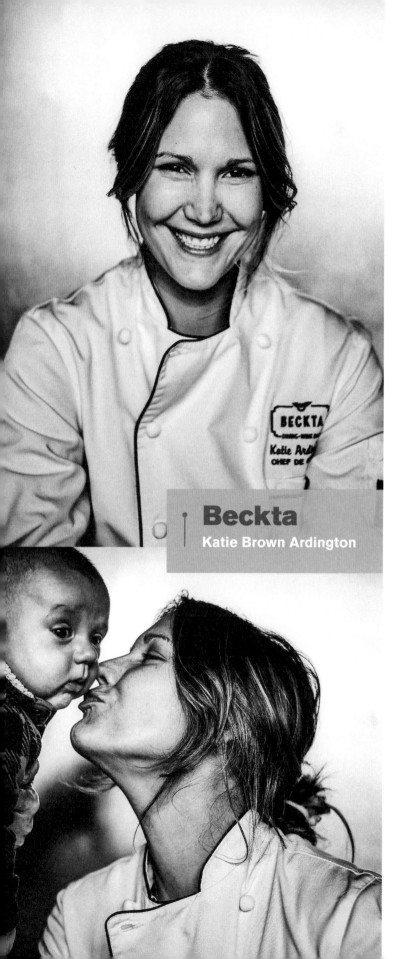

Beckta
Katie Brown Ardington

EIGHTY KILOS of rich organic dirt were delivered this spring to the seventh-floor rooftop patio at 150 Elgin, high above Beckta's new home. This summer the greens on Beckta plates had a special sort of smack, plucked as they were from an urban garden overhead. A smash hit from its first day of service (in its first, more modest home on Nepean Street), Stephen Beckta's flagship restaurant shows no evidence of resting on its considerable laurels. In a time that seems less enamoured with fine dining and gracious service, Beckta continues to deliver on both. If anything, it is doubling down, having restored a beautiful heritage mansion in dire need of some loving. You come to the new Beckta as you've always come to Beckta—to be wined, dined and tended to extremely well. Nobody does the trinity better. The service may be old-school, but the food is thoroughly modern. The kitchen brigade, led by executive chef Michael Moffatt and chef de cuisine Katie Brown Ardington, secures the finest ingredients and plates them in delicious, sophisticated ways, constantly conjuring dishes that subtly push the boundaries. Settle in for Brown Ardington's innovative five-course tasting menu in the lovely front rooms, or snack on oysters, truffled devilled eggs, or a steak-frites in the more casual wine bar at the back.

150 ELGIN STREET, 613-238-7063

Lemon and herb risotto soup
8 cups vegetable stock
Sea salt and freshly ground black pepper
¼ cup unsalted butter, divided
2 shallots, finely diced
1 clove garlic, finely chopped
1¼ cups risotto rice (carnaroli is my
    favourite, arborio is fine)
¾ cup dry white wine
1 large bunch watercress, trimmed
Zest and juice of 4 lemons

1 cup fresh flat-leaf (Italian)
    parsley leaves
½ cup fresh mint leaves + a few
    delicate sprigs for garnish
1 cup freshly grated Parmesan
    cheese
4 sprigs fresh tarragon, leaves
    picked

Poached eggs
Splash of white wine vinegar
6 large eggs

Serves 6

Lemon and Herb Risotto Soup with Poached Eggs

Chef says: This dish offers everything I love to eat. It is hearty but fresh, with lots of herbs and citrus. Plus I like anything with a poached egg and sharp cheese! It is perfect for a light main with some bread and salad on the side, or make a smaller portion for an appetizer. I have made many versions of this dish with leftover risotto for family meals at Beckta.

Lemon and herb risotto soup In a large pot, bring stock to a boil. Season with salt and pepper to taste. Turn down the heat to keep the stock at a steady simmer.

In a large saucepan over medium heat, melt 3 Tbsp of the butter. Add shallots and sweat without colouring for 4 minutes. Stir in garlic and cook for 1 minute. Add rice and cook, stirring, until rice turns translucent and has a nice nutty aroma, about 3 minutes.

Pour in wine and cook, still stirring, until absorbed, about 3 minutes. Add hot stock, a couple of ladlefuls at a time, and cook, stirring, until absorbed. Repeat until stock is used up, rice is slightly firm to the bite and all the liquid absorbed, 20 to 25 minutes. Remove risotto from the heat and set aside.

In a large saucepan over medium heat, melt remaining butter. Add watercress, lemon juice (reserving zest for later), parsley and mint. Cook until watercress is just wilted. Pour in remaining stock and cook for 1 minute.

Transfer watercress mixture to a food processor fitted with the metal blade and process until watercress and herbs are finely chopped. Stir the purée into the risotto (the consistency should be nice and runny). Stir in half the Parmesan and lemon zest, salt and pepper to taste.

Poached eggs Have ready a large bowl of cool water. Bring a large saucepan of water to a boil. Add vinegar and turn down the heat to a simmer. Stirring the water with a fork to create a whirlpool, break eggs into the simmering water, 3 at a time. Once they rise to the surface, trim any wispy tails of white with a slotted spoon. Poach eggs for a total of 4 minutes. Using the slotted spoon, carefully transfer eggs to the bowl of cool water. Poach remaining eggs and transfer to the cool water.

To serve Warm six individual soup bowls in the oven. Gently rewarm the eggs in a large pan of simmering water for 1 minute. Ladle risotto soup into the warm bowls, place a poached egg in the centre of each bowl and sprinkle with remaining Parmesan. Garnish with more herbs, if desired.

Chef says: These bites are perfect for a dinner party if you just want something lovely to end the evening, or you can make them as a component of a larger dessert. At Beckta, we once put the peppermint patties on a New Year's Eve dessert tasting menu; since then, they have found their way back on the menu as petit-fours or part of other chocolate desserts. We usually make extra because they tend to disappear from our prep shelves as the day goes on. Serve the patties with chocolate ice cream or garnished with the lemon confit, or all on their own, sprinkled with sea salt.

Makes 25 to 30 small patties (or 15 to 20 larger ones)

Peppermint Patties with Lemon Confit

Lemon confit Using a vegetable peeler, zest lemons, then with a sharp knife slice zest into thin strips. Cut zested lemons in half and squeeze to make ½ cup juice.

In a small pot, combine water and salt and bring to a simmer, stirring to dissolve salt. Add lemon zest strips and remove from the heat.

In a second small pot over medium-high heat, bring sugar and lemon juice to a simmer and cook until reduced to a syrupy consistency, about 10 minutes. Stir in lemon zest and remove from the heat. Let cool completely.

Peppermint patties Line a large baking sheet with parchment paper. In the bowl of a stand mixer fitted with the whisk attachment, cream together butter, sugar and cream cheese. Add peppermint oil, evaporated milk and cream and beat at high speed until fluffy and smooth.

With a rubber spatula, scrape down the sides of the bowl and beat again for 30 seconds. Scrape the mixture onto the lined baking sheet. Cover with plastic wrap and refrigerate for about 2 hours, until stiffened to a workable paste.

Line another baking sheet with parchment paper. Divide chilled paste into ½-oz portions (about the size of a marble) if you are making them part of a dessert, or larger (about the size of a lime) if you plan to serve them on their own. Using your hands and wearing rubber gloves if possible, roll each portion into a ball, place it on the lined baking sheet and, using the back of a measuring cup or a steel bowl, flatten into a circle about ½ inch thick. Chill flattened patties for a further 30 minutes in the freezer.

Lemon confit
6 lemons
¼ cup water
Pinch of salt
½ cup white sugar

Peppermint patties
1 Tbsp unsalted butter
2 cups white sugar
1 Tbsp solid cream cheese
   (not spreadable)
1½ tsp pure peppermint oil
2 Tbsp evaporated milk
1 Tbsp whipping (35%) cream
9 oz good-quality semi-sweet
   (50 to 60% cocoa) chocolate
2 Tbsp solid coconut oil

In a stainless steel bowl set over a pot of simmering water, melt chocolate with coconut oil, stirring to blend well. Turn off the heat and keep chocolate warm by leaving the bowl over the pot of water (if it begins to stiffen, bring the water back up to a simmer).

Using a large fork or chopsticks, drop 2 patties into the melted chocolate, scoop them out and let the excess chocolate run off. Return them to the lined baking sheet to cool and dry (the patties should look matte, not glossy). Repeat with remaining patties, then loosely cover the baking sheet with parchment paper and refrigerate. (Will keep refrigerated in an airtight container for 3 to 4 days or frozen for 2 weeks.)

To serve Serve peppermint patties chilled, straight from the freezer or the fridge, or at room temperature. Arrange them on a platter, garnished with a couple of pieces of lemon confit, served at the same temperature as the patties.

Benny's Bistro
Scott Adams

WITH ITS COLOURFUL, art-filled walls and retro black 'n' white tiles, and with the gracious service of Yvon Foley, Benny's Bistro is an oasis of civility in the ByWard Market. Its fans use it for a morning meeting over cappuccino and a flaky croissant, for a mimosa-soused Sunday brunch that has few equals, or for one of the finest bistro lunches in the city. Devoted to local, seasonal, unhurried cooking, chef Scott Adams's dishes are still-life pleasures, exquisitely well made. Exacting, too. Just look at those shallots: you'd think a robot had churned out that perfect dice! It's a skill he holds dear, and one he instructs. Along with running The French Baker and Benny's Bistro, Adams is also a cooking teacher, working with children for a decade now. And I don't mean guiding them through the grilled cheese. These youngsters learn knife skills, make sausages from scratch and discover what yummy things can be made with a wonky-looking celery root. So it makes sense that Adams the teacher has given us a step-by-step recipe for translating stalks of rhubarb into a beautiful brunoise for a vibrant vinaigrette. And held our hand through the task of transforming raw duck legs into a sumptuous confit. Adams the bistro chef pairs an earthy tapenade with the salmon gravlax I could eat every day. His seared scallops are perfectly wobbly, gloriously bronzed, decked out with a sorrel crème fraîche. Eggs are elevated to art form, and vegetarians are well served, always.

119 MURRAY STREET, 613-789-6797

48

1 large or 2 small stalks fresh
  rhubarb
1 to 2 small shallots
3 to 4 sprigs fresh tarragon
¼ cup liquid honey
3 Tbsp white balsamic vinegar
1 tsp freshly cracked black pepper
¼ tsp kosher salt

Makes ¾ cup

Rhubarb, Honey and Tarragon Mignonette

Chef says: All Ottawa chefs eagerly await the arrival of spring. This recipe was inspired by the appearance of the first two signs of life in my garden: rhubarb and tarragon. The success of this simple and versatile mignonette relies greatly on the precision of your cuts, so make them count! A sharp knife, a good-quality cutting board and patience will make all the difference. This condiment is great with fish, raw oysters, grilled pork and duck. Although generally best served fresh, it can be refrigerated, covered, for up to one week.

To prepare rhubarb, wash stalk(s) under cold running water and pat dry with paper towels. Using a sharp knife, remove both the very top and bottom portions of the stalk. Begin by running the knife down the length of the rhubarb, spacing each consecutive cut 2 to 3 mm apart. Gather half of the slices into a stack and repeat, creating long sticks of rhubarb (this cut is called julienne). Repeat with remaining rhubarb. Align all of the julienned rhubarb and finish by cutting widthwise, using the same spacing, to create 2- to 3-mm cubes of rhubarb (this is called a brunoise). Measure ⅓ cup of the rhubarb brunoise and place in a medium bowl.

To prepare shallots, peel away the first 2 layers of skin. Using a sharp knife, remove approximately 1 cm from both the top and bottom portion of each lobe. Begin by running the knife lengthwise from the narrow to the fat end of each lobe, stopping just short of the end to prevent the shallots from falling apart completely. Space each consecutive cut 2 to 3 mm apart. While holding the shallot firmly in one hand, make several 2- to 3-mm horizontal slices, creating a uniform grid system. Lastly, slice widthwise along the length to create what should be a perfect brunoise of shallot. Measure 3 Tbsp of the shallots and add them to the bowl with the rhubarb.

To prepare the tarragon, remove the leaves from several stalks of tarragon. Loosely stack the leaves and carefully cut widthwise along the length of the stack, making even slices 2 to 3 mm apart. Measure 1 Tbsp of the chopped tarragon and add it to the rhubarb and shallots.

To the bowl, add honey, vinegar, cracked pepper and salt and gently combine. Transfer the mignonette to a small glass jar or ceramic bowl and refrigerate, uncovered, for 15 to 20 minutes before serving.

Chef says: This recipe requires advance planning, so give yourself plenty of time to source the ingredients. Duck legs and rendered duck fat can often be found in specialty butcher shops. Traditional recipes utilize a strictly salt-based curing method, but at Benny's we find that brown sugar adds a balanced and unique approach to this French bistro classic. Great served with summer salads or equally well with winter comforts such as braised white beans and creamed spinach. Total prep time: 36 hours + 1 week!

4 duck legs (including thighs)
1 cup kosher salt
1 cup packed brown sugar
½ tsp ground cinnamon
2 Tbsp black peppercorns
4 cups rendered duck fat
4 sprigs fresh thyme
2 fresh bay leaves

Serves 4

Duck Confit

Trim away any excess fat from duck legs and thighs (leave skin intact over the meat) and place on a clean work surface.

In a medium bowl, combine salt, sugar, cinnamon and black peppercorns and stir well. Using your hands, pack a generous and even amount of this spice mixture onto the meat side of each leg and place, meat side down, onto a dish. Leave enough room around each leg so it lays completely flat. Sprinkle remaining spice mixture evenly over the skin side of each leg. Cover and refrigerate for 24 hours.

Remove the duck legs from the dish and rinse them thoroughly under cold running water. Be careful to remove all of the curing mix from the entire leg, especially along the edges where the skin meets the meat, so there is no residual sugar to caramelize, scorch or even burn while cooking.

Preheat the oven to 275°F. In a medium saucepan, heat duck fat over medium heat just until it is completely liquefied. Place prepared duck legs, thyme and bay leaves into an ovenproof ceramic dish. Pour the duck fat over the legs until they are completely submerged. Cover and bake for 6 to 8 hours—the "low and slow" approach ensures that the duck will be tender and succulent.

Remove the duck from the oven and let cool completely in the fat at room temperature. Gently remove each leg from the fat and transfer it to a shallow, flat-bottomed ovenproof dish. Spoon the duck fat into a small saucepan and heat over medium heat. Set a fine-mesh sieve over a clean bowl and strain the duck fat; discard solids. Pour the strained duck fat over the duck legs, cover and refrigerate—ideally for a minimum of 1 week or up to 1 month—before using.

When ready to serve, preheat the oven to 400°F. Carefully remove the duck legs from the fat. Scrape off and, if you wish, reserve any excess fat that remains stuck to each leg. Place the duck legs, skin side down, in a non-stick ovenproof or cast-iron pan and bake for 20 to 25 minutes or until the skin has become crispy and the meat has warmed through. (The remaining duck fat can be kept for future use. Strain it through a fine-mesh sieve into an airtight container and keep for up to 3 months.)

To serve Enjoy duck confit in a multitude of ways. Serve the whole duck legs in their crispy skin warm with parsnip purée and caramelized apple, or remove the meat and toss it with crisp bitter greens, fresh pears and your favourite vinaigrette.

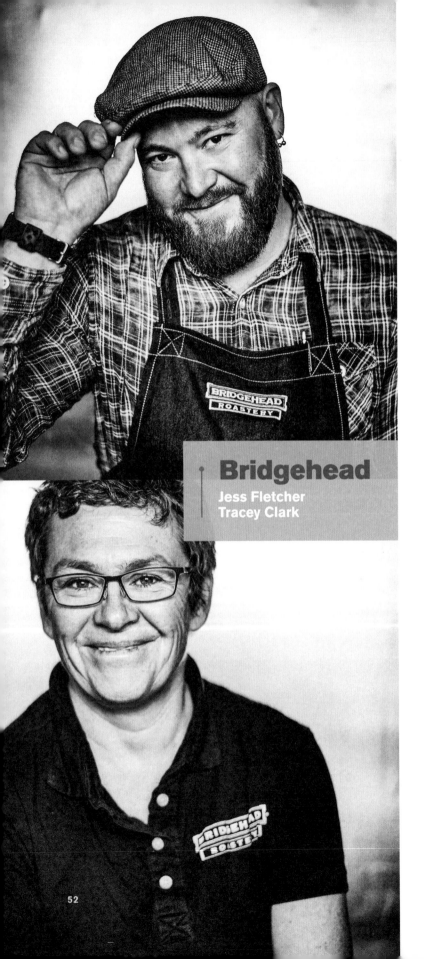

Bridgehead

Jess Fletcher
Tracey Clark

IT'S A COFFEE STORY with remarkable depth, and Ottawa is the richer for having Bridgehead to start its day. Few cities can boast a local coffeehouse chain so devoted to excellence, to sourcing coffee and teas from small-scale, co-operative and organic farms in far-flung places, and milk, cream, eggs, vegetables, herbs, honey, pork, maple syrup and beef from suppliers in its own backyard. It's mind-boggling how far the Bridgehead team, led by Tracey Clark, has come: from selling Nicaraguan beans in church basements to opening its twentieth coffeehouse by the time you've cooked its recipes. In 2012 Bridgehead also opened its own Roastery, and now roasts thousands of pounds of beans every week. Chef Jess Fletcher's ties to Bridgehead are deep—he was a teenager when his mother, Pam, and her friend Tracey Clark sat around the kitchen table, plotting the birth of Bridgehead. "So it's always been dear to my heart," he says. From Fletcher's scratch kitchen and the Roastery's glassed-in bakery, everything is made in-house: the popular breakfast wraps; the sandwiches on house-made seedy bread; the ginger cookies I am mad for; the rhubarb muffins; the big, filling salads with trumped-up flavours. And now beer! After years of collaborating with local craft breweries, Bridgehead is licensing some of its coffeehouses. Which means we can now enjoy draught beer, biodynamic Ontario wines or a glass of the tea-forward house kombucha, with a short menu of evening grazing plates.

BRIDGEHEAD.CA

Streusel topping

½ tsp ground cinnamon

¼ tsp salt

¾ cup + 1 Tbsp all-purpose flour

½ cup unsalted butter, room temperature

¼ cup cane sugar

⅛ cup brown sugar

Rhubarb muffins

4¼ cups unbleached all-purpose flour

½ Tbsp baking soda

⅛ tsp kosher salt

¾ cup canola oil

2¼ cups packed brown sugar

3 extra-large eggs

1¾ cups buttermilk

1 tsp pure vanilla extract

3¾ to 4 cups chopped fresh or frozen rhubarb (cut into 1-inch cubes)

Canola oil, for greasing pan

Makes 12 muffins

Rhubarb Streusel Muffins

Chef says: We love rhubarb—its vibrant colour, tart flavour and, most especially, how early it comes up in the garden. It's a spring treat that keeps on giving all summer long. In addition to making tarts, we like to bake up rhubarb muffins as soon as the season's upon us. We make the batter at least one day, and up to three days, before we bake the muffins so that the dry ingredients become well hydrated. The flavour and texture are worth the patience. All of our muffins and many of our scones make use of buttermilk. If you don't have buttermilk on hand, you can substitute 2% or whole milk cut with kefir or yogurt. The results are equally good. These are best freshly baked, but will keep for a day or two in an airtight container. At home, we reserve the batter in the fridge, and then bake a few each day.

Streusel topping In a small bowl, combine the cinnamon, salt and flour and set aside. In a second bowl, work the butter and sugars together by hand until combined (or briefly cream if using an electric stand mixer). Add the dry ingredients to the wet ingredients and mix until blended.

Rhubarb muffins In a large bowl, combine flour, baking soda and salt and set aside. In a second bowl, mix canola oil and brown sugar until well combined (at low speed if using a stand mixer). In a third bowl, blend eggs, buttermilk and vanilla, then add to the oil and brown sugar mixture. Add the dry ingredients to the wet ingredients and mix just until there are no lumps (by hand if using bowls, or at low speed if using a stand mixer). With a rubber spatula, fold in the rhubarb chunks and stir well so they are evenly distributed throughout the batter. If making ahead, refrigerate in an airtight container.

To bake, preheat the oven to 350°F. Lightly grease a 12-cup muffin pan with canola oil. Scoop the batter into the muffin cups, filling each about three-quarters full. Sprinkle each muffin with a good-size spoonful of streusel topping. Bake for 22 minutes or until a toothpick inserted into the centre of a muffin comes out clean. Transfer to a wire rack for 15 minutes before serving to cool slightly and let the flavours meld.

Quinoa salad

1½ cups quinoa, rinsed and drained

1 tsp salt

1½ cups cold water

1 large or 2 small butternut squash, peeled, seeded and cut into 1-inch cubes

1 red onion, diced

1 Tbsp olive oil

Salt and freshly ground black pepper

½ cup roughly crumbled feta cheese

½ cup dried cranberries (both sweetened and unsweetened work equally well)

2 Tbsp finely chopped fresh flat-leaf (Italian) parsley leaves

Spiced cider dressing

1 Tbsp ground cumin

1 Tbsp ground coriander

1 tsp ground turmeric

1 tsp sweet paprika

1 tsp ground cardamom

1 tsp ground nutmeg

2 tsp sea salt

2 tsp cane sugar

1 Tbsp Dijon mustard

¾ cup apple cider vinegar

1½ cups canola oil

Serves 8

Quinoa Salad with Butternut Squash, Feta and Cranberries

Chef says: Organic quinoa is a product we love and so do our Bridgehead customers. High in protein and amino acids, we use it as a base for salads, soups, vegetable patties and even in baking. Here, we pair the grain with local butternut squash. The squash is harvested in the fall and early winter, and we dice and freeze it for the spring and summer. We are also lucky to have a local cranberry supplier who provides us with amazing berries throughout the year. The sweetness of the butternut squash and cranberries, the complex spicing and acid from the dressing, and the creamy richness of the feta work together in ways we love. Cooked quinoa will continue to absorb moisture, so it is important to overdress it slightly to get the full flavour of the dressing as it sits.

Quinoa salad In a medium pot, combine quinoa, salt and water and bring to a boil. Turn down the heat and simmer for 12 to 15 minutes, until grains are cooked through and fluffy but still intact. Remove from the heat and let cool completely. (This step can be done ahead.)

Preheat the oven to 400°F. Place squash and onions in a large bowl, add olive oil and salt and pepper to taste and toss to coat. Arrange in a single layer on a baking sheet and roast in the centre of the oven for about 20 minutes or until the vegetables are golden brown and yield to a knife. While the vegetables are roasting, prepare the dressing.

Spiced cider dressing In a dry frying pan over medium heat, toast cumin, coriander, turmeric, paprika, cardamom and nutmeg until fragrant, 1 to 2 minutes. In a medium bowl, whisk together toasted spices, salt, sugar, mustard and vinegar. While still whisking, slowly drizzle in canola oil in a steady stream to create an emulsion.

To serve In a large bowl, combine the cooked quinoa with the roasted vegetables, feta, cranberries and parsley. Add dressing to taste, and toss gently. The quinoa will "soak up" the dressing. If keeping overnight, reserve some of the dressing to add just before serving.

le café at the National Arts Centre

John Morris

THERE'S AN international brigade of chefs in the le café kitchens, and a commitment from top chef John Morris to training young cooks. The National Arts Centre's culinary arm partners with Ottawa's three main cooking schools. It takes on students for seasonal work and for the series of NAC "Scene" festivals it runs, where Canadian cuisine from coast to coast to coast shares the stage with other arts. John Morris's role has been major in this: "I get chills when I think of all the things I've been taught along the way. I'm looking for ways to give back now. To help inspire and train another generation of Canadian cooks." Taking tea with Scottish-born Morris on the canal-side patio of le café, we're talking about his version of Canadian cuisine, how he honours and interprets it. "I try to respect the mosaic of cultures in my kitchen," he tells me. "The flavours of Canada, but with a global twist." Morris gets a kick from rebuilding, with all-Canadian materials, a dish associated with the cuisine of another. He sources freekeh and lentils from Saskatchewan for savoury pancakes that he overlays with a smoky pepper purée. He poaches eggs in Madras curry and places them on crunchy fritters of local zucchini. The classic Caprese salad takes Leamington tomatoes, first-press virgin canola oil from Alberta, basil from nearby Juniper Farm, and mozzarella di bufala from the largest water-buffalo herd in the country, in Saint-Charles-sur-Richelieu. "I call it the Canadese," he chuckles.

53 ELGIN STREET, 613-594-5127

Tarragon vinaigrette

¼ cup extra-virgin olive oil

4 cloves garlic

1 Tbsp Dijon mustard

⅓ cup champagne vinegar

2 Tbsp your favourite local liquid honey

1 bunch fresh tarragon leaves

⅔ cup cold-pressed sunflower oil

Sea salt

Black peppercorns, toasted and ground

Carrot, radish and watercress salad

8 young, colourful, medium carrots

8 whole radishes

¼ cup olive oil

Salt and freshly ground black pepper

¼ cup pine nuts

4 cups watercress leaves, trimmed to tender stems

1 Tbsp pink peppercorns, crushed with a mortar and pestle

Serves 4

Roasted Carrot, Radish and Watercress Salad

Chef says: I love this salad for its stunning colours, its textures and mostly for its flavours—the sweet earthiness of the carrots, further enhanced by roasting, the heat of the radish, the peppery watercress, the buttery pine nuts and the light licorice flavour the tarragon gives. And there are fringe benefits: watercress contains more Vitamin C than oranges, and four times more beta carotene and Vitamin A than apples. But nobody has to know that. Prepare the vinaigrette one day ahead to allow the flavours to mingle.

Tarragon vinaigrette In a small sauté pan, combine olive oil with garlic cloves and cook over low heat for 15 minutes or until garlic is lightly brown and fork-tender.

Transfer the garlic to a small bowl, mash with a fork, then add mustard, vinegar and honey. Roughly chop tarragon leaves, add to the bowl and whisk to combine. While whisking, add sunflower oil in a steady stream until fully emulsified. Season with salt and pepper to taste.

Carrot, radish and watercress salad Preheat the oven to 375°F. Cut carrots in half crosswise and quarter the radishes. In a medium bowl, toss carrots and radishes with olive oil and season with salt and pepper to taste. Arrange carrots and radishes in a single layer on a baking sheet and roast for 40 minutes or until fork-tender. Remove from the oven and set aside to cool.

Spread out pine nuts on a baking sheet and toast in the oven for 5 minutes or until golden brown. Remove from oven and set aside to cool.

To serve In a medium bowl, toss the roasted carrots and radishes with just enough of the tarragon vinaigrette to coat them. Arrange them on four plates or on a serving platter. In the same bowl, toss the watercress with just enough vinaigrette to coat the leaves. Arrange the greens atop the roasted vegetables. Garnish the salad(s) liberally with toasted pine nuts and crushed pink peppercorns. Serve immediately.

Smoked cheese

1 ball buffalo mozzarella (8 oz), cut into quarters

1 cup wood chips (readily available in BBQ supply aisles)

Confit cherry tomatoes

12 cherry tomatoes, rinsed and patted dry

1 cup olive oil

6 cloves garlic

4 sprigs fresh thyme

Sea salt

Black peppercorns, toasted and ground

Polenta

1 Tbsp reserved confit oil (see here)

6 confit garlic cloves (see here)

2 shallots, minced

1 bunch fresh thyme, leaves only, chopped

2 cups water

2 cups 2% milk

1 cup white cornmeal

½ cup butter, cut into cubes

1 cup freshly grated Parmigiano-Reggiano cheese

Sea salt

Black peppercorns, toasted and ground

Garnish

4 fresh basil leaves

2 Tbsp organic canola oil

Serves 4 as an appetizer

Smoked Buffalo Mozzarella and White Corn Polenta with Confit Cherry Tomatoes

Chef says: My goal with this recipe was to work that holy trinity of Italian flavours—the combination of buffalo mozzarella, tomatoes and basil—into an interesting starter. Smoking the cheese adds an intensity to those flavours.

Smoked cheese To create a stovetop smoker, spread the wood chips thinly in an even layer on an old stainless steel tray. Place the cheese on a wire rack that will sit inside the tray, ensuring the cheese does not touch the wood chips. Wrap the whole assembly tightly with foil and place it directly on a stovetop burner over high heat. When the wood chips start to smoke, remove the tray, set it on a cool but heatproof surface, and continue to smoke the cheese for another 10 minutes.

Confit cherry tomatoes Place tomatoes in a small pot with the olive oil, garlic and thyme and cook over low heat until soft, about 20 minutes.

Transfer tomatoes to a small bowl and season with salt and pepper to taste. Set aside. Reserve the confit oil and garlic, but discard the thyme.

Polenta Place a medium heavy-bottomed pot over high heat. Add reserved confit oil and garlic

cloves. Mash the garlic with a fork and then stir in shallots and thyme. Sauté quickly until the shallots are translucent but not brown. Pour in water and milk and bring to a boil.

Whisk in the cornmeal in a steady stream, whisking hard to prevent lumps from forming. Turn down the heat to the lowest setting and cook for about 20 minutes, stirring at least every 3 minutes with a wooden spoon.

Once cooked, stir in the butter and cheese. Season with salt and pepper to taste. Remove from the heat.

To serve Preheat the broiler in your oven to high. Divide the polenta among four heatproof bowls (or spoon it into a casserole dish). Unwrap the smoked cheese and nestle one quarter in the centre of each bowl. Set the bowls on a baking sheet and, watching carefully, broil for 3 to 5 minutes until the cheese is browned. Remove from the oven and divide the confit tomatoes over each serving. Tear a basil leaf over each bowl and drizzle with ½ Tbsp of canola oil. Season with salt and pepper to taste. Serve immediately.

Clover
West de Castro

WEST DE CASTRO'S copy of *The Flavor Bible* is torn, tattered, held together with tape. "It's my go-to," she tells me over the square of chicken liver pâté she's just delivered, exquisitely rich, served simply with green apple and crostini. Her food fits the décor—no-frills ("I really like plywood"), put together with creativity, hard work and humour. I love seeing the Bank Street suits slurping up her remarkably good corn soup while sitting on retro school chairs. "So why did you name your restaurant Clover?" I ask de Castro. "It sounded better than 'small potatoes.' That was the original idea." And why small potatoes? "Because I didn't want anyone to come in here with high expectations." Right. Well the trouble is, we have them now, and with good reason. De Castro is a self-described introvert, but there's nothing shy about her food. Flavours are confident, exuberant. Formerly cooking at the vegan powerhouse ZenKitchen, she brings a deep love to fresh vegetables. The brassicas dish she offers us comes from that love, each humble root treated with utmost respect. A power base of navy beans, hit with caper and lemon and some chili heat, drizzled with almond brown butter, it's a dish whose title sounds a bit like medicine ("No getting up from that table, young lady, till you've eaten your brassicas..."), but, my God, if my mother had cooked Brussels sprouts like this... Clover is a gem of a place, run by a gem of a woman: shy, modest—and no small potatoes. 155 BANK STREET, 613-680-8803

facing: **Roasted Brassicas with White Bean Purée and Almond "Brown Butter"**

White bean purée
½ cup extra-virgin olive oil
1 large shallot, thinly sliced
2 tsp chopped fresh thyme
1 large garlic clove, minced
1 cup cooked navy or cannellini beans
2 cups vegetable stock
2 tsp kosher salt or to taste
1 tsp freshly ground black pepper
  or to taste
1 tsp red chili flakes or to taste

Serves 4 as a main dish, 8 as a side

Roasted Brassicas with White Bean Purée and Almond "Brown Butter"

White bean purée In a small saucepan, heat 2 Tbsp of the olive oil over medium heat. Add shallots, thyme and garlic and sauté until soft, about 3 minutes. Stir in beans, stock, salt, black pepper and red chili flakes and bring to a simmer. Turn down the heat to low and cook until beans are very soft and stock is reduced by half. Remove from the heat and allow the mixture to cool slightly.

Transfer the bean mixture to a blender and purée at high speed until very smooth. With the motor running at low speed, add remaining olive oil in a slow, steady stream until well combined (the purée should be pourable but thick enough to hold its shape; if too thick, add a bit more stock or water and mix well). Season to taste, as needed, with salt, pepper and/or chilies. Strain the purée through a fine-mesh sieve into a small pot; discard solids. Cover with a lid and keep warm.

Roasted vegetables Preheat the oven to 375°F. Heat 2 Tbsp of grapeseed oil in a large ovenproof pan over high heat. When the oil starts to smoke, place cauliflower wedges, cut side down, in the pan and sear until golden brown. Turn cauliflower over, season with salt and pepper to taste and bake in the oven until the tip of a knife inserted in the thickest part of the core has slight resistance, 10 to 12 minutes. Remove from the oven and set aside.

Heat another 2 Tbsp of grapeseed oil in a second large ovenproof pan over high heat. Add pearl onions and Brussels sprouts, cut side down, and sear carefully until golden brown. Stir in broccoli, tossing to coat with the oil, and season with salt and pepper. Bake in the oven until Brussels sprouts are knife-tender, 3 to 4 minutes. Set aside.

Roasted vegetables

6 Tbsp grapeseed oil, divided

1 small cauliflower, cut into 4 wedges, core trimmed but left intact

Kosher salt and freshly ground black pepper

6 pearl onions, blanched and peeled, cut in half crosswise

10 to 12 medium Brussels sprouts, trimmed and cut in half

1 to 2 heads broccoli, florets separated and stems reserved for garnish

1 small celeriac, peeled and julienned (cut into matchsticks)

1 leek, white parts only, cut into ⅛-inch half-moon slices

1 small head Savoy cabbage, cut into ⅛-inch slices (and outer leaves reserved for garnish)

White Bean Purée (see here)

Almond "Brown Butter" (see here)

Almond "brown butter" sauce

¼ cup extra-virgin olive oil

2 Tbsp finely chopped shallots

2 Tbsp capers, drained

1 Tbsp whole unblanched almonds, toasted and finely ground

2 Tbsp freshly squeezed lemon juice

Kosher salt and freshly ground black pepper

Garnish

12 pieces thinly sliced cauliflower (or romanesco broccoli)

1 to 2 broccoli stems, peeled and sliced into ¼-inch-thick rounds

12 rounds cut from larger Savoy cabbage leaves, each 1½ to 2 inches in diameter

20 pickled pearl onion "petals" (individual leaves)

¼ cup finely grated toasted almonds (almond dust)

4 kale chips

Heat 2 Tbsp of grapeseed oil in a third large sauté pan over high heat. Add celeriac and leeks and sauté for about 1 minute. Add cabbage and cook for another minute. Season with more salt and pepper to taste. Remove from the heat and set aside.

Almond "brown butter" sauce Heat olive oil in a small sauté pan over medium heat. Add shallots and cook until soft and lightly browned on edges. Stir in capers and sauté for 30 seconds. Remove from the heat and stir in almonds, lemon juice and salt and pepper to taste. Set aside.

To serve Warm four plates. Spread a quarter of the warm bean purée in the centre of each plate. Top with equal amounts of the leek, celeriac and cabbage mixture. Set a cauliflower wedge on top of the leek mixture and arrange the pearl onions, Brussels sprouts and broccoli florets around the cauliflower. Tuck the raw cauliflower slices, broccoli stem pucks and cabbage rounds around the dish as a garnish. Drizzle with warm almond "brown butter" sauce, especially over the cauliflower wedges and raw vegetables. Finish with pickled pearl onion petals, a sprinkle of toasted almond dust and a kale chip, and serve warm.

Corn stock

2 medium onions, quartered

1 fennel bulb, roughly chopped

4 stalks celery, cut into 2-inch pieces

2 bay leaves

1 tsp black peppercorns

4 sprigs fresh thyme

4 ears corn, kernels removed and reserved for chowder

12 cups cold water

Corn chowder

¼ cup butter, divided

¼ cup grapeseed oil, divided

1 small onion, thinly sliced

1 leek, white and light green parts, thinly sliced

1 medium shallot, thinly sliced

2 celery stalks, thinly sliced

1 Tbsp fresh thyme leaves

1 Tbsp salt

1 tsp freshly ground black pepper

2 bay leaves

8 cups Corn Stock (see here)

10 to 12 white pearl onions, blanched, peeled and cut in half

¼ lb waxy yellow potatoes, cut into ½-inch cubes and parboiled in salted water

¼ lb slab bacon, cut into lardons, cooked and rendered fat reserved

2 ears corn, charred on the grill, then kernels removed

4 cups reserved raw corn kernels (see here)

½ cup evaporated milk

2 green onions, white and green parts, sliced thinly on a bias, for garnish

Serves 6 as an appetizer, 4 as a main course

Corn Chowder

Chef says: This is a lighter version of a classic, with smoky bacon, caramelized pearl onions, golden potatoes and charred sweet corn bobbing about. It's the kind of soup I enjoy, thin and almost brothy, contrasted with hearty bits for a little chew.

Corn stock In a large, heavy-bottomed pot, bring all of the ingredients to a boil. Turn down the heat to low and simmer for 1 hour. Using a fine-mesh sieve, strain into a clean bowl; discard solids. Set aside.

Corn chowder In a large, heavy-bottomed pot, melt 2 Tbsp of the butter with 2 Tbsp of the grapeseed oil over medium heat. Stir in onions, leeks, shallots, celery and thyme and cook until soft, 8 to 10 minutes. Add salt, pepper, bay leaves and corn stock and simmer for 15 minutes.

While soup is simmering, prepare the garnish. In a large sauté pan on medium-high heat, melt remaining 2 Tbsp of butter with 2 Tbsp of the grapeseed oil until frothy. Add pearl onions, cut side down, and cook until caramelized, 1 to 3 minutes. Stir in potatoes and sauté until golden,

2 to 3 minutes. Add cooked bacon, some of the rendered fat if you wish, and charred corn kernels. Set garnish aside.

Remove bay leaves from the soup pot. Stir in reserved raw corn kernels, and remove chowder from the heat. Let cool slightly, then transfer the soup to a blender. Purée at high speed until very smooth. Strain soup through a fine-mesh sieve into a clean pot, using the back of a spoon to push the softer solids through the sieve; discard solids. Stir in evaporated milk until well combined. Season with salt and pepper to taste.

To serve Warm four or six soup bowls. Divide garnish among the soup bowls, ladle the chowder on top and sprinkle with green onions.

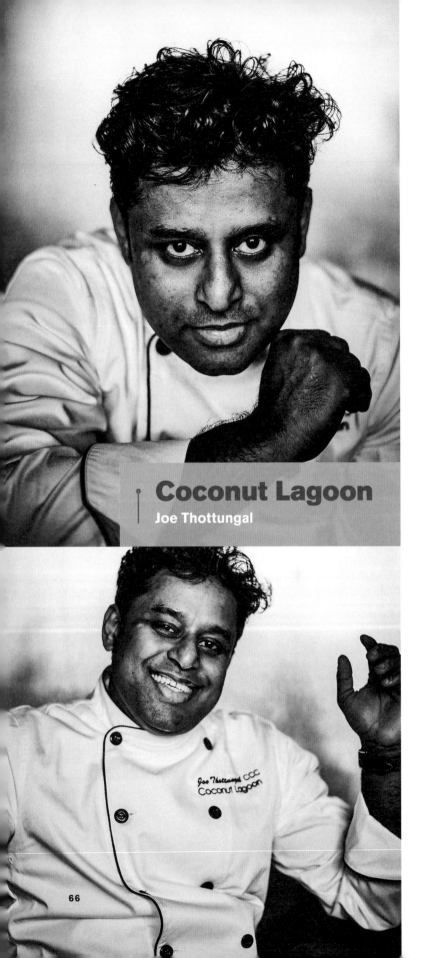

Coconut Lagoon

Joe Thottungal

I FIRST FELL HARD for the cuisine of Kerala at a harvest lunch. A yearly tradition at the Coconut Lagoon, the *Onam sadya* is a vegetarian smorgasbord of curries, chutneys, fruit and nuts, little hills of colour and flavour, presented in meticulous order on a banana leaf. Perpetually packed, on feast days and other days, the Coconut Lagoon is an oasis of calm, civilized service on busy St. Laurent Boulevard. It is also, inarguably, Ottawa's finest Indian restaurant. Chef Joe Thottungal comes to his own restaurant via Kerala, where he was born, and Mumbai, where he trained. Kitchen jobs took him to Saudi Arabia, and then to Toronto, where his first Canadian post was in chef David Lee's Centro. He worked his way up the food chain with sous chef jobs at the Royal York, Park Hyatt, Windsor Casino and finally at Ottawa's Crowne Plaza hotel, before the dream of his own place became real. Thottungal opened Coconut Lagoon in 2004, determined to imprint Kerala cuisine onto the palates (and hearts) of Ottawa. He does that with old-school hospitality and abundantly flavoured dishes—the vegetable *thali*; the great rounds of crisp dosa, served with sambar or filled with potato masala; the slow-baked Malabar-style biryanis. His Travancore fish curry with black tamarind is gloriously dark flavoured. And then there's the Ontario lamb Thottungal cocoons with Kerala spices in a banana leaf parcel, the dish that propelled him to the podium at the 2015 Gold Medal Plates culinary competition.

853 ST. LAURENT BOULEVARD, 613-742-4444

**Garam masala
(makes ½ cup)**

5 Tbsp fennel seeds

1 Tbsp whole cloves

1 Tbsp whole green
cardamom pods

2 pieces of cinnamon bark,
each 1 inch long

3 whole star anise

Kerala pepper lamb

2 lb boneless lamb leg, cut into
½-inch cubes

4 tsp Indian red chili powder,
divided

2 Tbsp ground turmeric, divided

¾ cup ground coriander, divided

3 Tbsp coarsely crushed black
peppercorns, divided

3 tsp Garam Masala (see here),
divided

1¼ tsp salt, divided

4 cups cold water

½ cup + 2 Tbsp vegetable oil
or more, divided

⅓ cup chopped peeled fresh
ginger

⅓ cup chopped garlic

5 cups chopped onions

3 sprigs fresh curry leaves

2 cups chopped tomatoes

3 Tbsp freshly squeezed lemon
juice

½ Tbsp white sugar

½ cup chopped fresh cilantro
leaves

Serves 4

Kerala Pepper Lamb

Chef says: One of our most popular dishes at the Coconut Lagoon, the lamb is flavoured with Malabar black pepper and served in a rich onion and tomato gravy. Indian curries taste much better if you cook them ahead of time and refrigerate them overnight to allow their flavours to develop. Serve with steamed basmati rice or matta rice (red Kerala), or with Indian flatbreads such as naan or Kerala *paratha*s.

Garam masala In a dry sauté pan, roast all of the spices over low heat for 3 minutes or until the spices become crispy. Transfer the spices to a clean coffee grinder and grind to a fine powder. Set aside. (Make garam masala in small batches so it retains its aroma.)

Kerala pepper lamb Pat lamb dry with paper towels and place the cubes in a large heavy-bottomed pot. Add 1 tsp of the chili powder, 1 Tbsp of the turmeric, ¼ cup of the coriander, 2 Tbsp of the black pepper, 2 tsp of the garam masala and 1 tsp of salt. Add the water and cook over medium heat, covered, for about 1 hour until meat is tender (or use a pressure cooker for faster results).

Heat ¼ cup of the vegetable oil in a sauté pan over medium heat. Add ginger and garlic and cook, stirring, for 1 minute. Add onions and curry leaves and cook, adding more oil as required, until onions are lightly brown. Stir in remaining chili powder, turmeric, coriander, black pepper, garam masala and salt. The vegetable oil will become cloudy. Keep stirring, and when the oil becomes clear, in about 2 minutes, the spices are cooked. Add tomatoes and cook for about 10 minutes. Stir in cooked lamb with about half the liquid, and let it simmer for another 15 minutes, until the sauce is thick. Add remaining stock. Cover and refrigerate the curry for 12 hours to allow the flavours to meld.

To serve Reheat the curry over medium heat until hot. Stir in lemon juice and sugar. Scoop the hot curry into a large serving dish and sprinkle with chopped cilantro. Serve family-style.

2 tsp salt, divided

3 Tbsp freshly squeezed lime juice, divided

2 lb fresh shrimp (16 to 21), peeled and deveined, tails on

½ cup coconut oil

1 Tbsp green cardamom seeds, cracked

¼ cup finely sliced (julienned) peeled fresh ginger

¼ cup finely sliced (julienned) garlic

2 to 4 Thai green chilies, cut in half lengthwise, with seeds or without (to taste)

2 sprigs fresh curry leaves, washed

2 onions, each cut into 4 wedges

½ Tbsp ground turmeric

1 cup cold water

2 cups coconut milk (preferably freshly made or organic)

1 tomato, cut into wedges

1 green bell pepper, cut into wedges

Serves 4

Shrimp Moilee

Chef says: Moilee is an authentic dish from Kerala, a mild ginger and coconut curry traditionally cooked with seafood and served with *appam*—a traditional thin and lacey rice flour pancake—or with Kerala rice. You can find red Kerala, or matta rice, in South Indian or Sri Lankan grocery stores or serve with steamed basmati rice instead. Start marinating the shrimp at least six hours before you want to serve the moilee.

In a medium bowl, combine 1 tsp of the salt and 1 Tbsp of the lime juice. Stir in the shrimp, cover and refrigerate for 6 hours.

In a large frying pan over medium heat, heat coconut oil. Add cardamom and cook for about 1 minute to infuse the oil with its flavour. Stir in ginger, garlic, chilies and curry leaves and, when slightly browned, add onions and cook until softened, about 5 minutes. Stir in turmeric until the raw smell disappears, about 30 seconds. Add

shrimp and water and cook just until the shrimp begin to turn pink, about 2 minutes. Pour in coconut milk and simmer for 2 minutes. Season with remaining 1 tsp of salt (or to taste) and remaining 2 Tbsp of lime juice. Add tomatoes and bell peppers and stir to combine. Arrange on a serving platter and serve family-style.

DiVino
Cristian Lepore

FOOD PLAYED second fiddle when DiVino first opened. The city's first enomatic took centre stage, as did the wine school and tasting rooms. Not so now. The cuisine at this wine bar has caught up in a big way. With chef Cristian Lepore on board, you might say DiVino is now a solidly good restaurant for wine lovers, its cuisine founded on a respect for regional Italian ingredients in dishes with thoroughly modern twists. Under the supervision of co-owner and sommelier Eric Diotte, each of those dishes is paired with a wine suggestion from a curated selection of Italian and Ontario bottles. It was DiVino's founder, Antonio Mauriello, who brought Lepore on board. He had met him as a toddler, making pasta with his mother in his family's trattoria in Ardea, south of Rome. After Lepore had been working for a year at a Michelin-starred restaurant in Rome, Mauriello sent for him. He arrived in Ottawa three years ago, speaking no English. Working in DiVino's open kitchen helps the English along and affords his fans a front-seat view of the kitchen team at work: plating crunchy-soft cuttlefish with a sharp caponata; seared scarmorza cheese and prosciutto di Parma with poached figs bathed in balsamic; and house-made fettuccine carbonara, the egg custard khakied with avocado. For dessert, Lepore delivers Ottawa Valley maple syrup to Italian custard, with a bronzed toque of rosemary meringue. And Diotte pours a complex vin santo to match. 225 PRESTON STREET, 613-221-9760

facing: **Avocado Gnocchi with Heirloom Tomato Velvet, Herb Pesto and Burrata**

Chef says: Gnocchi is an amazingly simple dish that is difficult to execute. It requires practice. This dish is a play on a few Italian classics melded together with flavours that complement each other... and with an avocado twist! Burrata is a cheese that can best be described as seductive, and one of our guilty pleasures at DiVino. It must be eaten fresh and can be found at most good Italian markets. Use the ripest tomatoes you can find for the sauce, and be sure to cook the gnocchi such that they hold their shape but are soft enough to be squished in your mouth without using your teeth. Practise!

Serves 4 as a main, 6 as a starter

Avocado Gnocchi with Heirloom Tomato Velvet, Herb Pesto and Burrata

Tomato velvet Fill a large bowl with ice water. Bring a medium pot of water to a boil. With a sharp knife, cut an X into the bottom of each tomato. Blanch the tomatoes in boiling water for about 1 minute, then using a slotted spoon, transfer them to the bowl of ice water. When they are cool enough to handle, peel and discard the skins.

Dice tomatoes and place them in a blender. Add olive oil and blend at medium speed until smooth and velvety. For an even smoother sauce, strain through a fine-mesh sieve into a clean pot; discard solids. If the sauce is a bit thin, set it over medium-low heat and cook for 2 minutes, until reduced slightly.

Herb pesto Using a mortar and pestle, pound all of the ingredients except olive oil until well mashed. Add olive oil and stir quickly until incorporated. Transfer to an airtight container and refrigerate until ready to use. (Will keep for a week.)

Avocado gnocchi On a clean work surface, make a well with the flour. Using a potato ricer, rice the avocado into the centre of the well. (If you don't have a ricer, use a food mill, or use a spatula to push the avocado through a colander. But a ricer will give the best results.) Add egg yolk and a pinch of salt.

Using your hands, slowly incorporate the flour into the avocado-egg mixture, kneading the dough just enough for it to come together (the dough should have a loose, airy texture; it should not be gooey or dense).

Divide the dough into 4 equal portions and coat each with a bit of flour. Using your hands, roll each part gently, with splayed fingers, into a rope about ½ inch in diameter.

Using a pastry cutter or a non-serrated knife, cut the dough ropes into ½-inch pieces (you should have about 15 pieces per rope). Toss the gnocchi with extra flour, place on a baking sheet and set aside in a cool place to prevent sticking. (Gnocchi can also be frozen. Arrange them in a

Tomato velvet

3 medium heirloom tomatoes

2 Tbsp olive oil

Herb pesto

15 fresh basil leaves

1 Tbsp chopped fresh cilantro
  leaves

1 clove garlic

1 Tbsp Parmigiano-Reggiano
  cheese

1 Tbsp pine nuts

3 Tbsp extra-virgin olive oil

Avocado gnocchi

1 cup all-purpose flour + more
  for dusting

4 medium avocados, pitted
  and peeled

1 egg yolk

Pinch of salt

Extra-virgin olive oil, for sautéing

Garnish

1 ball fresh Burrata cheese,
  torn or cut into small pieces

Highest-quality extra-virgin
  olive oil, for finishing

single layer on a baking sheet, freeze and then transfer to an airtight container. They can be kept frozen for up to 2 weeks.)

To cook the gnocchi, bring a large pot of salted water to a boil. Gently shake any excess flour from gnocchi, add them to the boiling water and cook until they float to the top, 2 to 4 minutes. With a slotted spoon, gently transfer cooked gnocchi to a colander and drain well. Reserve some of the cooking water for the sauce.

To assemble Reheat tomato velvet in a small pot until warmed through. Remove the pesto from the fridge. Heat a sauté pan over medium-high and add a splash of olive oil. Add gnocchi and a couple of spoonfuls of the reserved cooking water and toss until well coated. Turn down the heat to very low as you prepare plates.

To serve Divide the hot tomato velvet among warmed, shallow bowls. Arrange gnocchi around the velvet. Drizzle with the pesto, add three to five pieces of Burrata and finish with a drizzle of the olive oil.

Chef says: The fall and winter months were on our minds when we created this dish. It's flavourful, warming and perfect for Sunday dinner with the family. It may take eight hours to cook the ribs, but most of the work can be done ahead so you can enjoy your company. The recipe serves four, but it can easily be multiplied to feed a bigger family!

Serves 4

Espresso-Cocoa Braised Short Ribs with Roasted Onions and Maple Sweet Potato Mash

Rubbed beef ribs Preheat the oven to 250°F. Remove and discard the silverskin—pull it off yourself or ask your butcher to do this. In a small bowl, combine espresso and cocoa powder and stir well. Using your hands, rub over the ribs to coat.

Heat olive oil in a heavy frying pan over medium-high heat. Add ribs and sear for about 2 minutes per side. Transfer to a large roasting pan.

To the frying pan, add onions, celery and carrots and sauté for about 2 minutes. Deglaze the pan with ½ cup of the red wine, then pour the vegetables and wine on top of the ribs in the roasting pan. Season with salt and pepper to taste, pour in remaining wine and add sage and rosemary. Cover with a lid or a double layer of aluminum foil and roast for 8 hours.

Prepare the onions so you can add them to the oven during the last 4 hours that the beef is roasting.

Roasted onions If you are already roasting the beef, use a 250°F oven. If not, preheat the oven to 450°F. Have ready 4 pieces of aluminum foil, each 12 inches square.

Season onions with salt and pepper to taste. Place 2 onion halves on a clean work surface, cut side up, and place 1 Tbsp of butter and 2 sage leaves on top of each. Set the other halves on top of the butter, cut side down, sandwiching the butter and sage between the halves. Rub the outside of onions with olive oil and set each onion "sandwich" on 2 sheets of foil. Wrap each onion completely, sealing it well so the butter won't escape as it melts. Roast at 250°F for 4 hours or at 450°F for 50 minutes. Remove from the oven and keep warm in the foil.

Rubbed beef ribs

4 lb beef short ribs (1.6 kg),
    about 14 oz per chop
2 Tbsp freshly ground espresso beans
2 Tbsp unsweetened cocoa powder
¼ cup extra-virgin olive oil
1 onion, chopped
1 stalk celery, chopped
1 carrot, chopped
4¼ cups red wine, divided
Salt and freshly ground black pepper
8 fresh sage leaves
1 sprig of fresh rosemary

Roasted onions

2 medium onions, cut in half
Salt and freshly ground black
    pepper
2 Tbsp butter
4 fresh sage leaves
2 Tbsp olive oil

Sweet potato mash

3 sweet potatoes, peeled and cut
    into 1-inch cubes
2 Tbsp butter
3 Tbsp amber maple syrup
1 Tbsp finely chopped fresh sage
Salt and freshly ground black
    pepper

Garnish

Dark (60%) chocolate
Rock salt

Sweet potato mash Bring a medium pot of salted water to a boil. Add potatoes and cook until soft; drain excess water from the pot. Mash potatoes with a fork or using a ricer, and whisk in butter, maple syrup, sage and salt and pepper to taste. Cover with a lid or foil to keep warm.

To serve Place a scoop of the sweet potato mash in the centre of four warmed plates. Add a roasted onion half, a beef rib and a spoonful of the hot rib jus. Using a rasp, grate a bit of dark chocolate over each plate and finish with a sprinkle of rock salt.

Edgar
Marysol Foucault

EDGAR IS THE diminutive Gatineau restaurant owned by the diminutive Marysol Foucault, and both pack huge punches. Few eateries in the National Capital Region have so captured people's hearts. Be prepared to queue for one of Edgar's thirteen seats (twenty more on a summer patio), particularly for the walloping good brunch. When Foucault opened Edgar in 2010, it marked a return to her roots. She grew up in this Gatineau community and her goal was to give back. Edgar was her dad, whose work in restaurants secured her summer jobs. ("He knew which ones were nice, where he could trust they'd treat his eighty-pound daughter well.") Foucault delights in how the name confuses people. "So where's Edgar?" they ask, eyeing this teeny woman. They won't find any shortage of heart and soul poured into the food here. Every seasonally inspired, rooftop garden–sourced dish, every prim cookie and sticky bun, every wintry meat pie and summery salad on a menu that changes daily is utterly good. "A daily menu's important to me," the Gold Medal Plates winner says. "I don't like being comfortable." This extends to rising every weekend morning at four to start the work of churning out, in the cheek-by-jowl open kitchen, 165 brunches on any given Sunday. That's a kitchen Edgar would surely have trusted.

60 RUE BÉGIN, GATINEAU, QC, 819-205-1110

Pâte brisée

1¼ cups all-purpose flour
+ more for dusting

½ cup cold unsalted butter, cubed

Pinch of salt

½ cup iced water

2 sprigs fresh thyme, leaves picked

Tomato filling

5 medium to large ripe tomatoes

Freshly cracked black pepper

3 cups diced bread (multigrain, if possible, for added taste and texture)

4 cloves garlic

1 tsp kosher salt

1 cup fresh basil leaves

1 cup fresh flat-leaf (Italian) parsley leaves

¼ cup mixed fresh herbs (rosemary, thyme, tarragon are delicious)

⅓ cup good-quality olive oil

½ cup freshly grated Parmesan cheese

2 cups shredded mozzarella cheese, divided

Serves 4 to 6 as main course (Makes one 9-inch pie)

Rustic Tomato Tart

Chef says: This tart is best when made at peak tomato season, but it can also be made off-season with a firm tomato like a Roma. The recipe is extremely versatile: vary the herbs; add pine nuts or goat cheese; even substitute the tomatoes with zucchini squash!

Pâte brisée In the bowl of a food processor fitted with the blade, pulse flour, butter and salt until it resembles coarse meal. Slowly add some of the iced water through the feed tube and keep processing until the dough just starts to pull together and form a ball, about 1 minute. Add thyme and pulse one last time (the dough should still be lightly crumbly). Gather dough and shape into a ball. Wrap loosely in plastic wrap and flatten into a round disc. Refrigerate for at least 30 minutes before rolling. (This step can be done up to 2 days in advance.)

Line a clean work surface with parchment paper and lightly dust with flour. Have ready a 9-inch pie plate. Using a rolling pin dusted with flour, roll out the chilled dough into a circle about 14 inches in diameter and ¼ inch thick. Dust the rolling pin with more flour, so it doesn't stick to or tear the dough. Wrap the dough around the rolling pin, transfer it to the pie plate and gently press the dough into the sides and bottom to ensure it does not slide as you layer in the filling. If you are not ready to fill the tart, cover with plastic wrap and refrigerate the unbaked crust until ready.

Tomato filling Position a rack in the centre of the oven and preheat to 350°F. Line a baking sheet with parchment paper.

With a sharp knife, cut tomatoes into ½-inch slices. Arrange the slices in a single layer on the baking sheet, top with freshly cracked pepper and roast for 30 to 40 minutes or until the tomatoes start to dry out a bit. Remove from the oven and let cool on basin sheet at room temperature.

In the bowl of a food processor fitted with the metal blade, combine bread, garlic, salt, basil, parsley and mixed herbs. Pulse and slowly add olive oil until you have a crumbly paste (it should not be smooth). Divide the bread-herb paste evenly among 4 small bowls.

In another bowl, combine Parmesan and ½ cup of the mozzarella.

Spread the bread-herb paste from one bowl over the bottom of the tart shell, then top with one-third of the tomatoes followed by ½ cup of the mozzarella. Repeat this layering of bread-herb paste, tomatoes and mozzarella 2 more times. Finish with the reserved Parmesan-mozzarella mixture and remaining bowl of bread-herb paste. Bake the tart in the preheated oven for 30 to 45 minutes or until golden brown on top.

To serve Serve warm or at room temperature.

Brioche dough

2 cups all-purpose flour +
  more for dusting
1 tsp salt
1 Tbsp instant yeast
½ cup white sugar
4 large eggs
1 cup unsalted butter, room
  temperature, roughly chopped
  + extra for greasing the pan
Zest of 1 orange

Fig and pistachio filling

1½ cups chopped dried figs
1 cup raisins
¾ cup orange juice (freshly
  squeezed or store-bought)
1 cup chopped unsalted pistachios
½ cup chopped walnuts
Zest of 1 orange
Zest of 1 lemon
½ cup packed brown sugar
½ cup butter, room temperature, cubed
¼ cup chopped crystallized ginger
1 egg
½ cup liquid honey

Makes 12

Fig and Pistachio Brioches

Chef says: I love baklava, and I also love soft buttery brioche—this is the best of both worlds. Prepare the dough the day before you will serve these.

Brioche dough In the bowl of a stand mixer fitted with the hook attachment, blend flour, salt, yeast and sugar. With the motor running at low speed, incorporate eggs, one at a time, until the dough starts to form a ball, about 2 minutes. Add butter, one knob at a time, until the dough becomes smooth, about 5 minutes. Mix in orange zest. Cover the bowl and set aside in a warm place until the dough doubles in size, about 3 hours.

Have ready a 24-inch × 18-inch piece of plastic wrap, lightly dusted with flour. Lightly dust a clean work surface with flour. Remove the dough from the bowl, punch it down, shape it into a ball and place it on the plastic wrap. Wrap very loosely but completely (the dough will expand overnight) and refrigerate for at least 12 hours or for up to 3 days.

Fig and pistachio filling Place figs and raisins in an airtight container, add orange juice and refrigerate for at least 4 hours or, ideally, overnight. Drain.

In a medium bowl and using a wooden spoon, combine soaked figs and raisins, pistachios, walnuts, orange and lemon zests, brown sugar, butter and crystallized ginger and stir until well incorporated. Set aside.

Finish brioches Lightly grease a 12-cup muffin pan with butter. Dust a large clean work surface with flour. Remove and discard the plastic wrap from the dough.

Using a rolling pin, roll out the dough to an 18-inch × 16-inch rectangle, with a shorter edge facing you. Sprinkle the fig mixture evenly over the dough. Starting at the edge closest to you, roll up the dough as tightly as you can, enclosing the filling (you should have a log 16 inches long and about 3 inches in diameter). Using a very sharp knife, cut the dough into 12 even rounds. Gently place one round in each muffin cup. Let rise in a warm place for about 20 minutes or until the dough expands.

Preheat the oven to 350°F. In a small bowl, beat egg with about 1 Tbsp of water and gently brush the top of each brioche. Bake for 15 minutes or until the tops are golden brown. While the brioches are still warm and using an offset spatula, gently unmould the brioches from the muffin cups, transfer to a plate and drizzle with honey. Ideally, serve warm from the oven!

e18hteen
Kirk Morrison

WHEN YOU'RE in the mood for glamorous dining, head for this York Street beauty. Many restaurants swing in and out of vogue, but e18hteen has enduring appeal. Large, split-levelled, blessed with high ceilings and fine bones, it was a stunner from Day One, but its glamorous remodelling reminds us what a stunner it continues to be. E18hteen is simply one of the city's very finest places to eat and drink: chic, stylish, with calm, capable service, a very fine cellar and a seasonal cuisine that makes best use of superb ingredients. Chef de cuisine Kirk Morrison presents those ingredients in ways that make you rethink what you thought you knew about them. His food is ambitious, and sublimely artful in presentation. By way of prelude, order oysters with the kitchen's daily mignonette. And then head for the partridge, its gaminess intact in a rustic ballantine with walnuts and Brussels sprouts. Or lamb two ways, one of which comes as a rich stew spiked with Merguez sausage. The Reserve Angus Triple A beef tenderloin with classic bordelaise sauce is superb, ordered with a fragrant sauté of Le Coprin mushrooms and bang-on pommes frites—though it might not allow room for one of e18hteen's inventive desserts. Which would be a shame. 18 YORK STREET, 613-244-1188

facing: **Chicken Liver Mousse with Grilled Flatbread and Sprouted Salad**

Serves 8

Chicken Liver Mousse with Grilled Flatbread and Sprouted Salad

Sprouted salad Rinse legumes gently and separately under cold running water for 3 minutes. Place lentils in one Mason jar and pea seeds in another, filling each one no more than one-quarter full (using a second jar for each, if necessary). Fill each jar with cold filtered water to about three-quarters full. Seal the lids tightly and set the jars in a cool, dark place for 24 hours.

Have ready a large baking sheet, a tea towel and some plastic wrap for each Mason jar. Drain the lentils and peas, separately, in a colander, and rinse again under cold running water for 3 minutes. Soak the tea towels, wring them semi-dry and use them to line the baking sheets. Spread lentils and peas in a single layer on separate tea towels, using your fingers to gently space them apart. Wrap tightly with plastic wrap and poke a few holes in the top so that air can circulate. Place the baking sheets on a windowsill or in a place where they will receive some natural light for 24 hours.

After 24 hours, remove the plastic wrap. The legumes should be starting to sprout a little (you will notice a little white "arm" starting to push through the outer skin). Carefully repeat the process of rinsing, wrapping with fresh plastic wrap, poking holes for air circulation, and placing on a windowsill for a further 24 hours.

Rinse the legumes one final time. You can now place them in a resealable plastic bag with a dry paper towel inside. (Will keep refrigerated for about 1 week.)

Chicken liver mousse Heat a heavy-bottomed skillet or frying pan over medium heat. Add canola oil and 1 Tbsp of cold butter and heat until butter melts. Stir in onions and sage, turn down the heat to medium-low and cook, gently stirring with a wooden spoon, until onions are fully coated with the fat and turn soft and translucent, about 15 minutes. Transfer cooked onions to a small bowl and set aside.

Return the pan to the stove and increase the heat to medium-high. Add chicken livers and sear for about 2 minutes per side. Stir in cooked onions. Remove the pan from the heat, very carefully add brandy and return to the stove (removing the pan from the stove makes it less likely that the brandy will catch fire; however, if it does, wait for the alcohol to burn off and the flames will die down); cook until the liquid is reduced by half. Remove the pan from the stove and let mixture cool to room temperature.

Sprouted salad

½ cup organic beluga lentils
½ cup organic dried pea seeds, for planting
Cold water (filtered is best)
4 oz baby arugula
½ bunch fresh flat-leaf (Italian) parsley, large stems discarded
1 Tbsp good-quality olive oil + extra for dressing the greens

Chicken liver mousse

2 Tbsp canola oil
1 Tbsp cold unsalted butter and ¼ cup + 1 tsp unsalted butter, room temperature
1 medium onion, thinly sliced
5 large fresh sage leaves
4 oz (¼ lb) chicken livers, cleaned (ask your butcher to do this)
½ cup brandy
2 Tbsp red wine vinegar (or more to taste)
Salt and freshly ground black pepper
2 oz your favourite pickled vegetables (dills, asparagus, onions), for garnish

Flatbreads

½ tsp active dry yeast
⅛ cup warm water
1⅛ cups all-purpose flour + extra for dusting
½ tsp salt
2 Tbsp canola oil
1 tsp olive oil

Garnish

1 tsp aged balsamic vinegar (at least 8 to 10 years)
Large flake sea salt
Freshly cracked black pepper

Transfer the chicken liver mixture to a high-speed blender (or a food processor fitted with the metal blade). Add the room temperature butter and vinegar, and season with salt and pepper to taste; process at high speed until smooth. Using a spatula, scrape the mousse into a pastry bag fitted with the star nozzle, or a large resealable plastic bag. Refrigerate for at least 12 hours or, better, overnight.

Flatbreads In a small bowl, combine yeast and warm water. Let rest until you see little air bubbles and foam appear on the surface indicating the yeast has bloomed, about 5 minutes.

In the bowl of a stand mixer fitted with the dough hook, combine flour, salt and canola and olive oils. Mix at low speed for 2 minutes. Add the bloomed yeast and water and mix at low speed for another 3 minutes. (If you don't have a stand mixer, combine the ingredients in a bowl with a wooden spoon.)

Dust a clean work surface with flour. Place the dough on the floured surface and knead by hand for 3 to 5 minutes. Gently shape dough into a ball and cover with a dry tea towel; let rest for 9 to 12 minutes.

While the dough is resting, preheat an outdoor grill to medium-high. (If you don't have access to an outdoor grill, cook the flatbreads in a large non-stick pan on the stove over medium-high heat.)

Using a rolling pin, roll the dough into a rectangle, about ⅛ inch thick. Cut the dough into 3-inch squares, place them on the grill and cook for 2 to 3 minutes per side or until cooked through and lined with light char marks.

Finish sprouted salad In a medium bowl, combine the sprouted legumes, arugula, parsley leaves, a little drizzle of olive oil and salt until well mixed.

To serve With the pastry bag or the resealable plastic bag with a corner cut out, pipe three coin-size dollops of chicken liver mousse on one side of each plate. Arrange the pickled vegetables randomly around each plate. In the centre, place a tall mound of the salad. Break the flatbreads by hand into rough pieces and lean them up against the salad. Garnish each serving with a good drizzle of olive oil and aged balsamic, and season with salt and pepper to taste.

Chef says: If you are looking to make a great impression at your next dinner party or are hoping to woo your next date, this elegant soup is the right choice. It takes the familiar flavours of a great baked oyster and presents them in a new and playful way. Master this, and everyone will want to learn how you did it.

You can ask your local cheesemonger for Parmesan rinds or save up your own in a resealable plastic bag in the freezer. Check with your butcher for bacon ends or skin, which are usually cheaper to buy than the bacon itself. The consommé is best made the day before you plan to serve it.

Serves 8

Smoked Pork and Parmesan Consommé with Malpeque Oysters and Dill Purée

Consommé Place Parmesan rinds, bacon, celery, onions, carrots, bay leaves, peppercorns and garlic in a large heavy-bottomed stockpot and cover with water. Bring to a simmer over medium-high heat, being careful not to let it boil or consommé will turn cloudy. Turn down the heat to medium-low and simmer gently for 2 hours. Turn off the heat and let cool on the stovetop for 30 minutes.

Strain the mixture through a fine-mesh sieve into a clean bowl so that you are left with a beautifully clear golden liquid; discard solids. Season with salt and pepper to taste.

Dill purée Fill a third of a large pot with water and bring to a boil. While the water is heating, pick the dill fronds off their stems. Make an ice bath by placing equal parts cold water and ice in a large bowl.

Add dill to the boiling water and blanch for 20 seconds. Using a fine-mesh sieve, transfer dill first to the ice bath to cool, then to a high-speed blender. Add lemon zest and juice and blend at high speed until very smooth. If the dill is too thick to blend, add 1 tsp of cold water and blend again. If it is still too thick, add more water, 1 tsp at a time, until it's the desired consistency. Season with salt to taste. Scrape the purée into a kitchen squeeze bottle or a small bowl. Set aside until ready to use.

Consommé

2 lb Parmesan rinds
2 lb bacon ends and skin
2 stalks celery, roughly chopped
1 large yellow onion, roughly chopped
2 large carrots, roughly chopped
3 bay leaves
1 tsp black peppercorns
3 cloves garlic
1 gallon (16 cups) cold water
Salt and freshly ground white pepper

Dill purée

1 bunch fresh dill
Zest and juice of 1 lemon
Salt

Garnish

4 oz spinach, trimmed and thinly sliced
8 Malpeque oysters
Maldon sea salt
1 red radish, sliced very thinly with
   a knife or mandolin
4 tsp good-quality olive oil, divided

To serve Bring consommé to a gentle simmer over medium heat. In the bottom of eight soup bowls, make equal-size nests of spinach. Shuck oysters and place one on top of the spinach in each bowl, sprinkling the top of the oyster with a pinch of salt. Arrange two to three slices of radish around the oysters. Finish each serving with a half teaspoon of olive oil and four to six dots of the dill purée (from the squeeze bottle or with a teaspoon). Place the consommé in a heatproof decanter. Set the bowls in front of your guests and slowly pour in the hot consommé.

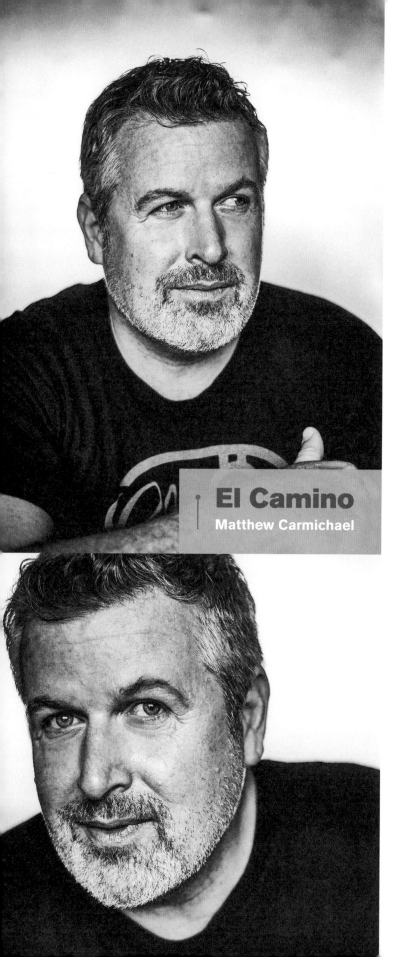

El Camino
Matthew Carmichael

THERE ARE TWO queues this fall night. One at El Camino's take-away, cash-only window, the other up the Elgin Street stairs awaiting a seat in the underground restaurant. El Camino serves creative Mexican food with Canadian content and dashing style from five thirty to close, and the city can't seem to get enough of it. After years of honing his craft with some of the culinary giants in the country—John Taylor, Susur Lee, David Lee—and running some of the most acclaimed restaurants in the city—notably e18hteen, Social and Sidedoor—Matt Carmichael switched gears. He opened a taqueria. Some of us were gob-smacked. For a guy known for some of the finest of fine dining in this town, this fork-optional basement thing didn't fit. And then we tasted the food, and it did. The rigorous technique learned in high-end kitchens was in clear evidence. With chef de cuisine Jordan Holley running the team, El Camino plates intensely flavoured takes on Mexican street food: summer squash blossoms stuffed with queso fresco and chorizo, served with revved-up corn sauce; chilaquiles topped with aromatic pork; albacore tuna ceviche with grilled coconut. Some come just for the crunchy-soft churros with salted caramel. The cocktail list is long and strong here, and the menu is constantly evolving. The El Camino team has now opened a second restaurant in the space next door. Named for another vintage car Carmichael's keen on, the new spot—Datsun—is no Edsel. 380 ELGIN STREET, 613-422-2800

Chef says: When we opened El Camino, we had some tongue in the walk-in fridge. Our plan was to make a taco with it, but we chickened out. We didn't think people would go for it. But a few early El Camino guests talked us back into the plan, so we ran an ox tongue taco as a special one day. It became apparent pretty fast that we had a winner, and now it's one of our most popular tacos. And also my favourite. Ox, by the way, is just another name for beef. Don't be confused—we just like the way "ox tongue" sounds on the menu!

Serves 4 to 6 (Makes 8 to 12 tacos)

Ox Tongue Tacos with Ranchero Sauce

Ranchero sauce Place ancho and guajillo peppers in a medium bowl, add just enough room temperature water to cover and soak for 1 hour or until chilies are soft. Transfer the chili peppers to a small bowl, squeezing out any extra liquid. Reserve this soaking water to thin out the blended sauce.

Preheat a barbecue or indoor grill to high. Place Roma tomatoes, onions and serrano peppers directly on the grill and cook, turning them several times, until blackened all over.

Place the rehydrated chili peppers and charred vegetables in a large bowl. Add canned tomatoes, bird's-eye chilies, garlic, cilantro, chipotle peppers and lime juice and stir until well combined. Season with salt to taste and let sit for 30 minutes.

Transfer the ranchero ingredients to a blender and process at medium speed until smooth (the sauce should have the consistency of a smoothie; if it is too thick, add a bit more of the reserved soaking water or the tomato juice). Refrigerate leftovers in an airtight container for up to 1 month or freeze for up to 3 months.

Ox tongue Place tongue in a large pot and fill with enough water to cover it by 2 inches. Simmer tongue over medium-low heat, adding more water if required, for 4 to 5 hours. The tongue should feel soft, giving easily to pressure from a finger. It shouldn't have a "rubbery" or bouncy feel when handled.

Ranchero sauce

6 to 8 dried ancho chili peppers

6 to 8 dried guajillo chili peppers

3 fresh ripe Roma tomatoes

2 sweet onions

4 serrano chili peppers

1 large can (28 oz) whole tomatoes, preferably San Marzano, drained but liquid reserved

8 bird's-eye chili peppers, chopped

6 cloves garlic (the best you can find)

½ cup chopped fresh cilantro leaves

½ can (7 oz) chipotle peppers in adobo, sauce reserved

½ cup freshly squeezed lime juice

Salt

Ox tongue tacos

1 large beef tongue, about 3 lb

Extra-virgin olive oil, for brushing

Salt and freshly cracked black pepper

8 to 12 store-bought corn tortillas (4 inches in diameter), from your local Latin mercado

Ranchero Sauce (see here)

1 avocado, sliced or mashed

Sliced, pickled jalapeño peppers, drained

1 radish, sliced

1 or 2 limes, cut into wedges

Lots of roughly chopped fresh cilantro leaves

Drain tongue, place in a bowl and cover with plastic wrap (this will help release the sheath, or outer layer of skin). While still warm but cool enough to handle, use your fingers to remove and discard all the outer membrane (it should peel away easily; if it does not, it has not been cooked enough). You can do this step a day ahead. If you are planning to use the tongue right away, chill it for at least 2 hours so the muscle completely cools and sets, which makes the meat firmer and easier to slice.

Place the cooled tongue on a cutting board. Using a sharp knife and beginning at the back (the thicker end), cut slices no thicker than ½ inch across the width of the tongue.

Preheat a barbecue or indoor grill to its highest temperature. Brush the tongue slices with a little olive oil, season with salt and pepper and grill on both sides until nicely coloured. Remove from the grill, and set aside.

Warm tortillas in a dry cast-iron skillet over medium heat, or toast them directly on the grill. If you are not using them immediately, wrap them in aluminum foil so they stay warm.

Have ready all of the taco fixings in individual bowls. Place warm tortillas on a clean work surface. Add a few slices of tongue and garnish with ranchero sauce, one or two slices of avocado (or mashed avocado), pickled jalapeño, sliced radish, lime juice and cilantro. Try to make sure every bite has a bit of everything in it. Serve immediately.

Avocado mash

3 to 4 medium avocados

Juice of 1 lime

1 shallot, very finely minced

1 bunch fresh cilantro, leaves picked and chopped

Maldon sea salt

Wild salmon tartare tostadas

8 to 18 oz sashimi-grade boneless wild BC Pacific salmon fillet, cut in large dice (2 to 3 oz per person)

Maldon sea salt

Juice of 1 lime

2 cups mayonnaise (we use Hellman's)

3 Tbsp (or to taste) fermented chili paste or *toban djan* (Sichuanese chili bean sauce)

1 small shallot, finely minced

Snipped fresh chives

4 to 6 corn tortillas, each 6 inches in diameter (buy pre-fried from your Latin mercado)

Handful of store-bought natural pickled ginger (not the pink stuff!)

1 radish, sliced into rounds

1 bunch fresh Thai basil leaves

Chopped fresh cilantro leaves

Lime wedges

Serves 4 to 6 as an appetizer

Wild Salmon Tartare Tostadas with Funky Chili Mayo

Chef says: We use whatever wild salmon we can get from our friends Handsome Frank and Sumo from Organic Oceans in British Columbia. We recommend searching for Ocean Wise—designated sustainably harvested fish, the freshest you can find. Ask the people at the fish counter what they recommend—if not salmon, this tartare recipe also works well with trout, mackerel and albacore tuna. I prefer to dice the flesh fairly large and hit it first with the salt, then after a few minutes I hit it again with the fresh lime juice and let it sit for 5 minutes or so. This method will quickly cure and season the fish before the mayonnaise is added. Keep the fish cold until you're ready to use it.

Avocado mash Cut avocados in half and scoop out the flesh into a medium bowl. With a fork, mash avocado until slightly chunky. Add lime juice, shallots and cilantro and stir until well combined. Season with salt to taste. Cover and refrigerate until needed.

Wild salmon tartare tostadas In a medium bowl, combine diced salmon and salt and let sit for 5 minutes. Stir in lime juice and let sit for a further 5 minutes.

In a second bowl, combine mayonnaise and 2 heaping Tbsp chili paste and mix well. Taste and add more chili paste, bit by bit, mixing well after each addition, until you have a good balance of hot and salty (the mixture should be a salmon colour).

When the raw salmon has turned slightly opaque and "cooked" in the lime juice, gently stir in the chili mayonnaise, shallots and chives.

Warm tortillas in a dry pan over medium-low heat until lightly crispy.

To assemble Set the warm, crispy tortillas on a clean work surface. Spread a thin layer of the avocado mash on each, followed by a few dollops of the salmon mixture. Place some pickled ginger on top so that each bite gets a push from the sweet and spicy ginger. Garnish with a few slices of radish, followed by a few sprigs of basil and some cilantro. Be sure there isn't too much on each tortilla, as you don't want the flavour of the corn and the crunch to get lost. Serve with a wedge of lime.

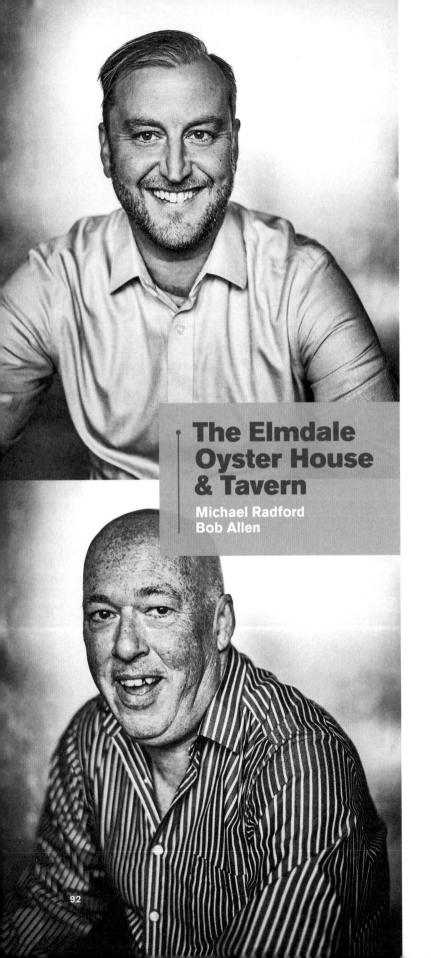

The Elmdale Oyster House & Tavern

**Michael Radford
Bob Allen**

YOU CAN FEEL the ghosts at this tavern—though thankfully just in the building, not in the grub it offers. The spirits are welcome, though: they keep alive the eight-decade story of this place. When the owners of The Elmdale House were ready to hang up the tavern towel, they approached the crew from The Whalesbone (page 214). Its co-owner Joshua Bishop had a long-held affection for the old place and its Hintonburg 'hood. The team rebuilt the bar and put in a proper kitchen, giving the old rooms a bit of a redirect, but otherwise this is still The Elmdale House Tavern, only now with food worth honouring—a craft beer list, too, and Bloody Caesars that double as meal replacements. Executive chef Michael Radford splits his time running both oyster houses. The starters he and day cook Bob Allen dream up run from luscious salmon gravlax to steamed mussels paddling in a citrus-soy bath. Oysters, of course, served on metal trays with yummy potions. Or go straight to the 'Tasty Fried Stuff' section of the menu—saltfish fritters, crunchy-coated shrimp and beer-battered fish. There's a hanger steak and a lovely braised lamb dish for the "no fish, thanks" folk. The live music tradition lives on, five days a week, as do the dance parties (shall we "Shuck 'n Strut"?), and every Saturday night, a different DJ takes the stage. If this is the modern tavern, I'm a believer, and would you please pass the mignonette? 1084 WELLINGTON STREET WEST, 613-728-2848

facing: **Bob's Kickass Lobster Roll and Kettle Chips**

Chef says: I first met Bob Allen when I was just a young cook, keen to learn, and Bob was Chef. We worked alongside each other for many years, Bob always challenging me to push myself. He's been a huge influence in my life as a cook and a friend, and he's taught me more than he'll ever know. We lost touch through the times, but a guy like Bob, you don't forget. About three years ago we became reacquainted; he had taken a break from working in kitchens but thought that he'd like to get back at it. I was just leaving one kitchen for another, but about six months later I gave Bob a call. We've been working together ever since—though this time I'm Chef. Bob always made kickass sandwiches. He still does… This is his kickass lobster roll. (Chef's note: Leftover lobster salad is great served with some iceberg lettuce, avocado, tomato, a little Thousand Islands dressing and some sourdough croutons.)

Serves 12 for lunch (Makes 12 sandwiches)

Bob's Kickass Lobster Roll and Kettle Chips

Brioches In the bowl of a stand mixer fitted with the hook attachment, combine warm milk, sugar, salt and yeast. Let stand for 10 minutes to activate yeast. With the motor running at low speed, add egg and flour and mix for about 5 minutes, until dough starts to come together. Turn off the mixer, cover with a kitchen towel and let the dough proof in the bowl for about 20 minutes.

With the motor running at low speed, start adding butter, a knob at a time, until butter is incorporated and dough is smooth.

Have ready 2 brioche loaf pans, each 10½ inches × 4½ inches × 3½ inches, and 2 large, clear plastic bags. Lightly dust a clean work surface with flour. Turn the dough out and divide it into 2 equal pieces. Shape each piece into a loaf, place it into a pan, wrap in a plastic bag and proof in a warm place until the dough has doubled in size, about 1 hour.

Preheat the oven to 350°F. Brush the proofed loaves with egg wash and bake for 15 minutes. Rotate the pans and continue to bake for another 10 to 15 minutes, until crust is golden brown. Remove pans from the oven and let cool on wire racks. Once cool, cut each loaf into 6 pieces, each the size of a hot dog bun.

Mayonnaise Combine egg yolks, mustard, lemon juice, vinegar and salt in a medium bowl and whisk well for about 30 seconds. Slowly incorporate about ½ cup of the canola oil, a few drops at a time, whisking constantly. (Tip: Place the bowl over a folded kitchen towel to keep it in place while you whisk in the oil.) Whisking continuously, add remaining canola oil in a very steady stream until mayonnaise is thick, about 10 minutes. Season with more salt and Tabasco sauce to taste, and a touch more lemon juice to make it all pop. (Will keep refrigerated in an airtight container for up to 3 days.)

Brioches

330 mL (1⅓ cups) 2% milk, warmed to just below body temperature

27 g (scant 2 Tbsp) white sugar

10 g (2 tsp) salt

10 g (2 tsp) active dry yeast

1 egg, room temperature

550 g (2⅓ cups) all-purpose flour

45 g (3 Tbsp) unsalted butter, room temperature + more for buttering cooked brioches

Egg wash (1 egg + ¼ cup milk), for brushing loaves

Mayonnaise

2 egg yolks

1 tsp Dijon mustard

1 Tbsp freshly squeezed lemon juice, or more to taste

2 tsp white vinegar

1 tsp salt + to taste

2 cups canola oil

Dash of red Tabasco sauce

Lobster salad

1 cup kosher salt, for boiling lobsters

4 fresh Atlantic lobsters, each 1¼ lb

1 cup minced celery

1 cup peeled, cored and diced apples

½ cup chopped mixed fresh herbs (any combination of chervil, dill, parsley, tarragon, chives)

¼ cup minced shallots

¾ cup Mayonnaise (see here)

Salt and freshly ground black pepper

Freshly squeezed lemon juice

Kettle chips

6 medium russet potatoes, washed well

3 Tbsp kosher salt + more for seasoning

2 qt canola oil, for deep-frying

Lobster salad To cook lobsters, fill a large stockpot (12 to 15 qt) three-quarters full with water, add kosher salt and bring to a hard boil. Fill a second large stockpot or roasting pan with ice water.

Once the water comes to a hard boil, set a timer for 8 minutes. Place lobsters in the pot and immediately remove the pot from the heat. Once the timer dings, place lobsters in the ice bath to shock them and stop the meat from cooking further. Let cool completely in the water.

Using lobster crackers, remove the meat from the tails, knuckles and claws (suck all yummy juices off the little legs while you're doing this—chefs need to taste what they're cooking, after all). Place the lobster meat in a bowl and refrigerate while you assemble remaining ingredients for the lobster salad.

To assemble the salad, remove the bowl of lobster meat from the fridge. Add celery, apple, chopped herbs, shallots and mayonnaise. Stir until just combined and season with salt and pepper to taste and a splash of lemon juice. Refrigerate until ready to serve.

Kettle chips Fill a large bowl with ice water. Using a food processor fitted with the slicer attachment (or using a mandolin), slice potatoes paper thin into the ice water. Drain and rinse potato slices. Fill a large bowl with cold water, add 3 Tbsp of salt and potato slices and let soak for about 30 minutes. Drain potatoes and pat dry as best you can.

Heat canola oil in a medium, heavy-bottomed pot over medium-high heat until it reaches 325°F (use a deep-fry thermometer to test the temperature). Line a large plate with paper towels. When the oil is ready, add potatoes in small batches and fry until golden brown. Using a slotted spoon, transfer chips to the lined plate to drain. Continue frying potatoes in batches until all of them are cooked. Season chips with a few dashes of salt.

To serve Lightly butter the cut sides of the brioche buns and toast until golden brown and crispy. Cut a shallow V-shaped wedge the length of each bun, then spoon in the lobster salad. Serve with kettle chips.

3 cups kosher salt, for lining
   the baking sheet
2 to 3 dozen oysters, freshly shucked
1 cup butter, softened
3 Tbsp minced garlic
⅔ cup minced shallots
¼ cup chopped mixed fresh herbs
   (flat-leaf/Italian parsley, tarragon,
   chervil, dill)
3 oz bourbon (Wild Turkey or other,
   or an Irish whiskey such as Jameson)
1 cup freshly grated cheese (we use
   Monterey Jack and 2-year-old cheddar)
½ cup unseasoned panko bread crumbs

Garnish
¼ cup chopped fresh chives
Lemon wedges
Freshly cracked black pepper

Serves 4 to 6 as an appetizer

Bourbon Butter-Baked Oysters

Chef says: As the executive chef of two Ottawa oyster houses, I generally prefer my oysters raw and naked on the half shell. But when the mood hits me for something a little more decadent, this is what I do. For baked oysters, look for a good meaty, briny East Coast variety with a nice deep cup, like a Cascumpec Bay or Foxley River from PEI, or if you'd prefer something with even more of a punch try oysters from the West Coast, a little less briny but full of amazing sea flavours, like a Marina's Gold or a Sea Angel. West Coast oysters tend to be a little more delicate and brittle, so be careful of the shells when you are popping the hinges.

Position a rack in the middle of the oven and preheat the broiler. In a large bowl, combine salt with ½ cup water to make "wet salt." Spread this wet salt over a baking sheet and place shucked oysters (in their shells) on top (the wet salt will help keep the oysters upright so they don't lose any of their precious oyster liquor).

In a small bowl, combine butter, garlic, shallots and mixed herbs. Place a small knob (about 1 tsp) of this compound butter over each oyster. Sprinkle a dash of bourbon over all of the oysters and top with cheese. Lightly sprinkle with panko and broil the oysters for 5 minutes or until golden brown and glistening.

To serve Arrange the cooked oysters on a serving platter (or mix up another batch of "wet salt" to anchor the baked oysters to the platter). Garnish with chives, lemon wedges and pepper. Eat them while they're hot.

Erling's Variety

**Jeff Bradfield
Liam Vainola**

Special note: Erling's lost a much-loved member of our kitchen team last year. We dedicate these recipes to Deepak.

A TUCKED-AWAY treat off Bank Street (found if you're clever enough to peek around corners), Erling's is a most welcome addition to the Glebe dining- and drinking-out options. Opened in 2014, the restaurant is named in honour of owner Liam Vainola's Norwegian grandfather. Before running the restaurant, Vainola was a rap musician (formerly known as Flip Kuma) on the local club scene, and though it had been a long-held dream of his to open a restaurant, he first needed to learn the ropes. So he began to flip things other than records, working his way up the ladder in a bunch of Ottawa restaurants until he felt ready to run his own show. Tall and handsome, Erling's Variety is well windowed, warmed with blond wood and good lighting. The eye is drawn to the big art, the fanciful wall of bric-a-brac and the open kitchen show. In that kitchen is Jeff Bradfield, who avails himself of Vainola's kitchen garden, of forest foraging and frog legs (his amphibian play on jerked chicken wings—ooh la la!). Sit at the raw-edged bar and order up his cured meats, including the richly flavoured head cheese served with stylish condiments. There's always a chef's choice scallop dish, or an elegant tartare of beast or fish, and if they ever take the fat, juicy pork chop (brined, smoked and caramelized) off the menu, well... I don't even want to think about it.

225 STRATHCONA AVENUE, 613-231-8484

Jerk sauce

¼ cup freshly squeezed lime juice

¼ cup freshly squeezed orange juice

¼ cup soy sauce

4 green onions, white and green parts, roughly chopped

3 Scotch bonnet peppers, stemmed, seeded and roughly chopped

4 cloves garlic, chopped

1 Tbsp minced peeled ginger

2 Tbsp chopped fresh thyme

2 Tbsp chopped fresh cilantro leaves

2 Tbsp chopped fresh Thai basil leaves

1 Tbsp chopped fresh mint leaves

1½ Tbsp brown sugar

2 tsp ground allspice

½ tsp ground cinnamon

½ tsp ground cloves

1 tsp kosher salt

½ tsp freshly ground black pepper

2 Tbsp apple cider vinegar

Sweet potato purée

1 lb sweet potatoes, peeled and cut in large dice (roughly 3 to 4 medium)

1 Tbsp minced peeled ginger

2 cups coconut milk

1 vanilla bean, split lengthwise and seeds scraped

2 tsp salt

½ tsp freshly ground black pepper

4 oz (½ cup) unsalted butter, cut into cubes

Minted peas

2 cups fresh or thawed frozen peas

2 Tbsp unsalted butter

2 Tbsp very thinly sliced (chiffonade) fresh mint

Salt and freshly ground black pepper

Jerk pork chops

4 pork chops (each 6 oz), bone in or out

Salt and freshly ground black pepper

2 Tbsp canola oil

2 Tbsp unsalted butter

3 Tbsp Jerk Sauce (see here)

Serves 4 to 6

Jerk Pork Chops with Vanilla Sweet Potato and Minted Peas

Chef says: This is a play on several dishes I've made at Erling's, and one of my favourite creations to execute in a home setting.

Jerk sauce Place all of the ingredients in a food processor fitted with the metal blade or blender and process at high speed until smooth.

Sweet potato purée Place sweet potatoes, ginger, coconut milk and vanilla seeds in a medium pot over medium heat. Simmer until sweet potatoes are soft and breaking up. Transfer to a food processor fitted with the metal blade or blender and add salt and pepper. With the motor running at low speed, add butter cubes one at a time, gradually increasing speed, and purée until smooth.

Minted peas In a sauté pan over medium heat, sauté peas with butter, mint and salt and pepper to taste for about 3 minutes. Set aside.

Jerk pork chops Heat a large cast-iron skillet over high heat. Season pork chops liberally with salt and pepper. Turn down the heat to medium, add canola oil and pork chops and sear for about 4 minutes. Turn chops over, add butter and jerk sauce, and cook for another 4 minutes, basting with the butter and sauce. Remove from the heat and let chops rest for 6 minutes.

To serve Warm four to six plates. Make a swoosh with the sweet potatoes on each plate, place the peas inside the swoosh and position the pork chops over top.

Avocado crema

3 medium avocados, cut lengthwise and pitted (reserve pits)
1½ cups chopped fresh cilantro leaves
¾ cup sour cream
3 Tbsp freshly squeezed lime juice
3 Tbsp freshly squeezed orange juice
3 Tbsp olive oil
1½ tsp kosher salt

Blood orange salsa

2 blood oranges, peeled, segmented and juice reserved
½ cup finely diced (brunoise) red onions
½ jalapeño pepper, seeded and minced
2 Tbsp chopped fresh Thai basil leaves
1 Tbsp freshly squeezed lime juice
Salt

Brussels sprouts and edamame

1½ Tbsp canola oil
10 Brussels sprouts, trimmed and cut lengthwise
¼ cup vegetable stock
1 Tbsp unsalted butter
2 cups shelled edamame

Pan-fried pickerel

4 pickerel fillets (each 6 oz), skin on
Salt and freshly ground black pepper
2 Tbsp canola oil
2 Tbsp butter

Serves 4 to 6

Pickerel with Avocado Crema and a Blood Orange Salsa

Chef says: Growing up a fisherman, I fell in love with pickerel at a young age. I still consider it one of the finest eating fish in Ontario lakes. This is my absolute favourite fish dish to prepare at home.

Avocado crema Scoop avocado flesh into a food processor fitted with the metal blade. Add cilantro, sour cream, lime juice, orange juice, olive oil and salt and process until smooth. Scoop the crema into an airtight container, add reserved avocado pits to deter oxidization and refrigerate until needed.

Blood orange salsa Place orange segments and juice, onions, jalapeño, basil, lime juice and salt in a medium bowl and stir gently. Cover and refrigerate until ready to serve.

Brussels sprouts and edamame Heat canola oil in a sauté pan over medium heat. Add Brussels sprouts, cut side down, and sear for about 4 minutes, until golden brown. Stir in vegetable stock and cook until fully reduced. Add butter and edamame and cook for another minute. Remove from the heat and set aside.

Pan-fried pickerel Season fish liberally on skin and flesh with salt and pepper. Heat a non-stick pan over medium heat, add canola oil and pickerel, skin side down, and cook for 4 to 5 minutes, until pickerel skin is crispy. Turn fish over, add butter and baste for about 1 minute. Remove from the heat and let rest for 3 minutes.

To serve Make a swoosh of avocado crema on each plate. Top with the Brussels sprouts and edamame, a piece of pickerel and a dollop of salsa. Garnish the plate with more salsa.

Fauna
Jon Svazas

ANY CHEF WITH means can buy superb ingredients. What he does with them, how he looks at them with fresh eyes, that's what sets him apart. Jon Svazas is such a chef. His raw materials are very fine, his rustic-modern style distinguished. There's an interest in kitchen science at play on his plates, and his grasp of how to blend cultures is impressive. The team of Jon Svazas, chef de cuisine Billy Khoo and sommelier/general manager Alex McMahon is a solid one, and Fauna has been a go-to from the get-go. Tastefully modern, boisterous and buzzing, this soaring space may be the best reuse of an old shoe store I've ever come across. Skills extend to the zinc bar, and Fauna's is as much a draw as its tables. The menu offers Mediterranean, Middle Eastern and Asian flavours applied to local ingredients, with most dishes meant to be shared. If you've a hankering for emu, it will be amply satisfied in a carpaccio of the rich meat, with black garlic crackers and house pickles. Japanese eggplant is treated with a tempura bath and served with Lankaaster gouda. The Quebec lamb tartare with puffed wild rice has all the gaminess of raw lamb perked with pickled shallot and punched with the heat of harissa, the pungency of preserved lemon and the freshness of mint. It comes balanced with a rich aioli and bound with a quail egg. Tough to share... 425 BANK STREET, 613-563-2862

facing: **Lamb Tartare with Puffed Wild Rice, Harissa, Preserved Lemon and Mint**

Chef says: I love working with raw meat, making tartare and carpaccio, but in this dish I wanted the richness of roasted lamb to balance the subtle taste and texture of raw lamb, so I added the roasted lamb aioli. I chose Middle Eastern and North African garnishes, as I think they best complement the gamey flavour of the lamb. It can be time consuming to prepare the garnishes (lemon purée, harissa, aioli), but they can be made well in advance, keep well in the refrigerator and can be used for many other applications as well. Harissa is also available at most grocery stores.

Preserved lemon purée

1 cup white sugar

1 cup water

Zest of 2 lemons, peeled with a vegetable peeler

Pinch of saffron

6 lemons, segmented (skin, pith and seeds removed)

2 preserved lemons, seeded (look for them in Middle Eastern grocers)

½ tsp xanthan gum

Serves 4 to 6

Lamb Tartare with Puffed Wild Rice, Harissa, Preserved Lemon and Mint

Preserved lemon purée Place sugar and water in a small heavy-bottomed saucepan and bring to a boil. Turn down the heat to medium, add lemon zest and saffron and simmer until zest is translucent, about 10 minutes.

Place lemon segments and preserved lemons in a blender, pour in lemon syrup and purée at high speed. With the motor running, carefully add xanthan gum and mix until well combined. Strain the purée through a fine-mesh sieve into a clean, airtight container and refrigerate; discard solids. (Will keep refrigerated for 1 to 2 weeks, or longer, and can be used to finish sauces or salad dressings or as a garnish for raw and cooked fish and seafood.)

Harissa Preheat the broiler to high. Line a baking sheet with aluminum foil.

In a large bowl, toss bell peppers and chili peppers with 2 Tbsp of the olive oil. Arrange peppers in a single layer on the baking sheet and broil, rotating them to ensure an even char, until blackened. Return peppers to the bowl, cover with plastic wrap and let cool.

While peppers are cooling, toast coriander, cinnamon stick, cumin and caraway seeds in a dry pan over medium heat until fragrant and lightly smoking, 3 to 5 minutes. Transfer the seeds to a small bowl and set aside.

Wearing latex or vinyl gloves, peel and seed peppers, discarding skins and seeds (reserve seeds if you like a very spicy sauce). Transfer prepared peppers and their juice to a blender and add lemon juice, honey, toasted spices, remaining olive oil and garlic. Purée at the highest speed until completely smooth and emulsified. Season with salt to taste. Strain through a fine-mesh sieve into an airtight container and refrigerate; discard solids.

Lamb aioli Place lamb fat in a heavy-bottomed saucepan over medium-low heat and cook, stirring occasionally, until completely rendered (the fat should be crispy and brown). Let cool and then carefully strain through a fine-mesh sieve into a clean bowl; discard solids.

Place garlic cloves into the pot, pour the rendered lamb fat over them and cook over low heat to confit until completely tender and slightly browned, 15 to 20 minutes. With a slotted spoon, transfer confit garlic to a small bowl and set aside. Let the rendered fat cool to room temperature.

Harissa

2 red bell peppers
6 long hot red chili peppers, such as red serranos, Espelettes, red habaneros (I like a mix)
¼ cup olive oil, divided
1 tsp coriander seeds
¼ cinnamon stick, crushed
1 tsp cumin seeds
1 tsp caraway seeds
¼ cup freshly squeezed lemon juice
1 Tbsp liquid honey
2 cloves garlic
Salt

Lamb aioli

1 lb diced lamb fat
10 cloves garlic
3 egg yolks
2 Tbsp smooth Dijon mustard
1 Tbsp red wine vinegar
2 cups olive oil (preferably Arbequina or another light, grassy olive oil)
Salt and freshly ground black pepper

Puffed rice

½ cup Canadian black wild rice
1 cup (or more) canola oil
Salt

Lamb tartare

1⅓ lb lamb loin, fat removed (ask your butcher to do this or cut the loin from the rack)
2 large shallots, very finely chopped
½ bunch mint, picked and finely chopped (set aside whole small leaves for garnish)
2 Tbsp small capers, drained, patted dry and finely chopped
2 Tbsp Lamb Aioli (see here)
Kosher salt
Freshly cracked black pepper
Maldon sea salt
12 quail egg yolks, separated, yolks reserved and whites discarded
Black Niçoise olives, pitted
Fresh mint leaves, for garnish

Place confit garlic, egg yolks, mustard and vinegar in a blender and purée at medium speed until combined. Add olive oil to the rendered fat. With the motor running, slowly pour the fat mixture into the blender in a slow, steady stream to emulsify. Season with salt and pepper to taste. (Will keep refrigerated in an airtight container for 2 to 3 days. Leftover lamb aioli is really good on a sandwich or served with roasted lamb or a dip for pretty much anything.)

Puffed rice Line a plate or baking sheet with paper towels. Divide rice into 3 equal portions. Heat canola oil in a frying pan to 350°F (use a deep-fry thermometer to test the temperature). Carefully add one portion of rice to the pan and swirl gently until rice has puffed (be careful not to burn the rice, as it will taste bitter). Using a slotted spoon, transfer the rice to the lined plate (or baking sheet) to drain. Season with salt to taste. Repeat with remaining portions of rice, reusing the canola oil (you may have to top up oil to ensure there is enough in the pan).

Lamb tartare Slice lamb loin into rounds about ⅛ inch thick. Stack 4 slices and cut into ⅛-inch strips. Rotate strips 90 degrees and cut into ⅛-inch cubes. Repeat until all of the lamb is chopped.

Fill a large bowl with ice. Set a stainless steel bowl over the ice and add the chopped meat. Stir in shallots, mint, capers and aioli and stir thoroughly until well combined. Season with kosher salt and pepper to taste, cover and refrigerate until ready to use.

To serve Divide the lamb tartare into six even portions and allow them to come to room temperature. Place a teaspoon of harissa in the centre of each plate and spread it around with a small spatula or the back of a spoon. Place a 3-inch ring mould on top of the harissa and fill it with a portion of the lamb tartare, smoothing the top evenly. Gently remove the mould. Repeat for each portion. Drizzle olive oil over the meat and season with Maldon salt, then scatter puffed rice over each plate. Place small dots of preserved lemon purée around each plate and on the tartare, and gently place two quail yolks on each portion of tartare. Garnish with olives and mint leaves around the plate.

Chef says: This dish is spring. All the vegetables used are the first things out of the ground when the snow melts, and as a chef in Ottawa I am always excited for this time of year after our long winter. I enjoy foraging ingredients (morels, fiddleheads and ramps) to use in the restaurant or around the dinner table at home. I like to keep the flavours of the ingredients pure and simple. I hope you enjoy them.

Note that you can confit the rabbit legs up to a week in advance. Just make sure the legs are completely covered in fat.

Serves 6

Confit Rabbit Legs with Morels, Ramps and Fiddleheads

Cured and confit rabbit legs Place a wire cooling rack over a large baking sheet. In a medium bowl, stir together sugar, salt and pepper until well combined. Toss rabbit legs in the cure mixture until they are evenly coated, and place them on the wire rack. Spread half of the thyme, sage and rosemary sprigs over the legs and then cover the herbs in more of the cure mixture. Cover and refrigerate for 12 hours, reserving remaining herbs for the confit process.

Position the rack in the middle of the oven and preheat to 300°F. Rinse the cure mixture from the rabbit legs under cold water and pat them with a clean cloth until completely dry.

In wide, deep, heavy-bottomed ovenproof pot with a snug-fitting lid, warm duck fat over medium-low heat. Once the fat has melted, add shallots, garlic and remaining herbs and place the rabbit legs on top, ensuring that the fat completely covers the legs and that there is at least 3 inches between the fat and the top of the pot. Allow the fat to come to a gentle bubble, then cover and place in the oven for 2½ to 3 hours. To test for doneness, gently move the joint on the rabbit legs. If the meat looks ready to fall apart, it is ready. Remove from the oven, uncover and let the fat cool to a safe handling temperature on the counter.

Using a slotted spoon and tongs, carefully transfer rabbit legs to a container and refrigerate. Once completely cooled, place lid on container. Refrigerate until needed, or serve the rabbit straight out of the fat. Let fat cool to room temperature, strain through a fine-mesh sieve and refrigerate for another use; discard solids. (Will keep refrigerated for up to 2 months.)

Ramp purée Fill a large bowl with ice water. Bring a medium pot of salted water to a boil. Add ramp leaves and count to 10. Using a small strainer, transfer the ramp leaves to the ice bath to stop the cooking. Squeeze any excess water from the ramp leaves, transfer them to an airtight container and refrigerate.

Slice half of the ramp bulbs into small thin rounds and set aside (reserve remaining bulbs for the morels and fiddleheads). In a medium saucepan over medium heat, add butter. When it is foaming, add sliced ramp bulbs and cook for 10 minutes. Pour in chicken stock and cook until reduced by half. Stir in cream and cook until reduced by half again. Pour this mixture into an airtight container and let cool to room temperature.

Coarsely chop chilled ramp leaves and place in a blender. Pour in cream mixture and quickly

Cured and confit rabbit legs

3 cups packed light brown sugar
2 cups kosher salt
7 Tbsp freshly toasted and cracked black pepper
6 hind rabbit legs (available at most butcher shops with advance notice)
1 bunch fresh thyme
1 bunch fresh sage
1 bunch fresh rosemary
4½ lb duck fat (available at most butcher shops with advance notice)
8 shallots, cut in half
8 cloves garlic, smashed
2 Tbsp butter
1 Tbsp olive oil
1 bunch fresh tarragon, leaves picked and washed
Maldon sea salt

Ramp purée

2 lb ramps, leaves and bulbs separated and washed thoroughly (ramps are available at farmers' markets in mid-May–early June)
2 Tbsp butter
1 cup chicken stock
2 cups whipping (35%) cream
Salt and freshly ground black pepper

Israeli couscous risotto

2 Tbsp olive oil
2 cups Israeli couscous
6 shallots, finely chopped
8 cups chicken stock
1 cup Ramp Purée (see here)
2 Tbsp butter

2 cups finely grated Tomme de Kamouraska cheese (or use Parmigiano-Reggiano)
Salt and freshly ground black pepper

Morels and fiddleheads

2 lb local morels (found in local markets between May and June)
½ lb fiddleheads, washed and stems trimmed (or use trimmed asparagus)
1 Tbsp olive oil
2 Tbsp butter
Reserved ramp bulbs, sliced into thin rounds
½ cup Pinot Noir
½ cup chicken stock
Salt and freshly ground black pepper

---

purée at high speed (do not purée for long, as the heat of the blender will brown the leaves). Strain purée through a fine-mesh sieve into a small bowl and set aside; discard solids.

Couscous risotto In a large, heavy-bottomed pot, heat olive oil over medium-high heat. Add Israeli couscous, stirring to toast lightly, then add shallots and cook for 5 minutes, stirring constantly with a wooden spoon. Slowly add chicken stock, ½ cup at a time, adding more only once the previous addition is nearly absorbed. Repeat this process until the couscous is al dente, 20 to 25 minutes. Stir in ramp purée, butter and cheese until desired consistency is reached (if the couscous is too thick, add a splash of water or stock). Season with salt and pepper to taste.

Morels and fiddleheads Set a wire cooling rack on the counter and cover it with a kitchen towel. Wash morels thoroughly in lukewarm salted water and place on the towel to dry.

Fill a large bowl with ice water. Bring a small pot of water to a boil. Add fiddleheads and blanch for about 1 minute. Transfer the fiddleheads to the ice bath to stop the cooking. Remove and set aside.

In a sauté pan over medium-high heat, combine olive oil and 1 Tbsp of the butter. When butter is foaming, add morels; increase the heat to high and sauté for 2 minutes. Add ramps and cook until slightly browned and caramelized. Deglaze the pan with the wine (if the alcohol ignites, allow it to burn off), and then pour in chicken stock and cook until reduced by half. Add remaining butter to glaze the mushrooms. Add fiddleheads at the last minute and cook until heated through. Season with salt and freshly ground pepper to taste.

Finish rabbit legs Preheat the oven to 350°C. Place a large ovenproof sauté pan over medium heat, and heat butter and olive oil until foamy. Set rabbit legs, flesh side down, in the pan and cook in the oven until the meat reaches 150°F, 10 to 15 minutes (check the temperature of the meat by inserting an instant-read thermometer into the thickest part of the leg).

To serve Divide the risotto equally among six bowls or plates and top with one confit rabbit leg per serving. Garnish with morels and fiddleheads, spooning some of the pan sauce over each portion. Finish with a few leaves of fresh tarragon and a sprinkle of Maldon salt.

Les Fougères

Charles Part
Jennifer Warren Part

I THINK I LOVE Les Fougères best in that fleeting period between winter and spring. In the city, the snow piles are as black as our mood, but mere minutes from Parliament Hill the Chelsea chickadees are still darting from Fougères' feeders. Gooseberry bushes and raspberry canes are being pruned. Soon the gardens will be tilled and seeded. On chef Charlie Part's menu the venison with Wassail jus is replaced with Quebec foie gras with a compote of rhubarb and rosemary. With luck there'll be maple syrup *pouding chômeur*. In the summer, when the gooseberry bushes are ripe and the gardens in their glory, Part might pair the tart berries with Lake Winnipeg pickerel. He'll show a bird the team of chanterelles, raspberries, thyme and luscious Laliberté cheese, and chicken will never have had it so good. His wife, Jennifer Warren Part, and the entire Les Fougères family are big-time believers in slow, seasonal cooking, and in using product from the backyard, locally raised, thoughtfully sourced. They are also devotees of the homemade-everything ethic—there are constantly bones simmering, vegetables pickling, sauces burbling, for both the recently remodelled restaurant and the extensive take-away shop. Les Fougères is a national treasure. Now well into its third decade, it shows no sign of resting on its considerable laurels.

783 ROUTE 105, CHELSEA, QC, 819-827-8942

2 Tbsp butter

2 Tbsp olive oil

6 grain-fed boneless chicken breasts, skin on

2 cups fresh chanterelles, sliced if large

1 onion, diced

½ cup dry white wine

1 cup chicken stock

¼ cup raspberry vinegar

6 oz Laliberté cheese, cut into 12 slices (or other creamy Quebec cheese, such as Verdict d'Alexina or La Sauvagine)

18 fresh raspberries

½ Tbsp fresh lemon thyme leaves

Serves 6

Chicken with Chanterelles, Raspberries, Laliberté Cheese and Lemon Thyme

Chef says: Chanterelles and raspberries usually peak together in July, and their earthy, sweet, tangy flavours work beautifully together, especially when paired with succulent grain-fed chicken from nearby Ferme Aux Saveurs des Monts and oozing Laliberté cheese from Fromagerie du Presbytère in Sainte-Elisabeth-de-Warwick, Quebec. A Yukon Gold potato purée with sweet corn stirred in, and sautéed Toscano kale or other summer green would be delicious with the chicken.

Preheat the oven to 375°F. Melt butter with olive oil in a large frying pan over medium heat. Add chicken breasts and sear until golden brown on both sides, about 5 minutes. Transfer the chicken breasts to a baking sheet (reserve the pan) and cook in the oven for 14 minutes, until cooked through and firm to the touch.

To the reserved pan, add chanterelles and onions and sauté gently over medium heat until tender, about 4 minutes. Deglaze the pan with the wine, stock and vinegar, scraping the brown bits from the bottom of the pan. Using a slotted spoon, transfer chanterelles to a bowl and keep warm. Continue to simmer the liquid in the pan until reduced to a loose glaze, about 10 minutes.

To serve Warm six plates in the oven. Slice each chicken breast into three pieces. Tuck a slice of Laliberté cheese between each piece of chicken and place a chicken breast on each plate. Spoon some of the glaze over top and finish with the warm chanterelles, fresh raspberries and lemon thyme.

Chef says: I love the deep essence of the sea that salt cod and mussel fumet offer. Start this recipe the night before you want to serve it, to allow the salt cod its soaking time.

Serves 6 as an appetizer

Salt Cod Ravioli with Mussel Fumet

Salt cod ravioli Drain salt cod fillets and rinse well under cold running water. Set aside.

Place onions, 6 garlic cloves, celery, potatoes, peppercorns, bay leaves, lemon quarters, wine and water in a heavy-bottomed pot with a lid and steam gently over medium-low heat until the potato is cooked and soft. Arrange salt cod fillets on top of the potato mixture, cover with the lid and continue to steam until cod is cooked and fork-tender, about 10 minutes.

Remove and discard the bay leaves. Using a slotted spoon, transfer the solids (reserving the cooking liquid) from the pot to a food processor fitted with the metal blade. Add remaining clove of garlic and lemon juice, and pulse until the mixture is smooth.

Return the cooking liquid to medium heat and reduce to a syrup. Add this syrup to the salt cod mixture and process to combine. With the motor running at medium speed, slowly pour in olive oil followed by the cubes of cream cheese until the mixture is well combined. Taste and adjust the seasoning as necessary. Cover and refrigerate the mixture until cool.

To make the ravioli, set pasta squares on a clean, dry work surface. Brush 12 squares with beaten egg. Using a small ice-cream scoop, mound 2 Tbsp of the cooled salt cod mixture in the centre of each of these 12 squares. Place one of the remaining 12 pasta squares over each mound and, using your fingers, press the edges together around the filling to seal them. Using a round cookie cutter slightly bigger than the filling, punch out a neat circular ravioli. Repeat until you have 12 ravioli. (Filled ravioli can be placed on a baking sheet, lightly covered with waxed paper and refrigerated for 1 day.)

Mussel fumet Clean mussels in cold water and discard any with broken or cracked shells and that do not close tightly when tapped against a hard surface.

Salt cod ravioli

1 lb boneless salt cod fillets, covered with cold water and soaked overnight

1 onion, chopped

7 cloves garlic

2 stalks celery, chopped

1 large potato, peeled and chopped

6 black peppercorns

4 bay leaves

1 lemon, cut into quarters, seeded

2 cups dry white wine

1 cup water

Juice of ½ lemon

1 cup extra-virgin olive oil

1½ cups solid cream cheese, cubed

Salt and freshly ground black pepper

24 fresh pasta squares, each 3½ inches square, cut from homemade or (Italian specialty) store-bought fresh pasta sheets

1 egg, beaten

1 Tbsp melted butter, for finishing (optional)

Mussel fumet

2 lb fresh mussels

3 Tbsp butter

1 onion, sliced

1 fennel bulb, sliced

1 cup dry white wine

¾ cup grape tomatoes, sliced in half

2 Tbsp chopped fresh flat-leaf (Italian) parsley leaves

Garnish

Chopped fresh dill

Lemon zest

Chili oil and truffle oil (optional)

In a wide pot, melt butter over medium-low heat. Add onions and fennel and sauté gently until soft and translucent. Stir in the mussels and wine, increase the heat to medium-high and cook, covered, until the shells open and the mussels are cooked, about 5 minutes (discard any mussels that do not open). Add tomatoes and parsley and toss to combine.

Using a slotted spoon, transfer mussels to a bowl. Remove mussels from their shells and return to the fumet; discard shells. (Fumet will keep refrigerated in an airtight container for 1 day.)

Finish ravioli Bring a large pot of lightly salted water to a boil. Drop the ravioli into the boiling water and cook until pasta is tender, about 5 minutes.

To brown them, place the melted butter in a large, heavy-bottomed saucepan over medium-high heat, add the cooked ravioli and allow to brown on one side, about 2 minutes.

To serve Warm the fumet gently over low heat and ladle equal amounts into six warmed soup bowls. Place two ravioli on top of each serving. Garnish with dill, a bit of lemon zest, and a few drops of chili oil and/or truffle oil (if using).

Fraser Café
Simon and Ross Fraser

THE FRASER BROTHERS, Simon and Ross, have been the darlings of Ottawa East for seven years. From their wee starter restaurant on Putman Avenue, they sourced a larger space on Springfield Road, opened up the kitchen and invited more of their New Edinburgh neighbours. And didn't they come in droves! So they expanded again, into an empty shop next door, calling the space Table 40. It's used for private parties but also serves family meals in the style of "this is dinner, come and get it," and the chefs' choice meal is always inspired. The vibe in their restaurants is casual, open and welcoming. The food follows the seasons and their fancies, and seems precisely what the neighbours want to eat. Brunch might be huevos rancheros or a panzanella salad with Mariposa Farm tomatoes and a splendid Scotch egg. We tend to start dinner here with Whalesbone oysters and Jacobson's cheese while we consider what next. The rich shrimp bisque with warm Thai flavours? The grilled halloumi and melon salad sharpened with cacciatorino and soothed with a yogurt dressing? Or maybe just the comfort of lamb meatballs with pappardelle noodles. You will not look up until they have vanished. House-churned ice cream to end. If surprise is in order, there is the Kitchen's Choice, and most of the neighbours go that route. No surprise, these brothers now have a third act: The Rowan is their modern British restaurant, opened last summer in the Glebe. A new neighbourhood to feed well. 7 SPRINGFIELD ROAD, 613-749-1444

Preserved lemon mayonnaise

2 egg yolks

2 tsp Dijon mustard

Juice of 1 lemon

2 Tbsp white vinegar

2 cups canola oil

3 Tbsp chopped preserved lemons

15 large green olives, pitted and chopped

Salt

Shrimp and tomato ragù

3 Tbsp olive oil

½ lb fresh chorizo sausage, sliced

2 shallots, finely diced

3 cloves garlic, finely sliced

1 small red chili pepper, chopped

1 red bell pepper, cut in small dice

½ cup white wine

1 cup tomato passata (homemade or good-quality store-bought)

1 pt cherry tomatoes, halved (20 to 25)

1 lb sidestripe shrimp, peeled, cleaned, tails on (10 to 12 per person)

Salt and freshly ground black pepper

Garnish

Chopped fresh basil and dill

Olive oil

Freshly squeezed lemon juice

Chopped red chili pepper (optional)

Serves 4 as an appetizer or a small plate

Sidestripe Shrimp with Chorizo, Tomatoes and Preserved Lemon Mayo

Chef says: This dish has a Mediterranean influence and is made using Ocean Wise–sustainable British Columbia shrimp. It works as a simple appetizer, which can be made in one pan (with the exception of the mayo). It should be served hot with slices of baguette spread with olive oil and toasted.

Preserved lemon mayonnaise In a medium bowl, whisk egg yolks, then add mustard, lemon juice and vinegar and whisk to combine. Whisking continuously, gradually add canola oil in a slow stream until the mayonnaise is emulsified and thickened, 3 to 5 minutes. Mix in preserved lemons, green olives and salt to taste. Set aside. (Will keep refrigerated in an airtight container for up to 1 week.)

Shrimp and tomato ragù Heat olive oil in a large saucepan over medium heat. Add sausage, shallots, garlic, chili peppers and red bell peppers and sauté gently for 2 to 3 minutes. Deglaze the pan with white wine and cook until reduced by half. Stir in passata and cook for an additional 5 to 10 minutes or until you have a thick sauce. Add cherry tomatoes and shrimp and cook until shrimp are slightly opaque, 2 to 5 minutes (do not overcook!). Season with salt and pepper to taste.

To serve Divide the shrimp and tomato ragù evenly among four small side dishes. Top each serving with basil and dill, a drizzle of olive oil, a squeeze of lemon juice and extra chilies (if desired). Serve the preserved lemon mayo in a small ramekin on the side.

Spice mix

1 Tbsp yellow mustard seeds
1 Tbsp coriander seeds
1 Tbsp fennel seeds
1 Tbsp dill seeds
1 Tbsp caraway seeds
1 Tbsp salt
1 Tbsp freshly cracked black pepper
2 tsp smoked paprika
2 tsp red chili flakes
3 Tbsp liquid honey
3 Tbsp brown sugar
¼ cup warm water

Slow-roasted pork shoulder sandwiches

4 to 6 lb pork shoulder or pork loin, trimmed of fat if desired
1 recipe Spice Mix (see here)
2 Tbsp olive oil
1 recipe Peach BBQ Sauce (see here)
8 soft rolls, sliced open and lightly toasted
4 fresh peaches, sliced
½ to 1 cup coleslaw (your favourite homemade recipe or good-quality store-bought)
8 to 16 sprigs fresh cilantro

Peach BBQ sauce

1 medium onion, diced
3 cloves garlic, crushed
1 red bell pepper, diced
3 to 4 ripe peaches, diced
½ cup tomato paste
1 cup water
3 Tbsp apple cider vinegar
3 Tbsp Worcestershire sauce
3 Tbsp apple cider
2 Tbsp light (fancy) molasses
3 Tbsp brown sugar
2 dried ancho chili peppers
2 Tbsp Dijon mustard
Pinch of red chili flakes
Salt and freshly ground black pepper
Juice of 1 lime, or to taste

Serves 8

Slow-Roasted Pork Shoulder Sandwiches with Peach BBQ Sauce

Chef says: When we first opened our little café, pulled pork was—and still is—all the rage. We wanted to do something a little different, but still keep it recognizable. This is what we came up with. We served the porchetta at the first Canadian Chefs' Congress on Michael Stadtländer's Eigensinn Farm, cooked outdoors over a fire pit. We'll never forget the smell of the smoky pork over the open flames. This is just one way of using the pork. There are so many others!

Spice mix Place all of the ingredients in a large bowl and stir until well combined. (Will keep refrigerated in an airtight container for 1 week.)

Slow-roasted pork shoulder sandwiches Place pork in a large bowl. Using your hands, coat pork in spice mix and let sit for 1 to 1½ hours at room temperature, turning it a couple of times.

Preheat the oven to 275°F. Roast the pork uncovered for about 90 minutes, turning it once or twice while it cooks (the sugars in the marinade should be nice and brown and the pork cooked through to medium-well). Remove from the oven and let cool to room temperature. Cover and

refrigerate for an hour to cool fully. While the pork is cooling, prepare the BBQ sauce.

Peach BBQ sauce In a medium saucepan, combine all of the ingredients. Simmer over medium-low heat until soft, 20 to 25 minutes. Transfer the mixture to a food processor fitted with the metal blade and process until still slightly chunky. Season with salt and pepper to taste and a squeeze of lime juice. (Will keep refrigerated in an airtight container for up to 7 days.)

Finish sandwiches Cut the pork into slices of whatever thickness you prefer. Heat olive oil in a cast-iron frying pan over medium to medium-high heat, add the pork slices and sear both sides until hot and slightly crispy in some places.

Place the warm BBQ sauce in a small bowl. Add the fried pork slices to coat.

To serve Arrange a lightly toasted bun on each plate. Top with pork slices, a couple of slices of fresh peach and a little dressed coleslaw. Garnish with sprigs of fresh cilantro.

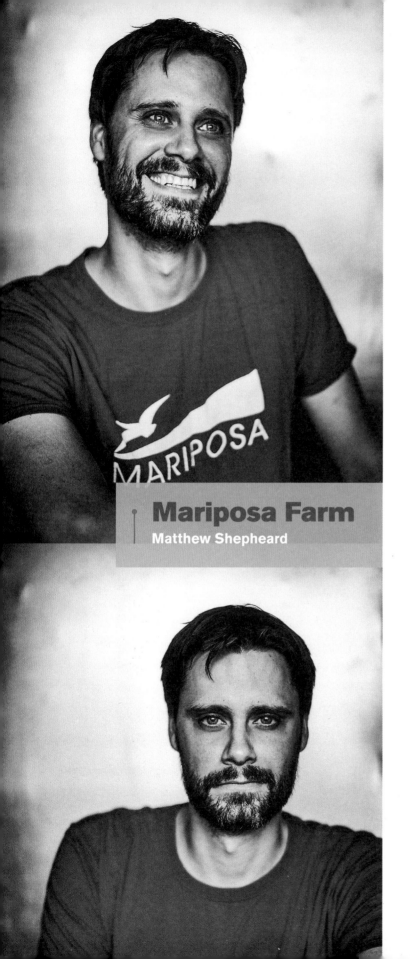

Mariposa Farm
Matthew Shepheard

IAN WALKER bought the Plantagenet property and worked "the helloutofit" when he was barely out of his teens. Thirty some years later, Mariposa Farm owners Walker and Suzanne Lavoie raise ducks, geese and crossbred pigs (fed on kitchen scraps from twenty-eight regional restaurants and spent grains from a local brewery). They keep chickens, milk a cow and grow vegetables. A small farm store sells their products. And you find their Mariposa duck, pork and produce on the menu at dozens of the city's finest restaurants (many of them in these pages). Sixteen years ago, the couple converted a barn into a dining room, and on Sundays they serve lunch. You make a reservation by picking up the phone and talking to a real live farmer. You'll be greeted by that real live farmer and a pair of Bouviers lounging on the front porch, and then by a pretty plate of foie gras. There is always foie gras on the menu, along with mains showcasing duck and goose. And then perhaps a carrot salad, the star ingredient just-plucked a hundred paces from the kitchen. Matthew Shepheard's been in that kitchen since 2012. A ragout of Mariposa pork is an homage to his grandmother. The roast Mariposa goose to his mother. (Gotta love this guy...) Shepheard puts a spin on the classic beets-with-chèvre pairing by adding summer strawberries, ground cherries and lavender in a stunner of a summer salad. The Mariposa menu follows the rhythm of life on the farm, and the farm-to-table feast is mighty fine. 6468 COUNTY ROAD 17, PLANTAGENET, 613-673-5881

Beet and strawberry salad

24 small or 12 medium beets (use a mix of red, golden, candy cane)

Salt

2 cups strawberries, hulled and sliced

1 cup ground cherries, papery outer shells removed, left whole or cut in half

10 oz mixed salad greens

Wildflower honey vinaigrette

2 Tbsp wildflower honey

2 Tbsp rice wine vinegar or freshly squeezed lemon juice

¼ cup hot water

¼ cup safflower, sunflower or canola oil

Salt and freshly ground black pepper

Lavender goat cheese

½ cup whipping (35%) cream

2 tsp fresh culinary lavender flowers (or 1 tsp dried)

1 cup goat cheese, softened (we use C'est Bon)

Serves 6

Beet and Strawberry Salad with Lavender Goat Cheese

Chef says: By using seasonal and locally grown ingredients, we prepare creative, fresh food for our Mariposa guests. This classic dish of beets and goat cheese sees the start of the beet and ground cherry season here at the farm, adds late-summer strawberries and our garden-fresh lavender. It's a great example of how we think of food at Mariposa, starting with what's growing in our gardens, then adding a modern twist!

Beet and strawberry salad Preheat the oven to 400°F.

Divide beets by colour and wrap in separate aluminum foil packages (so the colours don't bleed), adding a pinch of salt to each. Roast for 40 to 75 minutes, depending on their size, until a sharp knife pierces their centre without resistance. Set aside to cool, opening the foil packages just enough to let out a little steam. When cool enough to handle, peel beets and shape as desired. (I like to leave them whole if they're small and cut them in half if they're larger.)

Wildflower honey vinaigrette Combine honey, vinegar (or lemon juice) and hot water with the oil and salt and pepper to taste and give it a good whisk.

Lavender goat cheese In a small pot, heat cream over medium-high heat until bubbling. Remove from the heat, add lavender, setting aside a few flowers for the garnish, and let steep for 10 minutes. Place goat cheese in a bowl. With a fine-mesh sieve, strain the lavender-infused cream over the goat cheese; discard flowers. Using a whisk, whip until well combined.

To serve Divide the infused goat cheese evenly among six plates, placing it in the centre of each one. With the back of a soupspoon, form it into a large circle-like nest or border. Arrange the beets around the outside of this cheese border. Add strawberries and ground cherries. Toss the mixed greens with vinaigrette and pile some in the middle of each plate. Sprinkle a few reserved lavender flowers on top and serve immediately.

Serves 6

Roasted Goose with Pan Gravy

Chicken stock Place all of the ingredients in a large stockpot and bring to a boil. Turn down the heat and simmer for 2 to 3 hours, uncovered, occasionally using a spoon to skim off any foam from the surface. Strain the stock through a fine-mesh sieve into a clean bowl or pot; discard solids. Let stock cool, then cover and refrigerate for up to 3 days.

Roasted goose with pan gravy Preheat the oven to 450°F. Place a wire rack in a large roasting pan. Wipe the goose inside and out with paper towels and season it inside and out with salt and pepper to taste. Place apples, onions, thyme, bay leaves, cinnamon stick and juniper berries inside. Truss the goose, if you wish, to keep its legs together and wings in tight (see next).

To truss the goose, have ready a roll of kitchen twine and some scissors. On a clean work surface, position the goose, breast side up, with its legs facing you. Cut a good length of twine about 3 feet long and slide it under the bird so its centre sits directly beneath the tailbone of the goose with the ends extending left and right. Lift the twine, loop each end around the legs and then reverse

the twine to make a cross. Pull tightly on both ends of the twine so that the legs come together. Pull the ends of the twine away from you, loop them around the front of the goose and over the wings. Then flip the goose over so that the neck is now facing you, keeping the twine pulled tight. Now you can just tie a knot so that the twine stays secured beneath the neckbone. Trim any excess twine and turn the goose onto its back again.

To roast the goose, place it on the wire rack in the roasting pan and roast in the oven until it starts to brown, about 40 minutes. Turn down the temperature to 350°F. Prick the goose skin all over to release the fat underneath it, taking care not to prick too deeply into the flesh. Using tongs and oven mitts or towels, carefully turn the bird breast side down and baste it with the pan juices. Continue roasting the goose at 350°F, basting often, for 1 hour.

Remove the bird from the oven, drain and reserve the fat (there will be a lot of it). Turn the goose breast side up, add the cranberry juice to the roasting pan and cover loosely with the foil. Return the goose to the oven and continue

Chicken stock

1½ lb chicken bones and carcass, including goose neck and wing tips

2 cups mirepoix (combination of chopped onions, celery and carrots)

1 bouquet garni (fresh thyme, parsley, bay leaf)

2 cloves garlic, chopped (optional)

6 black peppercorns

8 cups water (or slightly more if necessary to cover bones)

Roasted goose with pan gravy

1 goose, 9 to 10 lb

Salt and freshly ground black pepper

3 tart apples (Empire, Northern Spy), peeled, cored and cut in half

2 medium onions, chopped

2 sprigs fresh thyme

2 bay leaves

6-inch cinnamon stick

6 dried juniper berries

2 cups unsweetened cranberry juice

2 Tbsp butter

4 cups Chicken Stock (see here)

roasting for a further 1 to 1½ hours. You want the meat to easily pull away from the drumstick and a thermometer inserted in the thigh, away from the bone, to register 165°F. When the goose is cooked, remove it from the oven. Increase the oven temperature to 450°F.

Line a baking sheet with aluminum foil and set the goose, breast side up, on top. Set the roasting pan aside. Rub the goose with butter and return it to the hot oven for 5 to 10 minutes to crisp the skin.

Transfer the goose to a large platter and cover loosely with aluminum foil to keep warm. Let rest for 20 to 30 minutes before carving.

Make the pan gravy while the goose is resting. Pour the roasting juices into a medium pot and skim as much fat from the surface as you can (reserve this fat for another use). Bring the juices to a boil, then turn down the heat to medium and simmer until reduced by at least half. Add chicken stock and reduce again by at least half or until well flavoured and concentrated. Adjust the seasoning. Strain the gravy through a fine-mesh sieve into a bowl (discard solids) or, if you prefer a thicker gravy, into a smaller pot so you can reduce it further.

To serve Scoop the apple-onion mixture from the cavity inside the goose. Discard the bay leaves, thyme sprigs, cinnamon stick and juniper berries and set the stuffing in a small serving dish. Carve the goose, arranging the slices on a serving platter, and serve with the gravy alongside.

MēNa
James Bratsberg

IT WAS THE *amuse* that spoke volumes—my introduction to MēNa and to its gifted young chef. James Bratsberg sent out a boutonnière, a delicate sprig of chickweed that tasted of freshly shucked corn, sharpened with a spear of wild onion looped together and served with a striking citrus vinaigrette. If the purpose of an amuse-bouche is to please the eye, whet the appetite and remind us of the season, this one did just that. From there, the potato soup poured tableside over a bowl full of treats was pure genius, and (hurrah!) the recipe for it is provided here. This 2014 addition to the Little Italy neighbourhood is owned by Bryan Livingston. His MēNa is modern, minimalist, with white-washed barn boards, white flowers on black tables, and dozens of hanging filament bulbs lending mood and warmth. It's a space that suits the food: it commands the attention. Bratsberg has an artist's eye. His seasonal menu of modern French dishes is plump with striking-looking plates. Scallops arrive on a white bean purée, with a snowy cascade of fresh horseradish, served with four types of pickled beet, each delivering its own flavour and colour. His Quebec lamb five ways is a tour de force. And when's the last time we tasted such a perfect pommes Anna? What fun that it comes with ribs. MēNa is a young restaurant run by young men with old souls who understand the ageless art of gracious hospitality. 276 PRESTON STREET, 613-233-6462

facing: **Quail Confit with Beets and a Jicama-Treviso Salad**

Chef says: You will need to start this recipe at least two days ahead, to give the quail time to cure and confit. The quail cure makes more than you'll need for this recipe, but the spice mix is also good with things like roasted squash in the fall. And a note on semi-boneless quail: you can often find whole quail and debone the breasts yourself, much like you would a chicken. Or most good butcher shops will either carry boned quail or be happy to do it for you. As for the white chocolate, it pairs remarkably well with beets!

Serves 4 as appetizer

Quail Confit with Beets and a Jicama-Treviso Salad

Quail legs and breasts For the quail cure, in a dry pan over medium-low heat, toast cinnamon sticks, cloves, star anise and black peppercorns for roughly 5 minutes. Grind the spices in a clean coffee or spice grinder. Combine sugar and salt in a medium bowl, add the ground spices and mix thoroughly.

Line an airtight container large enough to hold the quail breasts with paper towels. Place the breasts on top, seal tightly and refrigerate.

Using your hands, rub each of the quail legs with about 1 tsp of the quail cure, working it into the skin. Arrange the legs in single layer in a baking dish, cover tightly and refrigerate for at least 6 hours or overnight.

Rinse the cured quail legs under cold running water and pat dry with paper towels. Preheat the oven to 190°F. Warm duck fat in a large ovenproof sauté pan over medium-low heat. Add the quail legs, cover with a lid or aluminum foil, and cook for 2 hours in the oven. Once the meat is soft but not falling off the bone, remove from the oven and let cool in the pan, uncovered. Once cool, cover the pan and refrigerate overnight to build the flavour.

Pickled beets Dice beets into medium cubes (you will need at least 24, or 6 per person); reserve the beet scraps for the purée.

Place cubed beets in a small pot, cover halfway with water, then add enough vinegar to cover them fully. Season with salt and sugar and simmer over medium-low heat for about 20 minutes, until soft but firm to the bite. Serve immediately or let cool in their cooking liquid.

Beet purée Place beet scraps in a pot, cover with water and season with a bit of salt and sugar. Simmer over medium heat until the beets are soft and breaking down. Using a slotted spoon, transfer beet scraps to a blender; reserve half of the cooking liquid.

Blend beets at low speed (if they are not blending easily, add a small amount of the cooking liquid, a bit at a time, until you have a smooth purée). Adjust the seasoning. Strain the purée through a fine-mesh sieve into a small pot; discard solids. Place over very low heat and add butter and vinegar.

Quail legs and breasts

3 cinnamon sticks, broken into pieces
½ Tbsp whole cloves
1 Tbsp whole star anise
1 Tbsp black peppercorns
2 cups packed brown sugar
1 cup sea salt or kosher salt
4 semi-boneless quail, breasts and legs separated
3 cups duck fat
Butter, for basting
¼ cup melted white chocolate, for finishing the dish

Pickled beets

2 to 3 medium red beets, peeled
Red wine vinegar
Pinch of salt
1 Tbsp white sugar

Beet purée

Beet scraps, cut into pieces of similar size (see here)
Salt
White sugar
1 Tbsp butter
Red wine vinegar

Jicama-Treviso salad

1 Tbsp grated peeled fresh ginger
⅓ cup white wine vinegar
1 cup canola oil
1 jicama, peeled and sliced thinly in diamonds
1 radicchio Treviso, or substitute the more commonly available radicchio Verona
Salt

Jicama-Treviso salad Place ginger in a small bowl, cover with vinegar and let marinate for 5 minutes. While whisking constantly, add canola oil in a slow, steady stream until emulsified. Set aside.

Remove outer, thicker leaves of the radicchio and discard, or save for another use. Trim the inside, softer leaves into bite-size pieces, similar in size to the jicama triangles. Combine jicama and Treviso in a bowl and season with salt to taste. Set aside.

Finish quail Preheat the oven to 350°F. Place the pan of confit quail legs in the oven and warm until you are able to lift the legs out of the fat. Dry the legs with paper towels to remove the excess fat; discard fat.

Line a plate with paper towels. Heat a cast-iron or heavy-bottomed pan over medium-high heat. Remove the quail breasts from the fridge and season them and the confit legs with more of the quail spice, about a pinch each. Place them in the pan, skin side down, and sear for 1 minute until the skin starts to get crispy. Baste with butter and cook for a further minute. (The breast will take about 2 minutes to cook. When you press

your fingertip against the flesh, the meat should spring back a little. If it is still very soft, cook for a little longer; you don't want it to feel very firm.) Transfer the quail to the lined plate to rest for 2 minutes before serving.

To serve Place a dollop of the warm beet purée off centre on each of four warmed plates, either creating a "splat" with the back of a spoon or a long swipe with either a spoon or a palate knife. Arrange six beet cubes in groups on the purée. Set a quail breast and legs against or on the cubes. Drizzle a tablespoon of the melted white chocolate close to the quail. Gently toss the salad with the vinaigrette and place it around but not directly on top of the quail, so the lettuce stays crisp.

Chef says: The inspiration for this dish didn't actually come from a baked potato but from one of my favourite kitchen snacks. When we make gnocchi or pommes purée at MēNa, we bake potatoes on a bed of salt. The fluffy flesh gets used, and the skins always seem to make their way into the fryer for a little snack that is salty, crunchy and absolutely delicious. I wanted to share with you something that we would eat on a regular basis in the kitchen, but dressed up a bit. So we made a soup with all the flavours of a baked potato. Start the crème fraîche the day before, or purchase it or a good-quality sour cream, if you prefer. Prepare the confit and the garnishes while the potatoes are baking.

Serves 4 as an appetizer

Baked Potato Soup

Crème fraîche In a non-reactive container, combine cream, sour cream and pinch of salt, cover with plastic wrap, poke a few holes in it and let sit at room temperature for 24 hours. It should start to get thick, and tangy. Once it's ready, cover and refrigerate until ready to use.

Baked potato soup Preheat the oven to 450°F. Cover a baking sheet with ¼ inch of extra-coarse salt.

Wash potatoes thoroughly, and while still wet, roll them around in the salt so the salt sticks to their skins. Set potatoes on top of the salt-lined baking sheet and bake for roughly 2 ½ hours or until the tip of a knife inserted in the flesh comes out easily.

Remove the potatoes from the oven, cut them in half and let cool for 1 minute. Using a spoon, scoop the potato flesh directly into a large pot, reserving the skins. Add bacon trimmings, cover with stock and bring to a simmer over medium heat. Add cream and butter and simmer for another 10 minutes.

Let soup cool for a few minutes, then transfer it to a high-speed blender. Starting at low speed and working up to high, blend the soup until smooth (if you are having a hard time blending it, add more chicken stock or water to coax it along).

Strain the soup through a fine-mesh sieve into a clean pot; discard solids. Season with salt and white pepper to taste.

Potato confit In a medium pot over medium-low heat, warm fat to about 250°F (use a deep-fry thermometer to test the temperature). Gently place potatoes into the warm fat and season with salt to taste. Cook, stirring gently and often so they don't stick to the bottom of the pot, for 30 to 45 minutes or until soft but still retain their shape.

Line a plate with paper towels. Using a slotted spoon, carefully transfer the potatoes to the lined plate to drain. Reserve the duck fat for rewarming.

Bacon and leeks Line a plate with paper towels. In a frying pan over medium heat, cook bacon, stirring often, until crispy. Drain off the fat and spoon the lardons onto the lined plate. Set aside.

Crème fraîche
2 cups whipping (35%) cream
1 Tbsp sour cream
Pinch of salt

Baked potato soup
Extra-coarse salt, for baking the potatoes
6 Yukon Gold potatoes (roughly 2½ lb)
6 oz good-quality bacon trimmings (about ¾ cup)
8½ cups chicken stock (or vegetable stock)

1 cup whipping (35%) cream
½ cup butter
Salt
Freshly ground white pepper
1 bunch fresh chives, for garnish

Potato confit
2 cups duck or bacon fat
2 Yukon Gold potatoes, peeled and cut in medium dice (do not store in water)
Salt

Bacon and leeks
½ lb good-quality thick bacon, cut in large dice
2 leeks, white and light green parts only, cut into ¼-inch rounds

Crispy potato skins
Canola oil, for deep-frying
Reserved potato skins (see here)
Salt and freshly ground black pepper

Fill a medium bowl with ice water. Bring a small pot of salted water to a boil. Rinse leeks under cold water to remove any dirt, then drop them into the pot and blanch for about 2 minutes, until soft but not falling apart. Drain and transfer leeks to the ice water to cool. Set aside.

Crispy potato skins Just before serving, preheat oil in a deep fryer, or a sturdy pot, to 375°F, using a deep-fry thermometer to check the temperature. Line a plate with paper towels. Once the oil is hot, carefully drop in potato skins, stir gently and fry until crispy, about 2 minutes. Using a slotted spoon, transfer the potato skins to the lined plate to drain. Season lightly with salt and pepper to taste and set aside.

To serve Warm the soup over medium heat, stirring often so it doesn't scorch. In a small pot over medium-high heat, warm a bit of the reserved duck fat and sear the confit potatoes. Turn down the heat to medium, and add bacon to rewarm it. Place cooked leeks in another small pot, add butter and a small amount of water just to cover, and warm over medium heat.

Ladle the warmed soup into four warmed bowls. Garnish with the crispy potatoes, confit potatoes, bacon and leeks. Finish with a dollop of the crème fraîche and snip some fresh chives over top. Serve immediately.

Nat's Bread Company
Natali Harea

I MET NATALI HAREA at a coffee shop at ten in the morning. I was still waking up. She was ready for bed. Her day's work starts as most of us are ending ours, delivering her artisanal loaves at daybreak to a dozen retail stores and a dozen more restaurants, before calling it a night. Or a day. The Venezuelan-born, Algonquin-trained Harea's cheffing cv was lengthy before she decided to focus on bread and set a new course. She opened up Nat's Bread Company in 2013, first working in the basement of gezellig, a Stephen Beckta–run restaurant in Westboro. For a while, she moved to the basement of Beckta's Nepean Street location, arriving as the cooks were leaving, and baking the night through. But when Beckta moved to its new home (page 42), she did too—to the kitchen at St. Paul's University where she's finally above ground. "I can see the trees now!" I ask her, Why bread? "I was always into it. I learned bread baking from my grandmother," she replies. It's the routine of bread baking she loves. How it commands full attention: "You need to know how to read it, notice how it changes with humidity, temperature, altitude, flour type. Especially the sourdoughs. I love that." Her particular sourdough starter is called Stan. And Stan gets around, spreading the joy of superb bread to restaurant baskets across the city. NATSBREADCOMPANY.COM

Chef says: This bread is a fan favourite at Nat's Bread Company. It's versatile enough to be used for everything from sandwiches to French toast!

4⅛ cups unbleached all-purpose flour + more for dusting
1¼ cups whole wheat flour
1¼ tsp active dry yeast
⅓ cup white sesame seeds, toasted (optional)
⅓ cup poppy seeds
⅓ cup unsalted hulled sunflower seeds (raw or roasted)

⅓ cup whole flax seeds
2¾ cups + 1 Tbsp room temperature water
1 Tbsp extra-virgin olive oil + more for greasing
2 tsp kosher salt

Makes 2 loaves

Four Seed Bread

In the bowl of a stand mixer, combine both flours, yeast and all of the seeds. Using your hand, mix to ensure seeds are evenly dispersed throughout the flour. Add most of the water and the olive oil and, using your hands, mix just to combine (add more water as needed to hold the dough together, ensuring that no dry flour remains). Let dough rest in the bowl of the stand mixer covered with a clean, dry kitchen towel for 20 minutes.

Fit stand mixer with the dough hook. Add salt to the dough and mix at low speed for 10 minutes, until the dough looks smooth and starts to pull away from the sides of the bowl (it will still feel sticky to the touch; if the dough hasn't started pulling away from the sides of the bowl, continue mixing, checking every few minutes, until it has).

Lightly grease a large metal or glass bowl (it should be twice as large as the ball of dough) with olive oil. Place the dough in the bowl, cover with a clean, dry kitchen towel and let rise in a warm, draft-free location until doubled in size, 1 to 1½ hours.

Line a rimless baking sheet with parchment paper. Cut a sheet of plastic wrap slightly larger than the baking sheet and grease it lightly with olive oil; set aside. Lightly dust a clean work surface with flour and turn the dough onto it. Using a bench scraper or a dull knife, cut the

dough into 2 equal portions. Using your hands, shape each portion into a round boule, set it on the baking sheet and cover loosely with the plastic wrap, greased side down. Let rise in a warm, draft-free location until doubled in size, about 45 minutes.

While the dough is rising, position the oven racks in the middle and lower third of the oven. Place a clean, empty roasting pan or rimmed baking sheet on the lower rack. Preheat the oven to 450°F. Have ready about half a tray of ice cubes in a bowl.

Once the dough has doubled in size, use a serrated knife to score an X, about 1 inch deep, across the top of each loaf. Set the tray with the loaves on the upper rack and, working quickly, toss the ice cubes onto the hot tray on the bottom rack. (This creates instant steam in your oven, and this steam is crucial to the formation of a nice crust on your baked loaf of bread.) Close the oven door and immediately turn the oven temperature down to 400°F. Bake for 15 minutes, rotate the tray 180° and cook for another 15 to 25 minutes, until the bread is golden brown and sounds hollow inside when tapped on the bottom.

Remove the pan from the oven, transfer the bread to wire racks and let cool completely before serving (this is the hardest part!).

Lime vinaigrette

Zest of 1 lime
Juice of 2 limes
2 Tbsp rice wine vinegar
2 Tbsp liquid honey
¾ cup extra-virgin olive oil
Kosher salt
Freshly cracked black pepper

Bread salad

¼ cup unsalted butter
1 large clove garlic, minced
½ loaf day-old Four Seed Bread, cut into 1-inch slices
1 pint cherry tomatoes, halved
1 medium shallot, minced
1 bunch of fresh mint, leaves picked and thinly sliced
½ bunch of fresh flat-leaf (Italian) parsley, leaves only
Lime Vinaigrette (see here)
Kosher salt
Freshly cracked black pepper
1 ball Burrata cheese
Extra-virgin olive oil
Maldon sea salt (or other finishing salt)

Serves 4

Four Seed Bread Salad

Chef says: There are so many ways to use up day-old bread that it should never end up in the trash! This is one of our favourite uses for yesterday's Four Seed Bread: a fresh, tasty salad that allows lots of room for improvisation. Play around with the ingredients, using seasonal vegetables and herbs, making the bread and vinaigrette the constants.

Lime vinaigrette In a medium bowl, whisk together lime zest and juice, vinegar and honey. Whisking continuously, slowly add olive oil and whisk until it has emulsified. Season with salt and pepper to taste. Set aside. (This recipe makes more than you need: refrigerate leftover vinaigrette in an airtight container and use it to dress other salads, to marinate meat or to toss with roasted vegetables.)

Bread salad Preheat a barbecue or stovetop grill to medium heat. In a small saucepan, melt butter over low heat. Add garlic and cook for 5 minutes, then remove from the heat.

Brush the bread slices on both sides with the garlic butter. Grill bread on one side until grill marks appear, then flip over and grill the other side until grill marks appear. Let cool for 10 minutes, then cut into bite-size cubes. Set aside.

In a large bowl, combine tomatoes, shallots, mint and parsley. Toss with lime vinaigrette. Add the grilled bread cubes and toss until all of the ingredients are well combined and evenly distributed. Season with salt and pepper to taste.

To serve Transfer the salad to a serving bowl or four individual salad plates. Cut or gently tear the Burrata into 1-inch pieces and disperse them across the top of the salad. Drizzle with olive oil and season with Maldon salt.

NeXT
Michael Blackie

IT'S EIGHT THIRTY in Stittsville, Ontario, and Michael Blackie's walking his dining room. He's a chef who likes to come out of the kitchen. A chef who's never met a mic he doesn't like, or a food event he hasn't wanted to organize: the bigger the cause, the better; the more chefs, the merrier. His energy and generous spirit have made him something of a rock star chef in this town. Now, after years of working for others, he runs his own show. "So what will you do next?" people kept asking him, and the question answered itself. NeXT is a lounge-restaurant with thirteen-foot coffered ceilings, an open kitchen, an intimate bar, a patio for the gentle months and a fireplace for the brutal ones. Blackie has a clear affinity for the flavours of Mexico—where he lived on a sandbar, where his kids were born—and for Asia and the South Pacific, where he spent years of his career. His menu categories set the stage: "Nibbly Bits," "Cold Stuff," "Hot Stuff," "Dirty Stuff," which include tempura cheese curds, green papaya salad, lobster-stuffed steamed buns and his famous General Blackie's Chicken. These are plates that speak of his travels. Plates full of jumpy flavours that linger in the memory. Dinner at NeXT has impact. Michael Blackie wouldn't have it any other way. 6400 HAZELDEAN ROAD, STITTSVILLE, 613-836-8002

facing: Crispy Green Papaya Salad with Citrus Soaker and Peanut Crumble

Chef says: Green papaya is one of my go-to salads, a constant on my menus. It's a classic Thai dish, but this recipe is anything but traditional. And you will notice I do not use those nasty little dry shrimp. This papaya salad is all about layers of flavour and texture that will have your guests begging you to make it time and time again! You will need a granite mortar and pestle to do it justice. Most of the ingredients are available at Asian grocery stores.

Serves 4 to 6

Crispy Green Papaya Salad with Citrus Soaker and Peanut Crumble

Thai red curry paste In a dry heavy frying pan over medium heat, toast coriander seeds and black peppercorns until aromatic, about 1 minute. Using a mortar and pestle, crush the coriander and peppercorns. One by one, and working in 2 batches if necessary, add and grind the lemon grass, galangal, lime leaves, cilantro, shallots, garlic and chilies until you have a smooth, thick paste. Finish with salt and fish sauce. (Will keep refrigerated in an airtight container for up to 1 month.)

Spiced citrus soy soaker Combine all of the ingredients in a medium saucepan. Bring to a simmer over medium heat, stirring to ensure the miso is fully dissolved, and cook for 20 minutes. Strain the mixture through a fine-mesh sieve; discard solids. Let cool.

Vermicelli and taro root In a deep fryer or a large, flat-bottomed pot, heat vegetable oil to 350°F. Line 2 bowls with paper towels.

Have ready a fine-mesh strainer. Place taro root in a bowl and fill it with cold water. Swish the taro root around to remove the starch and drain it through the strainer. Repeat the rinsing and draining process twice more. (Taro root is an extremely starchy vegetable and rinsing it ensures that it does not clump when cooked.)

Pull raw vermicelli stick apart into strands. Carefully plunge the strands into the hot oil for no more than 10 seconds; using a slotted spoon, transfer the puffed noodles to one of the lined bowls.

Thai red curry paste

1 tsp coriander seeds

½ tsp black peppercorns

1 lemon grass stalk, bottom
    2 inches only, peeled and sliced
    in long, fine strips (chiffonade)

3 tsp finely chopped peeled galangal

2 lime leaves, finely chopped

3 Tbsp chopped fresh cilantro,
    leaves and stems

4 shallots, finely diced

6 cloves garlic, finely diced

2 bird's-eye red chili peppers, seeded

Kosher salt

⅛ cup fish sauce (I like Three Crabs
    brand)

Spiced citrus soy soaker

1 Tbsp white miso paste

Sriracha sauce

1 Tbsp minced peeled fresh ginger

1 cup freshly squeezed orange juice

3 Tbsp mirin

¼ cup kecap manis (Indonesian
    sweet soy sauce, I like ABC brand)

2 Tbsp kecap asin (Indonesian salty
    soy sauce, I like ABC brand)

Vermicelli and taro root

6 cups vegetable oil, for frying rice stick

1 medium taro root, peeled and finely
    sliced into thin strips

1 pkg (500 g/17.6 oz) Lung Chang rice
    vermicelli (be sure to buy this brand,
    as it is one of the few that actually
    puffs when fried)

Green papaya salad

2 Tbsp Thai Red Curry Paste
    (see here)

2 tsp palm sugar

Juice of 2 limes

1 medium green papaya, finely
    sliced into long strips

1 cup shaved Napa cabbage

3 Tbsp very, very finely sliced
    red bell peppers

¼ cup finely sliced carrots

¼ cup finely sliced daikon

12 to 14 sprigs fresh cilantro

3 Tbsp unsalted peanuts, toasted

Crispy vermicelli (see here)

½ cup finely sliced fried taro root
    (see here)

1 jalapeño pepper, finely sliced into
    wheels, for garnish (optional)

Using a slotted spoon or a "spider" (a wire mesh spoon with a long handle), add the taro to the hot oil, keeping it together as a mass and moving it around in the oil, and cook until it looks like fine angel hair. Transfer to the second lined bowl and set aside.

Green papaya salad Using a mortar and pestle, grind curry paste with sugar and lime juice until well combined. Add green papaya and pound it with the pestle to break it down.

In a medium bowl, combine the seasoned curry paste with cabbage, bell peppers, carrots, daikon, 6 or 7 of the cilantro sprigs and the peanuts. Add the crispy vermicelli and mix thoroughly with your hands.

To serve Set a pool of the spiced citrus soy soaker in the bottom of a large platter. Heap the salad in the centre. Garnish with the fried taro root, remaining cilantro and a few jalapeño wheels (if using) and serve immediately, preferably family style!

Crostini

1 fresh baguette, chilled in the freezer for 10 minutes

1 cup olive oil

Maldon sea salt

Steak tartare

14 oz rib-eye steak, centre cut, chilled for at least 2 hours

2 shallots, diced

2 Tbsp capers, drained and roughly chopped

½ bunch fresh chives, chopped

2 Tbsp Kozlik's Triple Crunch mustard

Juice of 2 limes (or to taste)

1 Tbsp kosher salt (or to taste)

2 Tbsp extra-virgin olive oil (or to taste)

Arugula salad

Juice of 2 lemons

¼ cup vegetable oil

2 cups arugula, trimmed

Maldon sea salt

Serves 4 to 6

Steak Tartare with Kozlik's Triple Crunch and Crostini

Chef says: Many people shy away from this classic dish for fear of handling raw meat and out of concern about its safety. This recipe has one critical thing missing from the classic and that is a raw egg yolk. The choice to leave it off has nothing whatsoever to do with safety; I just happen to hate creamy raw meat. The flavours in this recipe are all about bright and fresh! Once you taste this simple dish teamed up with "Triple Crunch" from Toronto's favourite mustard maker, Kozlik's, you will understand why I call this mustard "pop rock candy" for adults.

Crostini Preheat the oven to 350°F. Using a serrated knife, slice the chilled baguette into thin slices. (Placing the baguette in the freezer for 10 minutes allows you to cut paper-thin slices.)

Evenly coat a baking sheet with half of the oil. Place the bread slices on the baking sheet, drizzle remaining olive oil on top and season with salt to taste. Bake until golden brown. Remove from the oven and let cool.

Steak tartare Have ready a clean cutting board, sharp knife and chilled meat. Cut the meat in ¼-inch cubes (these should be clean little meat

parcels—if there are any tiny scraps of fat, remove and discard them—but avoid overworking the meat with the knife). Transfer the meat to an airtight container and refrigerate until ready to assemble.

Spoon the shallots, capers, chives, mustard and meat into a medium bowl and stir to combine (do not use your hands for this step, as it will heat up the meat). Pour in the lime juice, salt and olive oil to taste and mix gently again. The tartare should ball together smoothly and have a bright red sheen and finish.

Arugula salad In a small jar with a lid, shake together lemon juice and olive oil. Place arugula in a bowl, add the lemon–olive oil dressing and toss to just coat the leaves.

To serve Chill four to six plates in the fridge. Arrange a mound of arugula on each plate. Using a rectangular mould or with your hands, form the tartare into a cylinder and set it on the arugula. Garnish with crostini and season the plate with Maldon salt.

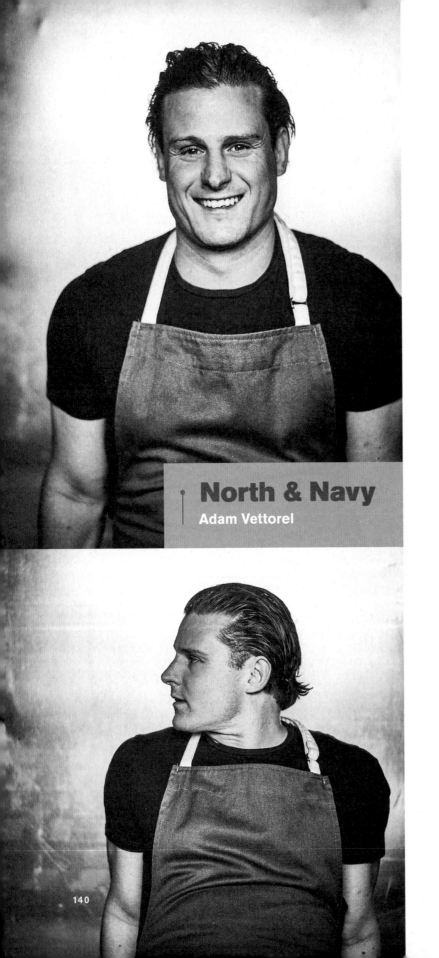

North & Navy
Adam Vettorel

THE SERVERS SEEM keenly aware that North & Navy newcomers, staring down an Italian menu that leads with *cichèti*, need some guidance. Like kind instructors taking ski-novices down the bunny hill, they cheerfully explain what bar snacking in Venice is about, that cichèti are small snacks served in *bàcari*, and why a 46-ounce Bistecca Fiorentina might be just the thing to order. Those expecting red-sauced Italian are in for a delicious awakening to the pleasures of bàcaro snacking: shimmering sardines on a tangled bed of onions sweetened with raisins; salt cod whipped to a frenzy with good oil; fragrant meatballs lolling in a tomato sauce. Chef Adam Vettorel's handmade tortelletti is just the right kind of chewy, stuffed with braised rabbit in a beurre blanc. It's my go-to on his menu of late, the richness cut with fresh plums and pickled shallots. Law school had been the plan, but while paying his way through with restaurant jobs, Vettorel changed direction. His food epiphany started at John Taylor's Domus Café and progressed through other fine restaurants in the city. When Beckta moved out of its Nepean Street home, Vettorel and his business partner, Chris Schlesak, moved in. They redesigned the space, opening the kitchen and extending the bar, and introduced Ottawa to the food and feel of Venice's wine bars. With some playfulness: check out Vettorel's version of the Whoopie pie, recipe provided.

226 NEPEAN STREET, 613-232-6289

facing: **Farfalle with Mushroom and Tomato Ragù**

140

Chef says: Making pasta at home is a bit of an undertaking, but the reward is worth the effort. High-quality dried pasta from Italian specialty shops can be used, but will never yield the perfect al dente that fresh pasta delivers. You can make the dough the day before.

A ragù generally refers to a slow-cooked Italian meat sauce, so the term may seem a little misleading in this recipe. I use it here because of the depth of flavour the mushrooms give the sauce. You can use oyster mushrooms or even button, but this dish is best when tomatoes are fresh from the vine and wild mushrooms are being foraged. The pasta water is an important element in this dish. At the restaurant we cook a lot of pasta and we take advantage of all the starch in the pasta water to thicken our sauces. At home you can create this effect by putting a small handful of semolina in the water when you add the salt.

Serves 4 to 6

Farfalle with Mushroom and Tomato Ragù

Pasta dough Before you begin, have ready a bench scraper (aka dough scraper), a squirt bottle filled with water and sheets of plastic wrap.

Clear a sturdy work surface and dust it lightly with flour. Mound the 1 ¾ cups of flour on the work surface and make a well in the middle, its walls high enough to contain the 12 egg yolks. Add the yolks and salt to the well and, using a fork, gently beat egg yolks until combined.

Working from the inside of the well, toward the outside, start incorporating small amounts of flour from the well walls to the yolks, being careful not to breach the perimeter or disturb the base. Eventually the yolks will have absorbed so much flour that the fork will become useless. Begin to use your hands and a bench scraper. At first the dough will feel too dry. If necessary, use the spray bottle to lightly mist it while you knead the mass. Be patient, it will come together! Use the bench scraper to lift any wet ingredients off the surface, and gather any crumbs that may try to escape. It is important that all the ingredients are incorporated, but resist the urge to use too much water. The dough is supposed to be dry. Shape the dough into a ball, wrap with plastic wrap and set aside at room temperature for 15 to 20 minutes.

Remove the plastic wrap and knead the dough again for at least 5 minutes. Notice how much the texture has changed now that the flour has had time to hydrate. Wrap the dough and let it rest again for another 15 to 20 minutes.

Remove the plastic wrap and knead the dough a third time for 5 minutes. Wrap the dough once more and refrigerate it for at least 2 hours, but preferably overnight.

Remove the dough from the fridge 20 minutes before you plan to work with it. Dust a few sheet pans with semolina. Lightly dust a clean work surface with flour. Have ready a pasta roller and a rolling pin or clean wine bottle. If you have a fluted roll cutter, keep that handy too.

Cut the chilled dough into 3 manageable pieces, set one of them on the counter and cover remaining chunks of dough with plastic wrap. With a rolling pin, roll out the dough into a long sheet. If you are using a hand-cranked pasta roller, set the rollers to the widest setting (usually "0") and feed the dough through the machine. Adjust the machine to the next narrowest setting (usually "1") and roll the dough through again. Continue to adjust the machine down a setting after each roll until you reach the second-to-last setting (often "7"). If you do not have a pasta machine,

Pasta dough

1¾ cups all-purpose flour
+ more for dusting
12 egg yolks
1 tsp salt
Semolina, for dusting

Mushroom and tomato ragù

20 cherry tomatoes
½ cup cold butter, cut into cubes
+ 2 Tbsp for cooking mushrooms
12 oz wild mushrooms (chanterelles,
morels and porcini, or use oyster
mushrooms, torn into large chunks,
4 to 5 per person), carefully cleaned
Salt and freshly cracked black pepper
2 cloves garlic, finely chopped
¼ cup dry white wine
6 perfect fresh basil leaves, for garnish
Freshly grated Parmesan cheese

keep rolling it out with a pin until you have a thin, almost translucent sheet of dough. Dust it lightly with flour, and repeat the rolling with remaining pasta dough.

Cut each sheet into rectangles, each 1½ × 2 inches. (If you have a fluted cutter, use it to cut the edges of the short sides.) You should have roughly 125 rectangles. Set the rectangles with the long edge parallel to the counter. Using your thumb and forefinger, pinch each rectangle in the middle of the long side, allowing the flanks to pucker so you have farfalle shaped like "butterfly wings" (ideally you should have 3 horizontal folds emanating from the centre on each side of the pinch). Place the farfalle on the semolina-dusted sheet pan. Repeat with remaining pasta until you have shaped all of the farfalle.

If you aren't using them right away, put the whole tray in the freezer so the farfalle freeze individually. Once frozen, place in resealable plastic bag(s) and store for up to 3 months.

Mushroom and tomato ragù Fill a large bowl with ice water. Bring a large pot of salted water to a boil. With a small sharp knife, score the bottom of the tomatoes with an X. Dunk tomatoes in the boiling water for 30 seconds, drain them and plunge them in the ice water to stop the cooking

and loosen the skins. Peel and discard the tomato skins. Set the tomatoes aside.

Finish pasta and ragù Bring a large pot with heavily salted water to a boil.

In another large saucepan big enough to hold the ragù and the cooked pasta, melt 2 Tbsp of the butter over medium-high heat. Add mushrooms, season with salt and pepper to taste and cook until mushrooms are browned, about 3 minutes. Stir in garlic and tomatoes and season again, to taste.

Drop the farfalle into the rapidly boiling water. It will take 4 to 5 minutes to cook. Return to the ragù, keeping an eye on the pasta while it cooks.

Once the garlic begins to colour slightly, add wine and reduce by half. As wine reduces, check the pasta for doneness. When the farfalle are about 80% cooked (nearly al dente but still a bit chewy), stir in the cubes of butter into the sauce, drain all but ½ cup of the pasta boiling water, then add the farfalle and reserved pasta water to the sauce (the starch in the water will help to thicken and emulsify the sauce). As soon as the last cube of butter melts, season the pasta and sauce to taste and remove from the heat.

To serve Divide the farfalle and ragù evenly among four to six individual bowls. Garnish with basil and Parmesan and serve immediately.

Makes 6 to 8

Giuseppe Luigi

Chocolate cakes Preheat the oven to 350°F. Line 2 baking sheets with parchment paper.

In a large bowl, whisk together flour, cocoa powder, salt, baking powder and baking soda.

In the bowl of a stand mixer fitted with the paddle attachment, cream butter and brown sugar at medium speed until fluffy, about 3 minutes. (If you do not have a stand mixer, just whisk the butter and sugar in a bowl and then continue adding remaining ingredients.) Add eggs, one at a time, and beat to combine. Add Nutella. Reduce the speed to low and add half of the flour mixture, mix to combine, and then add half of the milk and beat until incorporated. Repeat with remaining flour and milk, beating until all of the ingredients are well incorporated.

Scoop the cake batter into a piping bag with a non-fluted tip. Pipe (or just use a spoon) 12 to 16 mounds of batter, each 3 inches in diameter, onto the lined baking sheets, spacing 3 inches apart. Bake the cakes for 12 to 14 minutes or until a knife inserted in the centre comes out clean. Let cool on wire racks.

Cream cheese filling In the bowl of a stand mixer fitted with the paddle attachment, whip cream cheese with vanilla seeds at medium speed, about 1 minute. Add cream and sugar and beat until combined. Transfer the filling to a piping bag fitted with a non-fluted tip with a large opening (or to a resealable bag) and set aside while you prepare the salted caramel.

Chocolate cakes

1½ cups all-purpose flour

¾ cup unsweetened cocoa powder

1 tsp sea salt

1 tsp baking powder

½ tsp baking soda

½ cup unsalted butter, room temperature

1 cup loosely packed brown sugar

2 eggs

1 cup Nutella

1 cup whole milk

Cream cheese filling

¾ cup solid cream cheese
(not spreadable)

Seeds from 1 vanilla bean

¼ cup whipping (35%) cream

¼ cup icing sugar

Salted caramel

¾ cup white sugar

½ cup whipping (35%) cream

1 tsp sea salt

½ cup Nutella

Salted caramel In a tall-sided, heavy-bottomed saucepan over medium-high heat, melt sugar until it begins to turn a caramel colour, about 5 minutes. Once the sugar is golden-brown, remove it from the heat and slowly add cream (be careful!—there is no burn worse than a caramel burn). Whisk the cream into the caramel, then add salt and Nutella and whisk until combined. When the caramel has cooled enough that you can handle it, transfer half of the mixture to a piping bag fitted with a non-fluted tip with a large opening (or to a resealable plastic bag). Keep the other half warm over low heat.

To assemble Turn all of the cakes, flat side up, onto their baking sheets. Pipe (or spoon) the cream cheese filling in a ring around the perimeter of half of the cakes, then pipe (or spoon) the salted caramel into their centres. Gently place a second cake on top of each to form a sandwich. You should have 6 to 8 sandwiches.

To serve One by one, dip the cakes halfway into the warm caramel and transfer to individual plates. Serve at room temperature.

Ottawa STREAT Gourmet

Ben Baird
Elyse Pion

TALK ABOUT HITTING the road! If ever there was an example of the changing face of fine dining in this city, you need only point to the guy in the patriotically painted (an anthem to Ottawa) food truck feeding the downtown suits. Behind the wheel (or more likely standing over the propane stovetop) is where you'll find Ben Baird, a Stratford Chefs School grad, Sooke Harbour House alumnus, long-time owner of The Urban Pear restaurant and three-time Gold Medal Plates podium placer. In 2013 Baird sniffed the wind and smelled the coffee: the trend toward high-end vagabond cooking was on its way in and he wanted to be part of it. So he left his bricks-and-mortar restaurant and bought a truck. And now the short daily menu of Modern Canadian cuisine he was plating on bone china is a short daily menu of creative-gourmet street food handed out in compostable cartons. World flavours applied to local ingredients, dished up in every season and all weather, by Baird, his perpetually smiling partner Elyse Pion, and their small and mighty STREAT team. Why do they do it? "It's hard work, but it's fun. Every day is different." That's why. Chase them down.

PARKED WEEKDAYS AT THE CORNER OF ALBERT AND O'CONNOR.

facing: **Pulled Pork Fritters**

Chef says: This dish came to us accidentally. We were experimenting with a beer batter for a fried fish dish on the truck and we didn't want to use another portion of fish to test the batter. We had a small container of pulled pork left over from the day before and something delicious happened. Why hadn't we thought of this before? These fritters can be shaped into patties and put in a burger bun or made into small little bites for an hors d'oeuvre party. Start the pulled pork at least the day before you plan to serve these fritters.

Serves a crowd (12 to 15)

Pulled Pork Fritters

Pulled pork fritters Preheat the oven to 425°F. Arrange sliced onions in the bottom of a roasting pan large enough to hold all of the pork. Cut the pork into 4 to 6 fist-size pieces and place them in a large bowl. Set aside.

Place chipotle pepper and adobo sauce, garlic and cider vinegar in a blender and purée at medium-high speed for about 1 minute. Add cumin, coriander, paprika, fennel, thyme, oregano, salt, pepper and brown sugar and blend until smooth. Pour this paste over the pork and spread it over the meat with a spoon or spatula until evenly coated. Place on top of the onions in the pan and roast, uncovered, for 30 minutes. Turn down the oven temperature to 300°F, cover the pork with aluminum foil to seal, and cook for 4 to 6 hours until the pork pulls apart easily with a fork (if this doesn't happen, return it to the oven for another hour and test again). Remove from the oven, and let cool, uncovered, in the roasting pan.

Using a fork or your hands, pull the pork apart into long strands while in the roasting pan. Season with salt, pepper and more spice if desired. Transfer the pork to an airtight container and refrigerate overnight to cool completely. Using a spoon, remove and discard all of the congealed fat.

Beer batter Combine flour and baking powder in a large bowl. Add half of the beer and whisk until smooth. Add more beer as needed to obtain a thick pancake-like batter. (You will use about three-quarters of the bottle, which means you can drink the rest. You're welcome.) Refrigerate until ready to use.

Pulled pork fritters

6 onions, thinly sliced

1 boneless pork butt (shoulder), roughly 3 to 4 lb

1 chipotle pepper from a can + 1 Tbsp adobo sauce from same can

4 cloves garlic

¼ cup apple cider vinegar

3 Tbsp ground cumin

3 Tbsp ground coriander

1 Tbsp smoked paprika

1 Tbsp ground fennel

1 Tbsp dried thyme

1 Tbsp dried oregano

2 tsp sea salt

1 tsp freshly ground black pepper

¼ cup packed brown sugar

8 cups vegetable oil, for deep-frying

All-purpose flour, for dredging

1 recipe Beer Batter (see here)

Beer batter

1 cup all-purpose flour

2 heaping tsp baking powder

1 bottle (355 mL) good dark beer (I like to use Kichesippi 1855)

Garnish

1 head leaf or Bibb lettuce, leaves separated

½ bunch fresh parsley, chopped

½ cup mayonnaise mixed with ¼ cup Sriracha sauce (more or less to taste)

Finish fritters Heat vegetable oil in a deep fryer or a large heavy-bottomed saucepan until a deep-fry thermometer registers 375°F.

Place the flour for dredging in a shallow bowl. Remove the beer batter from the fridge. Line a plate with paper towels. With a spoon or an ice-cream scoop, shape pulled pork into balls or patties of equal size. Dredge the pork balls (or patties) in the flour and then dip them into the beer batter, making sure they are covered completely in batter. Let any excess batter drip off, then gently place into the hot oil and cook fritters, in batches or one at a time, if necessary, to a deep golden brown. Use a slotted spoon to transfer the fritter to the lined plate to drain. Season with salt and pepper to taste. Repeat with remaining pork and batter until you have fried all of the fritters.

To serve Arrange lettuce leaves on a large serving platter. Place the fritters on top and sprinkle with parsley. Wrap each fritter in a piece of lettuce, if you wish, and either drizzle with the spicy mayonnaise or serve the mayonnaise on the side.

Watermelon salsa

¼ seedless watermelon

Zest and juice of 1 lime

3 to 4 green onions, white and green parts, chopped

2 Tbsp chopped fresh mint leaves

1 clove garlic, finely chopped or puréed

Salt and freshly ground black pepper

Sugar or liquid honey (optional)

Guacamole

2 fresh ripe avocados

¼ cup chopped fresh cilantro leaves

1 Tbsp finely chopped red onions

1 tsp ground cumin

Juice of 1 lime

Salt and freshly ground black pepper

Tuna tostadas

Vegetable oil, for frying

4 to 6 fresh corn tortillas (each 3 or 4 inches in diameter)

Salt

8 oz fresh sushi-grade tuna, well chilled

1 tsp chili powder

1 tsp smoked paprika

Pinch of cayenne pepper

Juice of 2 to 3 fresh limes

2 Tbsp olive oil

Freshly ground black pepper

Garnish

4 sprigs fresh cilantro, leaves picked

1 jalapeño pepper, finely sliced into wheels

Serves 4 as appetizer or 2 as a main

Tuna Tostadas with Guacamole and Watermelon Salsa

Chef says: A great summer dish for when the days are sunny and hot and the watermelon are local, ripe and sweet. Source only the freshest sushi-grade fish for the tostadas. Serve the tostadas as is for an appetizer, make them more of a main course by adding beans and rice, or arrange them beside greens as a main-course salad.

Watermelon salsa Using a stainless steel spoon, scoop the flesh of the watermelon away from the skin. Cut the watermelon flesh in ¼-inch cubes and place it in a medium bowl. Add lime zest and juice, green onions, mint and garlic, toss gently to combine and season with salt and pepper to taste. If the watermelon is not quite ripe, add a touch of sugar or honey to sweeten, if desired.

Guacamole Cut the avocados in half, remove the pit and scoop the flesh into a large bowl. With a potato masher or a fork, break and mash the avocado. Add cilantro, red onions, cumin, lime juice and salt and pepper to taste and stir well. Transfer to a small, airtight container or cover well with plastic wrap and refrigerate for up to 1 hour.

Tuna tostadas Line a plate with paper towels. Heat 2 inches of vegetable oil in a large, heavy-bottomed pot until the temperature on a deep-fry thermometer registers 325°F to 350°F. Fry the tortillas one at a time in the hot oil until golden and crisp. Transfer the tostadas to the lined plate to drain, then season with salt to taste and set aside.

On a clean work surface and using a sharp knife, slice tuna into ¼-inch-thick strips. Place in a medium bowl, add chili powder, smoked paprika, cayenne, lime juice, olive oil and salt and pepper to taste, and toss gently to combine (do not overwork the tuna or it will turn mushy). Taste, and add more lime and salt if needed. Serve within 5 to 10 minutes of mixing.

To serve Spread a heaping spoonful of guacamole on each tostada, leaving a little divot in the middle. Arrange the tuna evenly over the guacamole, piling a little extra within the divot. Spoon the salsa on top and garnish with cilantro and the jalapeño wheels. Serve immediately on individual plates.

The Piggy Market

Warren Sutherland

WARREN SUTHERLAND came to cheffing with an engineering degree. After a year at Bombardier and with further support from his folks, he headed to the New England Culinary Institute to pursue a passion and then to acclaimed kitchens in New York and Phoenix. Sutherland first came to my attention at Sweetgrass, an aboriginal bistro with a menu that featured game, smoked fish, wild greens and native breads, along with culinary segues to his Jamaican roots—roast goose, followed by rum pudding. In 2009, with Sweetgrass sous chef Dave Neil, he opened The Piggy Market in Westboro Village. The team wanted a place "where food and community meet in old-fashioned ways," where all items were made in-house or sourced from artisanal suppliers and a spot that honoured the low-slow, fragrant food of Sutherland's childhood. The Piggy Market is exactly that place. Recent renovations have moved butchery and charcuterie downstairs, and freed up prep space for more in-house treats—sandwiches, soups, house pickles, braised beans dark with molasses and, hands down, the city's best Jamaican patties. This is where I buy my Thanksgiving turkey. This is where I send my sons for sausage-making classes or meet friends for cheese tastings. A few outdoor tables and rail seating along the front window mean you can eat in-house now, treated to the smells of chickens spit-roasting, sourdough baking and egg rolls frying. Yup, you heard me. This little piggy had three the other day.

400 WINSTON AVENUE, 613-371-6124

S1 sauce
1 Tbsp vegetable oil
1 onion, chopped
6 cloves garlic, minced
Kosher salt
3 cups balsamic vinegar
1 cup apple cider vinegar
1 cup Worcestershire sauce
½ cup raisins

½ cup tamarind paste
1½ cups packed brown sugar
1 tsp allspice berries
1 tsp yellow mustard seeds
1 tsp celery seeds
2 sprigs fresh rosemary
4 sprigs fresh thyme
1 bay leaf
1 cup ketchup

Spice-crusted steaks
2 Tbsp whole coffee beans
2 Tbsp black peppercorns
2 Tbsp dehydrated onions
1 Tbsp dried garlic
1 Tbsp red chili flakes
1 Tbsp dried thyme
1 Tbsp dried rosemary
1 Tbsp fennel seeds
4 rib-eye steaks, each about
  1-inch thick
Kosher salt
Vegetable oil, for greasing grill
Sea salt

Serves 4

Coffee- and Spice-Crusted Rib-Eye Steaks with S1 Sauce

Chef says: I love the combination of beef and coffee. In this recipe, the coffee flavour is subtle and, together with the spices, forms a nice crust, which pairs well with the fat of a rib-eye steak and with our Sutherland One (S1) Sauce. I have always been a sauce person, and I have always wanted to make my own version of things. Growing up in Jamaica, we had a spicy table sauce called Pickapeppa Sauce. When I was living in the States there was A1 Sauce, and in Canada we have HP. So I came up with my own sauce, inspired by all three, and as luck would have it, my first attempt turned out to be the tastiest! The S1 was born.

S1 sauce Heat vegetable oil in a stainless steel (or other non-reactive) pot over medium heat. Add onions and garlic and cook until fragrant, about 2 minutes. Season with salt to taste. Stir in vinegars, Worcestershire sauce, raisins, tamarind paste, brown sugar, allspice, mustard seeds, celery seeds, rosemary, thyme and bay leaf. Bring to a slow simmer and cook until reduced by half (to 2½ cups). Strain through a fine-mesh sieve into a clean non-reactive pot; discard solids. Stir in the ketchup, return the sauce to a simmer and let reduce to about 2 cups. Strain through a fine-mesh sieve into a clean bowl; discard solids. (Will keep refrigerated in an airtight container for up to 4 weeks.)

Spice-crusted steaks Preheat a grill or barbecue to high heat. In a coffee grinder or food processor fitted with the metal blade, coarsely grind coffee beans to about the size of the peppercorns. In a small bowl, combine ground coffee with peppercorns, onions, garlic, chili flakes, thyme, rosemary and fennel seeds. Transfer the spice mixture to a pepper mill set to a very coarse grind.

Season the steaks lightly with kosher salt to taste, and then grind the spice mix onto the steaks in a nice even coating.

Lightly brush the hot grill with vegetable oil, add the steaks and grill for 8 to 10 minutes per side for medium rare (or cook until your desired doneness). Sprinkle with sea salt. Remove the steaks from the grill and let rest for 4 to 5 minutes before serving or slicing.

To serve Serve steaks with a side of S1 sauce.

2-lb piece pork belly
Kosher salt
Freshly ground black pepper
3 cloves garlic, minced
1 onion, minced
1 Tbsp minced peeled fresh ginger
1 Tbsp Chinese five-spice powder
6 Tbsp soy sauce

3 Tbsp Jamaican rum
2 Tbsp hoisin sauce
1 Tbsp rice wine vinegar
1 whole star anise
2 lb taro root (dasheen), peeled (larger ones work best)
4 green onions, green parts only, chopped, for garnish

Serves 4 as a main or 6 as an appetizer

Pork and Yam

Chef says: Jamaican cuisine over the years has been heavily influenced by the island's large Chinese immigrant population. Throughout my world travels, some of the best Chinese cuisine I have eaten has been in Jamaica and this has heavily influenced my own cooking style. This recipe calls for taro root, but we call the dish "Pork and Yam" because, in Jamaica, all tubers other than potatoes are labelled "yam." Taro is sometimes also called dasheen. Pork and yam is one of my all-time favourite dishes that I have adjusted over the years to make my own. Serve with a side of sesame-seasoned garlic bok choy.

Preheat the oven to 350°F. Season pork belly with salt and pepper, place in a roasting pan and cook for 45 minutes. Turn pork belly over and cook for another 45 minutes, until golden brown on both sides. Remove from the oven and let cool to room temperature. Drain off the cooking juices into a small bowl and set aside. Place the pork belly in a bowl and refrigerate until completely cooled.

To the bowl with the cooled cooking juices, add garlic, onions, ginger, five-spice powder, soy sauce, rum, hoisin sauce, vinegar and star anise and stir well.

Remove and discard the skin from the cooked pork. Slice the meat into 2-inch × 4-inch rectangles. Cut the taro root into 2-inch × 4-inch rectangles to match the pork belly in size and shape.

In a medium stainless steel bowl, alternate pieces of taro and pork belly around the edges of the bowl, arranging them long sides up (like a row of dominoes). Arrange as many as you can upright, then pile the remainder in the centre. Pour the sauce over top, giving the bowl a gentle shake to allow the sauce to get between the layers. Place the bowl inside a pot large enough to hold it, fill the pot with just enough water to reach a bit above halfway up the side of the bowl and bring to a low simmer over medium heat. Cover the pot and simmer gently for 1½ hours, checking periodically to add more water and/or turn down the heat, if required. The pork is cooked when it is tender enough to cut with a fork. Remove the bowl from the pot and let sit for a few minutes before serving.

To serve Transfer the pork and taro to a serving bowl or a platter with sides high enough to hold the sauce. Garnish with green onions and serve.

Sidedoor
Jonathan Korecki

WHERE IN THIS CITY can you start with prawn dumplings and salt and pepper squid, move on to a Panaeng curry and Mapo tofu, and end with doughnuts filled with strawberry cream and iced with Olivia dark chocolate? Sidedoor, that's where. Some of the most innovative Asian food in the city is found here, in this underground restaurant in the oldest section of the ByWard Market, tucked beneath its big brother, e18hteen (page 80). Chef Jonathan Korecki runs the show at both restaurants. A Cordon Bleu grad who worked at Café Henry Burger until it closed and apprenticed with Toronto's Susur Lee, he also gave *Top Chef Canada* a whirl and has twice stood on the podium at Gold Medal Plates. For his knockout dishes, Korecki credits his team: "I've got the absolute best people around me." Those good people use top-notch ingredients in cunning ways, while those staples most chefs would outsource are all tackled in-house. They have a sizeable account with local farmers in the city. A 300-pound crop of Jerusalem artichokes at Acorn Creek Garden Farm? They'll take 'em all. On any given day there are 300 litres of pickles in the Sidedoor fridge. Walk by the open kitchen and gawk at the *mise en place.* Or stay put in the light-drenched solarium with your salmon sashimi (sharpened with pickled rhubarb) and your lineup of doughnuts. Your one mistake? Agreeing you'd share dessert.

18 YORK STREET, 613-562-9331

Chef says: When produce is abundantly available in Ottawa, with some diligence, our short growing season can be preserved and enjoyed all year long. This is a general recipe, but the beauty of pickling is that it's so versatile. You can vary the flavour of the brine and scale the quantity up or down to suit the amount of produce you have, as long as you keep the ratios the same (hence the "parts"). Capitalize on the peak of the growing season for the freshest and ripest produce—one week or two late and you can miss your chance!

When pickling anything, be sure to follow sanitary guidelines by using fresh snap lids or sealing bands for all of your jars, and washing and drying all of your produce before you begin.

Sidedoor's Master Pickling Recipe

Vegetables: Group 1

BEETS: Peel and cut into matchsticks

CARROTS: Peel and cut into rounds *or* peel into shavings

CAULIFLOWER: Cut into equal-size florets

CELERY: Break into stalks and dice

CUCUMBER: Scrub off bristles and cut into equal-size pieces

JALAPEÑO PEPPERS: Slice into thin rounds

KOHLRABI: Peel and cut into matchsticks

RED OR WHITE ONIONS: Peel and halve lengthwise, cut along ribs and rinse

SUNROOT (JERUSALEM ARTICHOKES): Slice into rounds and rinse

SWISS CHARD STEMS: Remove any green leaves (reserve them for another use) and dice the stems

MINI TURNIP: Peel and slice into quarters

WILD GARLIC (RAMPS): Cut into 2-inch-long pieces

Vegetables: Group 2

Increase the vinegar, salt and sugar in the Master Brine recipe by ½ part each (i.e., add ⅛ cup more vinegar, ¼ cup more salt, ¼ cup more sugar)

ASPARAGUS: Peel and discard the fibrous parts of stem and cut the spears to the length of the jar being used

BEANS: Trim off and discard the stems

BRUSSELS SPROUTS: Core and tear into leaves

GARLIC SCAPE BULBS: Trim off the greens (reserve them for another use), discard the root and use the clean bulbs

TOMATILLOS: Husk, wash and dice

WATERMELON RIND: Cut off skin and pith and slice into sticks (reserve the flesh for another use)

ZUCCHINI: Cut in half lengthwise, spoon out the seeds (reserve them for another use) and cut the flesh on a bias into half-moons

Master brine

12 parts (or 3 cups) water

4 parts (or 1 cup) any vinegar
with 7% acetic acid

1 part (or ½ cup) pickling or
kosher salt

1 part (or ½ cup) white,
palm or cane sugar

Classic

2 whole cloves

6 black peppercorns,

1 tsp coriander seeds

1 Tbsp yellow mustard seeds

1 bay leaf

Dilly

1 fresh dill flower

1 clove garlic (rinsed)

1 Tbsp yellow mustard seeds

Fresh

Peels from 1 lemon

4 whole star anise

Yellow

1 tsp freshly grated peeled
turmeric root (use gloves!)

1 tsp coriander seeds

1 Tbsp yellow mustard seeds

Relish

½ cup diced onions

2 Tbsp yellow mustard seeds

½ cup diced cabbage

1 hot chili pepper, split and
seeded if desired

Bring a large, deep pot of water to a boil over high heat. Add your 4-cup/1 L canning jar(s) to the water and boil for 5 minutes. Using tongs, transfer to a rack to drain and cool. Place the canning lid(s) and sealing band(s) in a large heatproof bowl and pour boiling water over them to cover. Let sit in the hot water for 5 minutes. Use tongs to transfer them to the rack to drain. Turn down the heat so the water remains at a low simmer.

Prepare the master brine by bringing the water, vinegar, salt and sugar to a boil in a large pot over medium-high heat.

Have ready a canning funnel. Pack your jar(s) with prepared vegetables and whichever variation of spices or aromatics you choose, leaving 2 inches between the vegetables and the top of the jar. (This is called the headspace, and it allows the food to expand as the jars are heated and then form a strong vacuum seal as they cool.) While the jar is still hot, pour the just-boiled brine through the canning funnel over the vegetables, leaving 1 inch of headspace. Place the snap lid or sealing band over the jar and screw on the lid until just tight.

If the jar(s) is still hot enough and the brine is poured in just-off-the-boil, the jar(s) should seal without further processing. To ensure a fail-safe seal after screwing on the lid, place a wire rack in the bottom of the pot of simmering water, increase the heat and bring the water back to a boil. Gently place the jar(s) in the pot of boiling water and process for 10 minutes.

Using tongs, remove the jar(s) from the water bath and let stand at room temperature. Within a few minutes and up to a few hours, you will start to hear the jar(s) pop, which means all is well and a proper seal has been made. Any jar that does not pop (meaning you can push on the lid and it will pop in and out) can be refrigerated or reprocessed in a boiling water bath.

Pickles usually take a good 3 weeks to mature, and sealed jars will keep in a cool dark place like a basement for up to 12 months. Unsealed pickles should be refrigerated and eaten within 3 months.

Grilled lamb
1 boneless leg of lamb (3 to 4 lb)
2 Tbsp olive oil
1 Tbsp kosher salt
1 tsp freshly cracked black pepper
2 cloves garlic, chopped
1 lemon, cut into 8 wedges

Thai pistou
2 cups fresh Thai basil leaves (about 1 bunch)
2 cups chopped fresh cilantro, leaves and stems (about 1 bunch)
2 cups fresh mint leaves (about 1 bunch)

1 bunch green onions, green parts only, thinly sliced (may reserve white parts, thinly sliced, for garnish)
1 bird's-eye chili pepper, seeded
2 Tbsp local liquid honey
Juice of 2 lemons and 1 lime
½ clove garlic
1 Tbsp fish sauce

Serves 4 to 6

Grilled Lamb with Thai Pistou

Chef says: With a few easy variations this recipe can brighten up a dreary winter day, become a light spring meal or part of an autumn harvest celebration. The technique for marinating and grilling the lamb leg can easily be applied to a spatchcock chicken, a tougher cut of beef (like flank, skirt or sirloin) or pork shoulder steaks. Start the marinade at least twelve hours before you plan to grill and serve the meat. When your herb garden is out of control, a pistou is a great way to preserve the fresh flavour of herbs instead of drying them. Garnish this dish with a mix of your favourite pickles and serve with steamed rice, boiled potatoes or some fresh lettuces.

Grilled lamb Trim and discard any sinew from the lamb and lay the meat flat on a large cutting board. Using a meat tenderizer, a pestle or your fist, lightly pound the flesh, being careful not to tear it, until it is an even thickness. In a large bowl, stir together olive oil, salt, pepper and garlic. Juice lemon, then add wedges to the bowl. Add lamb leg, using your hands to massage the marinade into the meat for 30 seconds. Cover and refrigerate the lamb in the marinade for 12 to 24 hours to mature.

Preheat a barbecue to medium-high heat, then turn down the heat on half the barbecue to low—this will be your cooking side. (If you are using charcoal, wait until lit coals have formed and then scatter them into a thin layer under the grill rack.) Remove the lamb from the marinade and set it, outer side down, on the cool side of the grill. Cook with the lid open for 6 to 8 minutes, turn once and cook for another 6 to 8 minutes. If you wish, use an instant-read thermometer to check the temperature of the meat: the centre should be cooked to medium-rare, or about 136°F. Remove the lamb from the heat, place on a serving platter and cover lightly with aluminum foil. Let rest for 10 minutes to ensure the blood or "juiciness" stays within the meat. While the meat is resting, prepare the pistou.

Thai pistou Place Thai basil, cilantro, mint and green onion in a blender with remaining ingredients and process at high speed for 30 seconds. Taste and adjust seasoning. (Will keep refrigerated in an airtight container for 4 days or frozen in resealable bags for up to 8 months. To reconstitute frozen pistou, thaw in the fridge overnight or on the counter for a few hours, then process in the blender for about 30 seconds, adding a bit more citrus juice to brighten the flavour.)

To serve Using a very sharp knife, carve the lamb across the grain and arrange slices on a large serving platter. Spoon the Thai pistou on top or serve it in a bowl on the side.

Soca Kitchen & Pub

**Daniela Manrique
Gustavo Belisario**

THE NAME SOCA comes from the Venezuelan word for the second harvest of the sugar cane crop. Gustavo Belisario knows about that: his family has been farming sugar cane for two hundred years. He met his wife in Caracas. Venezuelan-born, Montreal-raised and Miami-trained, Daniela Manrique is a young chef with a rustic-refined style all her own. For a newish addition to the Holland Avenue strip, the couple's Soca restaurant feels firmly part of its 'hood, and we feel good to be in it, tucked in and welcome. Where else are you greeted with a glass of freshly pressed sugar cane juice? Add rum and you're golden. Crisp arepitas come from the kitchen—something to give a sense of place and to nibble while you examine Manrique's short menu. On it are raw oysters and braised octopus, Catalonian seafood stew, steak with hazelnut romesco and a roasted black garlic mash. I am mad for her roasted cauliflower steak, sandwiched with a smoky red pepper coulis and a vibrant gremolata. We tend to start with one of the kitchen's sparkling crudos, or a plate of its Butifarra sausage with a lime-garbanzo stew—dishes that jump with irresistible flavours. But we can't help asking: why did this couple choose Ottawa as the city for Soca? Gustavo tells me he loves the snow; Daniela has enjoyed the welcoming warmth of the cooks' community here. Whatever the case, they are here and we are terribly pleased about that. 93 HOLLAND AVENUE, 613-695-9190

2 cups white sugar
1 can (14 oz) sweetened
    condensed milk
1¾ cups 2% milk
4 large eggs
2 large egg yolks
Seeds from ½ vanilla bean

Serves 6 to 10

Quesillo

Chef says: Quesillo is a traditional dessert from Venezuela similar to a crème caramel. This particular recipe comes from Gustavo's grandmother and has been passed down from generation to generation. At Soca, we use small Mason jars to serve our quesillos.

Quesillo Preheat the oven to 350°F. Have ready an 8-inch round, non-stick cake pan or 6 to 8 individual Mason jars and a large roasting pan.

In a heavy-bottomed pot over medium-low heat, melt sugar until it dissolves and turns a deep amber colour, about 8 minutes. Carefully pour the caramel into the cake pan (or Mason jars), covering the bottom to a depth of about ¼ inch. Set aside to cool and harden.

In a blender, combine condensed milk, 2% milk, eggs and egg yolks, and vanilla bean seeds, and blend at high speed for 2 to 3 minutes. Pour this custard over the hardened caramel and cover tightly with aluminum foil.

Place the cake pan (or Mason jars) in the roasting pan and fill the roasting pan with 1 to 2 inches of warm water to create a bain-marie. Bake for about 50 minutes (or about 25 minutes for the jars) or until the custard is set. To test for doneness, gently shake the cake pan (or jars) to see if the centre is still liquid or insert a knife into the centre: if it comes out clean, the custard is ready. If not yet set, return the pan to the oven and check every 5 minutes to see if the quesillo is cooked. Remove from the oven, take the pan (or jars) out of the bain-marie, and let cool to room temperature. Cover and refrigerate for 1 hour before serving.

To serve If you used a cake pan, run a butter knife around the pan to loosen the quesillo. Place a serving plate over the top of the pan and invert carefully. The caramel will have melted into the custard, and the syrup will pool around it. Serve chilled or at room temperature. If you used Mason jars, serve from the jar, chilled or at room temperature.

Pepper sauce
½ Tbsp canola oil
2 red bell peppers, diced
½ rocoto pepper (or other hot pepper), seeded
½ Spanish onion, diced
¼ cup freshly squeezed lemon juice
Salt

Scallop crudo
½ lb Nantucket Bay scallops (or other small scallops)
½ ripe tomato
½ cup natural Caesar juice (I prefer Walter All-Natural Craft Caesar Mix)
Juice of 1 lime
1 avocado, cut into ¼-inch cubes
1 small garlic clove (or ½ large clove), finely chopped

¼ bunch fresh cilantro, leaves picked and chopped
2 dashes Tabasco or homemade hot sauce
Salt
A few sprigs fresh micro cilantro or other microgreen, for garnish

Serves 4

Scallop Crudo

Chef says: This recipe is the combination of all the things we love to eat and what our food is all about: fresh seafood, spicy peppers, citrus, garden-fresh herbs and more. When buying scallops, make sure you smell them: they should smell like a fresh ocean. Serve the crudo with yucca chips, if you wish.

Pepper sauce Heat canola oil in a medium sauté pan over medium-low heat. Add bell and rocoto peppers and onions and cook until the vegetables are soft and onions are translucent, about 15 minutes. Add lemon juice and cook until juice is reduced by half, about 10 minutes. Transfer to a blender and process at medium speed, gradually increasing to high speed, until smooth. Season with salt to taste. Let cool. (Will keep refrigerated in an airtight container for about 3 days.)

Scallop crudo To clean the scallops, using your hands or with the help of a sharp knife, remove and discard the muscle attached to their sides, which tends to be tough.

Cut tomato in half and remove the seeds. Using a box grater over a bowl, grate the tomato, skin side out, until the flesh is completely grated and you are left with only the skins; discard skins. Add scallops to tomatoes, along with Caesar mix, lime juice, avocado, garlic, cilantro and Tabasco sauce and toss gently to combine. Season with salt to taste, cover and refrigerate for 20 minutes. The acid in the tomatoes and the lime juice will begin to "cook" the scallops.

To serve Refrigerate four bowls until well chilled. Spoon about a tablespoonful of the spicy pepper sauce in the bottom of each bowl, top with the scallop crudo and garnish with microgreens.

Social

Kyrn Stein

NOW IN ITS seventeenth year of service on Sussex Drive, Social's enduring beauty is prettier still after a 2015 facelift stripped its heavy drapes and red velvet. The old brick has been painted white, wallpaper evokes jungle life in the language of William Morris–meets-modernism, chairs are the yummy colour of grape jelly. Half-moon booths are just the thing for romantic dining, while the marble bar sets the scene for good long chats. Social's food has had a thorough rethink too. "I wanted something for everyone," chef Kyrn Stein tells me. "More democratic, more user-friendly." What does that look like? A burger and a dry-aged rib-eye next to bouillabaisse; fat-fried smelts with rémoulade, and the cure-everything-that-ails-you dish of mushy peas on toasted brioche with sous-vide runny eggs. Hunks of sweet lobster are poached in a remarkably layered green curry; and rabbit sits softly on pappardelle noodles with fava beans. Stein grew up in a house of cooks and bakers. His dad's family owned twenty kosher bakeries in Montreal. His mother was Cordon Bleu–trained. So, of course, the boy studied mathematics at U of O. And then gave his head a shake, enrolling at the Culinary Institute of America. Kitchen jobs took him to the States, the UK and Toronto, where he worked with luminaries like Jamie Kennedy and Mark McEwan. Stein's fish dishes are thoroughly modern: branzino beached on Juniper Farm's produce, set in a sherry-shiitake broth infused with lime leaf. His grandmother's plum cake plumbs the past.

537 SUSSEX DRIVE, 613-789-7355

Brioche

2 tsp (10 mL) active dry yeast

90 mL warm whole milk (about 6 Tbsp)

2 Tbsp (30 mL) white sugar

400 g white bread flour (about 3¼ cups)

13 g kosher salt (about 3 tsp)

100 g butter, room temperature (3½ oz)

4 eggs, lightly beaten

Vegetable oil, for greasing bowl

Goat's milk ricotta

8½ cups goat's milk

1 tsp sea salt

⅛ cup apple cider vinegar

Mushy peas and egg topping

4 cups shelled English peas, cooked and cooled (or use thawed frozen peas)

¼ bunch fresh mint, leaves picked and finely cut

Zest of 1 lemon

½ tsp salt

1 Tbsp olive oil + more for drizzling

4 eggs, poached

Mizuna, nasturtium leaves and/ or fennel fronds, for garnish

Serves 4

Mushy Peas on Toast

Chef says: This dish embodies the essence of spring, with fresh English peas, garden mint, farm-fresh hen eggs and homemade goat's milk ricotta. It's terrific as a brunch item—add hollandaise sauce with some fresh chives, dill and tarragon—or just as an afternoon snack! Start the brioche the day before.

Brioche Place yeast, warm milk and sugar into a bowl or jug, whisk together and let sit for 15 to 20 minutes. It should be nice and frothy.

In the bowl of a stand mixer fitted with the dough hook, combine flour and salt at low speed. Increase the speed to medium, add the yeasty milk mixture, butter and eggs, and knead until smooth and shiny, 8 to 9 minutes. Shape the dough into a round, place it in a large, greased bowl and cover tightly with plastic wrap. Refrigerate overnight.

Next day, have ready a 10½-inch × 4½-inch × 3½-inch brioche pan. Remove the dough from the fridge, shape into a rough loaf, place it into the loaf pan, cover with plastic wrap and let rise in a warm place until doubled in size, about 4 hours.

Preheat the oven to 400°F. Place loaf in oven and bake for 10 minutes, then turn down the heat to 350°F and bake for another 30 minutes, until golden brown. Remove the brioche from the loaf pan and let cool on a wire rack.

Goat's milk ricotta Line a large colander with cheesecloth or muslin. In a heavy pot over medium heat, heat goat's milk and salt to 195°F (check the temperature using an instant-read thermometer), being sure to stir every few minutes to prevent scorching. Add vinegar and continue stirring. The curd should start to separate at this point. If it doesn't, increase the heat slightly to bring the milk up to 205°F.

Place the lined colander in the sink and gently pour in the milk mixture, leaving the whey to drain away from the curds for 4 to 5 minutes. Refrigerate the curds while you prepare the peas and toast.

Mushy peas and egg topping Place peas into a food processor fitted with the metal blade and pulse until roughly chopped. Transfer peas to a bowl, add mint, lemon zest, salt and olive oil and stir gently.

To serve Cut four slices, each roughly an inch and a half thick, from the brioche loaf. Toast the bread and arrange one slice on each plate. Spread each slice with some of the pea mixture and top with a poached egg. Crumble ricotta over the egg, garnish with mizuna or nasturtium leaves and fennel fronds, and drizzle with oil. Serve immediately.

Chef says: This was a dessert that my grandmother Beatrice used to make me at the height of plum season when I was a child. I remember walking into her home, smelling the roasting plums and the cinnamon, and knowing instantly what she was up to! Feel free to replace the plums with seasonal berries: raspberries, blackberries, blueberries, strawberries or a mixture of all of them. Always goes well with vanilla ice cream, too.

Serves 4 to 8

Beatrice's Upside-Down Plum Cake with Warm Crème Anglaise

Upside-down plum cake Preheat the oven to 350°F. Lightly grease the bottom and sides of four 4-inch springform pans with butter, then sprinkle them evenly with sugar and cinnamon. Set aside.

In the bowl of a stand mixer fitted with the whisk attachment, beat egg whites, starting at low speed and gradually increasing the speed to high, until stiff peaks form. With a spatula, gently scrape the beaten egg whites into a clean bowl and set aside for later.

To the same mixer bowl, add butter and whisk at medium speed. With the motor running, slowly add sugar and beat for 15 minutes, until very light in colour and almost doubled in volume. Reduce the speed to low and, one at a time, with the motor running, slowly add buttermilk, water and vanilla and mix until well incorporated. Next, slowly add flour, baking powder and salt until well incorporated. Turn off the mixer and lightly fold in the whipped egg whites.

Arrange one sectioned plum (4 pieces) in the bottom of each springform pan. Divide the batter equally between the 4 pans, covering the plums but leaving a little room at the top for the batter to rise. Bake for 50 to 60 minutes or until a skewer inserted in the centre of the cake comes out clean. Remove from oven and place pans on wire racks to cool slightly.

Crème anglaise In a medium pot over medium heat, bring cream and vanilla seeds and bean to a boil. Remove from the heat and set aside to infuse for 10 minutes. Remove vanilla bean (can be washed and saved for another dish).

Upside-down plum cake

½ lb (1 cup) butter, room temperature + more for greasing baking pans

1¾ cups white sugar + more for lining baking pans

Ground cinnamon, for dusting baking pans

4 egg whites

1½ cups buttermilk

¼ cup water

1 tsp pure vanilla extract

1¾ cups all-purpose flour

2 tsp baking powder

2 tsp salt

4 ripe plums, pitted and quartered

Crème anglaise

2 cups table (18%) cream

1 vanilla bean, split lengthwise and seeds scraped (or use 3 cracked green cardamom seeds or a drop of orange blossom water or rosewater to change the flavour of the custard)

⅓ cup white sugar

5 egg yolks

In a medium bowl, whisk together sugar and egg yolks until well incorporated. Slowly add the hot cream to the yolk mixture, being careful not to scramble the eggs (this is called tempering). Once all of the cream has been tempered, return the custard to the pot over medium heat. With a rubber spatula, stir the custard continuously in a figure-eight motion, scraping the bottom of the pot to prevent scorching, and simmer until it reaches 175°F (the consistency should be *nappé*—when you run the spatula through the hot sauce it will leave a clear and distinct line where it passed). Set a fine-mesh sieve over a clean bowl and strain the custard through it; discard solids.

To serve Serve cakes warm with a dollop of crème anglaise, or cut them into wedges for smaller appetites.

Soif

Jamie Stunt
Véronique Rivest

GOSH, WE LOVE this story. It starts with the wine win in Quebec a few years ago. Véronique Rivest from Wakefield then moved on to top podium finishes at the national sommelier competition and at the Best Sommelier of the Americas. In 2013 she headed to Tokyo for the Meilleur Sommelier du Monde competition, where she made it to the finals (the only woman ever to reach that level) and ended up placing an unprecedented second. And now this remarkably accomplished woman has opened a wine bar in Gatineau, which snagged a spot on *enRoute* magazine's 2015 Top Ten list of Canada's best new restaurants. You find it in a handsome red-brick house, across the street from the park Rivest played in as a child. Soif it's called, which is how you are meant to arrive. (Something will be done about that!) Arrive *faim,* too. In the kitchen is Jamie Stunt, a chef with an impressive CV, including a Gold Medal Plates gold, and a silver medal from the Canadian Culinary Championships. Stunt has a laudable goal at Soif: to practise restraint. To keep the food wine-friendly. "Natural, simple dishes, without too much noise," as he puts it. Handmade bread with tapenade; house-smoked trout with crème fraîche; and a "Mushroom Melt" in which all the elements of a straightforward dish are utterly sound. Bison tartare vies for my affection with crispy smelts, served with rémoulade and a citrus salad. The star anise beef jus that pools beneath the grilled steak might make for a challenging wine pairing. The smart staff at Soif nails it, *bien sûr.* 88 RUE MONTCALM, GATINEAU, QC, 819-600-7643

Fried feta

½ cup fine or medium cornmeal

¼ tsp sweet or smoked paprika

¼ tsp garlic powder

¼ tsp onion powder

¼ tsp chili powder

¼ tsp ground coriander

¼ tsp ground cumin

¼ tsp ground fennel

Salt and freshly ground black pepper

2 Tbsp vegetable oil

8 oz good-quality feta cheese, cut into 4 rectangular pieces

Tomato and watermelon salad

1½ lb tomatoes, preferably in a variety of colours and shapes

1 lb watermelon (seedless or seeded)

2 Tbsp good-quality (first cold-pressed) canola oil

1 Tbsp sherry vinegar

Salt and freshly ground black pepper

Small handful each of fresh basil, flat-leaf (Italian) parsley, mint and chives

Serves 4 as an appetizer

Tomato and Watermelon Salad with Fried Feta

Chef says: This is a lovely recipe for mid- to late summer when tomatoes are at their peak. Try to use a variety of tomatoes to create a multicoloured summer mosaic. At Soif we use a nice sheep's milk feta from Quebec and cold-pressed canola oil, but the salad is good with cow's milk feta, and olive oil works as well.

Fried feta Combine cornmeal and all of the spices, including salt and pepper to taste, in a large shallow bowl.

Line a plate with paper towels. Heat vegetable oil in a large skillet over medium-high heat. Dredge feta in the cornmeal and spice mixture, shake off any excess and fry for 30 to 45 seconds per side. Transfer fried feta to the lined plate to drain.

Tomato and watermelon salad Chill 4 rimmed salad plates. Slice tomatoes and watermelon into bite-size pieces (don't worry too much about uniformity, but try to highlight the different sizes, colours and shapes of the tomatoes). Arrange tomatoes and watermelon on the chilled plates, drizzle with canola oil and vinegar and season with salt and pepper to taste.

To serve Place one piece of fried feta in the middle of each salad. Roughly tear the larger herb leaves (smaller leaves can be left whole) and scatter over the salad. Serve immediately.

Pickled cherries
1 lb fresh cherries
1 cup water
1 cup white wine vinegar
1 Tbsp salt
1 Tbsp white sugar

Grilled pork
1 lb pork neck or shoulder
1 tsp chopped garlic
1 tsp chopped fresh rosemary
½ tsp red chili flakes
1 Tbsp olive oil
2 cups beef or pork stock

Small handful of Pickled Cherries (see here)
1 tsp white wine vinegar
Salt
1 bunch fresh basil leaves, roughly torn, for finishing

Serves 4

Grilled Pork Neck with Pickled Cherries and Basil

Chef says: We were experimenting at the wine bar with different cuts of pork and discovered that the neck was a delicious and affordable one. It has a good meat-to-fat ratio, and when cut thin and grilled quick and hot is very tender and succulent. The marinade provides a little kick, the cherries add a touch of sweetness and acidity, the basil some freshness and the sauce brings all the components together. Most butchers will be able to get you some neck with a little notice, but pork shoulder works nicely as well. The recipe makes more pickled cherries than is needed, but fear not: they are great with cheese plates or other grilled or roasted meats, especially those with a bit of fat content.

Pickled cherries With a sharp paring knife and holding the stem to keep it intact, slice each cherry crosswise around the middle and carefully remove the pit without bruising the cherry. Repeat with remaining cherries until they have all been pitted; discard pits.

Bring water, vinegar, salt and sugar to a boil and cook until the sugar and salt have dissolved. Remove from the heat, add cherries and let cool in the pickling liquid until ready to use with the pork.

Grilled pork Wrap pork in plastic wrap or butcher paper and place in the freezer for 1 hour or until firm but not frozen. With a very sharp knife, cut across the muscle to make thin chops, no more than ¼ inch thick (the neck and shoulder can be chewy if they are not sliced thinly enough).

In a large bowl, combine pork with garlic, rosemary, chili flakes and olive oil and stir well, then cover and refrigerate while you make the sauce.

Place beef (or pork) stock and a small handful of the pickled cherries in a medium saucepan over medium-high heat and cook until reduced by half or until thick enough to coat the back of a spoon. Season with vinegar and salt. Strain through a fine-mesh sieve into a clean pot (discard solids) and keep sauce warm until ready to use.

Heat a grill to high. Season pork with salt to taste and grill until nicely charred and cooked to medium, about 1½ minutes per side.

To serve Divide the pork slices among four individual plates. Spoon some of the warm cherry sauce over the pork and garnish each plate with six or seven pickled cherries. Sprinkle with torn basil leaves.

Supply & Demand
Steve Wall

WE DEMAND OYSTERS at this West Wellington restaurant, and my God, they are supplied! Beauties washed up on crushed ice, all glistening on their half shells. Looking to blunt our hunger, we typically begin this way at the splendid Supply & Demand. But we save room—because we're smart and keen—for the many other pleasures on Steve Wall's menu. For the squid ink rigatoni with surf and turf meatballs; for grilled Humboldt squid with romesco and sea asparagus; and for the marvellous Mediterranean stew of slow-cooked lamb with crunchy farro. Vegetables are elevated to star status—anointed with such lovelies as brown butter and citrus, and the umami rightness of capers, anchovy oil and sharp cheese. The kale salad is legendary—the recipe kindly provided here—the greens almost buried under a snowy blanket of Pecorino Crotonese. Supply & Demand drew gasps of pleasure the first week it opened and was quickly noticed beyond the confines of its delighted neighbour-hood. *enRoute* magazine named it the fourth-best new restaurant in Canada; Gold Medal Plates put Wall on the podium. As much the pleasure of the place is Jennifer Wall, simply for her gentle command of the room, for the warmth and kindness she lends it. Notwithstanding its accolades, Supply & Demand still manages to feel like a terrific neighbour-hood hangout. 1335 WELLINGTON STREET WEST, 613-680-2949

Caper vinaigrette
2 anchovy fillets
1 Tbsp Dijon mustard
3 Tbsp capers and brine
1 shallot, cut in half
2 cloves garlic
⅓ cup white wine vinegar
¼ cup water
1¼ cups canola oil

Kale salad
1 bunch kale
2 cups chopped bacon
1 cup coarse bread crumbs
  (or finely chopped
  day-old baguette)
Pinch of salt
5 oz Pecorino Crotonese
  or Manchego cheese

Serves 4 as an appetizer

Kale Salad with Caper Vinaigrette, Crotonese and Bacon

Chef says: We created this salad on a whim! We read somewhere that people were massaging kale and obviously we found that funny and needed to try it out ourselves. We don't actually massage the kale and we are all tired of even looking at kale at this point, but this is the hospitality industry and here we are... offering you our most popular recipe because the fact is, it's delicious. At the restaurant we vacuum-seal the kale under high pressure with ice water, which allows us to process large amounts at once, but chances are you do not have a chamber sealer and will have to take the low-tech route, which is perfectly fine!

Caper vinaigrette Combine anchovies, mustard, capers and brine, shallots, garlic, vinegar and water in a blender and purée at high speed until smooth, about 2 minutes. With the motor running, slowly drizzle in canola oil until emulsified. (Will keep refrigerated in an airtight container for up to 2 weeks or until it splits, in which case you will just need to emulsify it again.)

Kale salad Pick the kale leaves from the stems, discarding any of the thicker stems you would not like to eat raw. As you do this, rub each leaf between your thumb and fingers until the leaves become tender and turn a darker green (massaging the greens will take about 3 minutes). Place in a large bowl.

Preheat the oven to 350°F. Place bacon on a baking sheet and cook until crisp, about 15 minutes. Drain off the fat into a frying pan. Set aside the bacon.

Set the frying pan of bacon fat over medium heat, add bread crumbs and sauté until golden and crunchy, about 1½ minutes.

To serve Toss the massaged kale with the caper vinaigrette, toasted bread crumbs, bacon and salt. Divide among serving bowls and, with a kitchen rasp, grate a large mound of light and fluffy Crotonese (or Manchego) over top.

Chef says: Gemelli means "twins" in Italian. To picture its shape think of the letter "s": as the noodle is pushed out of the extruder, the "s" becomes twisted and is cut fairly short, maybe three inches long. Chicken oysters are two small nuggets of meat located on the back where the leg bone joins. They have the flavour of dark meat and the tenderness of white meat… so the best of both worlds. We love using the oysters at Supply & Demand, but if you have difficulty sourcing them, use chicken thighs; I've included a recipe for braising them. We really love this pasta because it's all about layering flavours and it's incredibly easy to sneak in other seasonal ingredients.

Serves 4 as an appetizer or 2 as a main course

Gemelli with Chicken Oysters, English Peas and Rosemary

Onion purée In a small pot that will allow the onions to release lots of liquid as they cook, heat 2 Tbsp of the vegetable oil over medium-low heat. Add onions and cook slowly for a couple of hours until they reach a caramelized, jammy consistency. Transfer the caramelized onion mixture to a food processor fitted with the metal blade and pulse with just enough water (2 to 4 Tbsp) to make a thick purée. Season with salt and pepper to taste and set aside.

Gemelli with chicken oysters Using a paring knife, remove and discard any large veins from chicken livers, then season very well with salt. Heat about ½ Tbsp of the vegetable oil in a large sauté pan over medium-high heat. Add chicken livers and sear for 2 to 3 minutes per side, making sure they are still rare in the middle. Immediately transfer them to a plate and refrigerate to stop the cooking. Once cool, use a chef's knife to chop livers into a paste and set aside.

Bring a large pot of salted water to a boil. Season chicken oysters with salt. In a sauté pan big enough to hold the sauce and the cooked pasta, sear oysters in 2 Tbsp of the vegetable oil, skin side down, over medium-high heat until skin side is nicely coloured, about 3 minutes. Remove chicken from the pan, leaving one side raw. Transfer chicken to a plate and return the pan to the heat, deglazing it with white wine.

Drop the fresh pasta in the boiling water, then return to the sauce.

Cook the wine until most of it has evaporated and, when the pasta is nearly cooked, ladle it directly from the boiling water into the sauté pan, carrying lots of the water with it. Add the chicken oysters (or thighs if using the variation, see below) followed by the peas, chopped chicken livers, 2 Tbsp of the onion purée and the cubes of butter. Increase the heat to high and cook until the sauce is mostly reduced and glazy, about 2 minutes.

Onion purée

2 Tbsp vegetable oil
2 Spanish onions, sliced
   lengthwise with the grain
Salt and freshly ground
   black pepper

Gemelli with chicken oysters

2 Tbsp chicken livers
2½ Tbsp vegetable oil, divided
16 chicken oysters (or substitute
   4 braised chicken thighs—see here)
1 cup dry white wine
9 oz fresh gemelli pasta (or a similar
   shape, such as strozzapreti or
   casarecce)
½ cup shelled English peas
¼ cup cold butter, cubed
½ cup freshly grated Parmigiano-
   Reggiano cheese
1 Tbsp chopped fresh rosemary
2 Tbsp chopped fresh chervil

Variation: **Braised chicken thighs**

4 skinless, boneless chicken thighs
Salt and freshly ground black pepper
1 Tbsp vegetable oil
½ cup dry white wine
2 cups chicken stock

Variation: Braised chicken thighs Preheat the oven to 300°F. Have ready a large ovenproof dish with a lid. Heat a large sauté pan over medium-high heat. Season chicken thighs with salt and pepper to taste. Add vegetable oil to the pan, then chicken thighs and cook for about 1 minute per side or until nicely browned. Transfer chicken thighs to the ovenproof dish.

Deglaze the sauté pan with wine, then add chicken stock and bring to a simmer. Pour this hot liquid over chicken thighs, cover with the lid and braise in the oven for 1 hour. Allow thighs to cool completely in the liquid before using. Cut cooled thighs in small pieces for the pasta.

To serve Divide the pasta and sauce among individual plates or bowls. Finish with grated cheese, rosemary and chervil.

Suzy Q Doughnuts
Susan Hamer

YOU MIGHT SAY this city owes a debt to the postal strike of 2011. Without it there might never have been the Sugar Munkki and the little charmer known as Suzy Q. A former postal worker with a fine arts background and a deep pride in her Finnish roots, Susan Hamer used that summer strike to sell a family-favourite doughnut at the Sunday farmers' market. These were doughnuts she made for her children, from a recipe her family had passed down for generations. From sugary lips word spread, lines formed, and in one morning, her future work was figured out. Suzy Q Doughnuts found a home in a repurposed burger joint set back in a picnic-tabled parking lot in Hintonburg. It might have started with the Munkki, a golden ring of fried dough dusted with cardamom sugar, but on any given day Suzy Q offers a dozen creations, each hand-dipped or filled, the ingredients as natural and local as Hamer can muster. There seems only childlike pleasure on the face of grownups in the Suzy Q's queue, ordering a Cookies & Cream "for my children." My son is a slave to the Salty Caramel, my husband to the Maple Bacon. The Raspberry Cassis dressed with white chocolate is aimed at "those without a sweet tooth." For me, it's the Mango Lassi I moon over. Hamer's an Ottawa postie no more. But she still delivers in this town. And now from a shack no more—bigger digs have been secured. More to love.

969 WELLINGTON STREET WEST, 613-724-2451

1 cup whole milk
2 eggs
2 tsp white sugar
1 tsp freshly grated lemon zest
1½ tsp active dry yeast
2 Tbsp water (about 120°F)
2 cups all-purpose flour

1 tsp kosher salt
Icing sugar mixed with a
    pinch of ground cardamom
    (optional), for dusting cakes
Canola oil, for frying (we use
    palm shortening)

Makes 10 to 12 cakes

Tippaleipa (Finnish Lemon Funnel Cakes)

Chef says: Tippaleipa is a lemon funnel cake made of a thin batter piped into hot oil in figure eights, such that it resembles a bird's nest. These are served on Finland's May Day, or "Vappu," dusted with sugar and traditionally served with *sima,* a lemon-flavoured meade. You can fry these up freeform, or use a metal ring form or pastry cutter. And if you don't have a piping bag, use a resealable plastic bag. Makes clean-up pretty easy!

In a small pot, scald milk over high heat; remove from the heat and set aside to cool.

In a medium bowl, whisk together eggs, sugar and lemon zest until just combined (avoid beating them).

In a second bowl, dissolve yeast in warm water and then wait 5 to 10 minutes for the yeast to proof (become foamy or bubbly). Add to the cooled milk. Pour the milk mixture into the egg-sugar mixture and stir gently to combine. Add flour and salt and stir until a smooth batter forms. Cover and let the batter rest in a warm place for about 1 hour.

Line a plate with paper towels. Place sugar and cardamom in a bowl. Have ready either chopsticks or a slotted spoon for flipping the cakes (at

Suzy Q we use drum sticks!). Heat at least 2 inches of oil in a heavy-bottomed pan to 375°F (use a deep-fry thermometer to test the temperature). If you're using a 3-inch metal ring mould, add it to the oil.

Fill a piping bag fitted with the ¼-inch tip or a resealable plastic bag (snip off one small corner) with about 1 cup of the batter. Into the ring form or freeform into the hot oil, pipe a figure-eight shape of batter and wait a second until it floats to the surface. Continue piping figure eights, working in a "round" until you get a complete flower shape, a total of 6 figure eights. Fry for about 1 minute, very carefully flip the cake and fry for another minute until the cake is golden brown. Using a slotted spoon, transfer the cake to the lined plate. Repeat with remaining batter until you have 10 to 12 cakes. (Note that it takes practice to create the traditional shape. If your cakes look more like tangled bird's nests, not to worry: they will still taste delicious!)

To serve Dip the cakes in the sugar and cardamom, shaking off any excess, and serve immediately.

Elderflower-strawberry syrup
4 cups fresh strawberries, hulled and sliced in half
1 cup white sugar, divided
1 cup elderflower cordial

Pancake cake
6 eggs
2½ cups whole milk
2 Tbsp white sugar
½ tsp salt
1½ cups all-purpose flour

1 small jar rose hip jam (homemade or available at most Polish delis, or use apricot, raspberry, or strawberry jam or even Nutella)
Good-size knob butter, for greasing pan (replenish as needed)

Serves 6 (Makes one 6-inch cake)

Finnish Birthday Breakfast Cake with Elderflower-Strawberry Syrup

Chef says: My children are thrilled when they wake up on their birthday morning to this stacked cake. Pancakes were very important in my Finnish family. My dad would often wake me up Saturday mornings with a plate of them under my nose. If you don't have a birthday to celebrate, you can use this recipe and a nine-inch cast-iron skillet and eat pancakes for breakfast, rolled into a tube filled with jam and topped with berry syrup and whipped cream. Make your own elderflower cordial in the spring when the elder trees are in bloom, or Belvoir Fruit Farms (from the UK) makes a beautiful cordial that is available year-round.

Elderflower-strawberry syrup Place strawberries in a large heatproof bowl, add ½ cup of the sugar and toss gently to combine. Let strawberries macerate for 20 minutes.

In a medium pot over medium heat, combine cordial with remaining ½ cup of sugar and heat, stirring, until sugar is dissolved. Pour over the strawberries, stir well and return the strawberry mixture to the pot. Simmer over medium-low heat for 20 minutes, then allow the sauce to cool to room temperature.

Pour the cooled strawberries and syrup into a blender and process at high speed until very smooth and a light rose colour. Strain through a fine-mesh sieve if you like, but I prefer to see some strawberry pieces in my syrup. If you plan to serve the cake right away, pour the syrup into a small pot and keep it warm over low heat. The syrup can be made a day ahead and stored in the fridge in a Mason jar.

Pancake cake In a large bowl or in a blender, whisk or blend eggs with milk, sugar and salt. Add flour and blend until smooth. Cover the batter and refrigerate for at least 1 hour.

Have ready a cake plate (or serving platter) and place jam in a small bowl. Heat a 6-inch cast-iron skillet over medium-high heat. Add butter and when really sizzling, use a ¼-cup measure to drop the batter into the pan, tilting it to cover the bottom entirely. Cook the pancake for 30 to 40 seconds per side, using a thin offset spatula to flip the pancake and, once cooked, transfer it to the cake plate.

Continue making pancakes, one at a time, adding more butter as needed and making sure it is sizzling so the pancakes take on nice caramelized markings. Stack the cooked pancakes one on top of the other on the cake plate, spreading a layer of jam (or Nutella) over every second or third pancake. Keep going until you have used all of the batter (you should have about 20 pancakes).

To serve Slice the pancake cake into wedges and serve with a pitcher of warm elderflower-strawberry syrup.

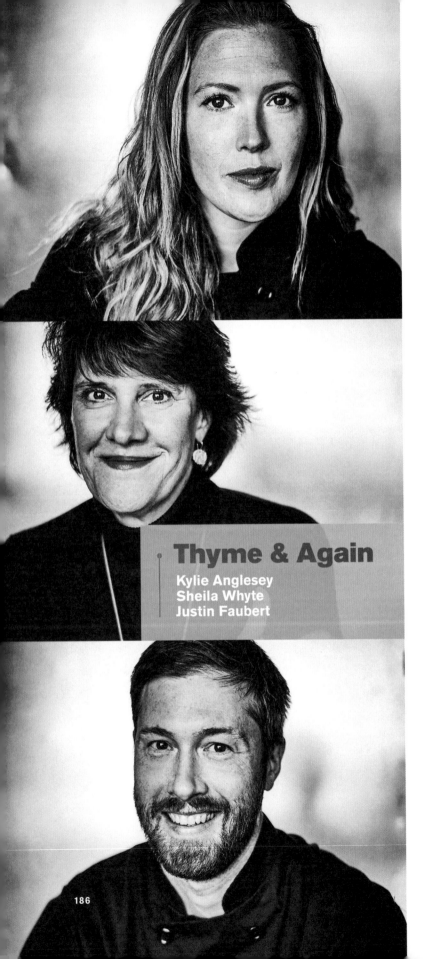

Thyme & Again

**Kylie Anglesey
Sheila Whyte
Justin Faubert**

I CAN'T TELL YOU how many times I've dashed over to Thyme & Again to pick up supper. Or nibbles for neighbours. Or spent a Saturday afternoon at a sunny table there with a friend, a coffee, a square. A fine catering company housed in a historic brownstone with event space, food shop and charming café, Thyme & Again has catered most of the biggies in this city, but also countless more intimate gatherings, dispensed with style and out-of-the-box thinking. Owned by the indefatigable Sheila Whyte, a generous community mover and shaker, she brings to events a can-do spirit and original mind. She also has a knack for hiring talent. The guy responsible for the inventive terrine is Justin Faubert, executive chef. Trained at Vancouver's Pacific Institute of Culinary Arts, he came to the capital after working in some of BC's finest restaurants. Faubert was part of the culinary crew during the Vancouver 2010 Olympics and was a private chef for a family on the Gulf Islands, where he commuted to work by floatplane. Planes are also part of pastry chef Kylie Anglesey's CV. A Stratford Chefs School grad, she created the confections for the expansion of the Ottawa airport. She also sweetened the Queen's visit in 2010. Her sweet potato cake with rum-raisin mousse is a fantastic twist on a rock-solid classic: fragrant, moist—and for me, now a Thanksgiving tradition. 1255 WELLINGTON STREET WEST, 613-722-6277

facing: **Sweet Potato Spice Cake with Rum-Raisin Mousse and Pecan Praline**

Chef says: With hints of traditional fall spices, fresh orange zest and a rum and raisin–infused mousse, this cake makes an impressive ending to any fall or winter dinner. The raisins in the mousse can be soaked in rum ahead of time for a more concentrated rum flavour. One word of warning: it's hard to resist snacking on the pecan praline while assembling the cake, so this recipe provides a little extra just in case!

Serves 6 to 8 (Makes one 9-inch cake)

Sweet Potato Spice Cake with Rum-Raisin Mousse and Pecan Praline

Rum and raisin mousse In a small pot, bring raisins, rum and water to a simmer over low heat. Turn off the heat and let cool completely in the pot for at least 2 hours. Strain through a fine-mesh sieve into a small bowl; reserve both the infused rum and raisins in separate bowls. (Raisins and rum liquid can be prepared ahead of time and refrigerated in an airtight container for up to 2 months.)

Measure 1 cup of reserved rum liquid and pour it into a small pot, then sprinkle gelatin over top. Over low heat, stir until the mixture has warmed and the gelatin has dissolved completely. Remove from the heat and set aside in a warm place.

In the bowl of a stand mixer fitted with the whisk attachment, whip cream at high speed until stiff, about 3 minutes. Scrape the whipped cream into a clean bowl, cover and refrigerate until needed.

Without cleaning the mixing bowl and still using the whisk attachment, add cream cheese, brown sugar and vanilla. Whip at high speed until fluffy, scraping the sides of the bowl every minute or so. Once the mixture is smooth and free of lumps, reduce the speed to medium. With

the motor running, add the warm rum-gelatin mixture in a slow steady stream. Turn off the mixer and quickly scrape the sides of the bowl, then turn the mixer back on and mix until everything is incorporated.

Add the whipped cream and raisins to the mixing bowl and, using a spatula, gently fold it into the cream cheese mixture until combined. Refrigerate in an airtight container for at least 2 hours or overnight.

Sweet potato spice cake Preheat the oven to 350°F. Lightly grease a 9-inch round springform pan and line the bottom with parchment paper.

In a large bowl, combine flour, baking soda, baking powder, cinnamon, ginger, cloves, nutmeg, cardamom, allspice and salt. Set aside.

In the bowl of a stand mixer fitted with the paddle attachment, combine sweet potatoes, sugar, orange zest and vanilla and beat at medium speed until smooth, about 1 minute. Add eggs, one at a time, incorporating each into the batter before adding the next. With the motor running, slowly add vegetable oil. Add the flour mixture and blend until just incorporated, scraping down the sides of the bowl once during mixing.

Rum and raisin mousse

1 cup raisins
1 cup dark rum
1 cup water
2 Tbsp powdered gelatin
4 cups whipping (35%) cream
8 oz solid cream cheese
   (not spreadable)
½ cup packed brown sugar
1 Tbsp pure vanilla extract

Sweet potato spice cake

Butter, for greasing pan
3 cups all-purpose flour
2 tsp baking soda
2 tsp baking powder
1 tsp ground cinnamon
½ tsp ground ginger
¼ tsp ground cloves
¼ tsp ground nutmeg
½ tsp ground cardamom
¼ tsp ground allspice
¼ tsp salt
2 cups cooked mashed
   sweet potatoes
1½ cups white sugar
2 tsp freshly grated orange zest
1 tsp pure vanilla extract
4 large eggs
1¼ cups vegetable oil
3 to 6 ground cherries (physalis),
   for garnish

Pecan praline

1 cup pecans
¾ cup white sugar
¾ cup packed brown sugar
½ cup whipping (35%) cream
2 Tbsp unsalted butter
½ tsp fleur de sel
1 Tbsp pure maple extract

Pour the batter into the springform pan and bake for about 45 minutes, until the cake begins to pull away from the sides of the pan and the centre has risen (it should spring back when lightly pressed). Transfer to a wire rack and let cool for 10 minutes in the pan, then unmould onto the rack and let cool completely. (The cake can be made ahead of time, wrapped and refrigerated for up to 3 days.)

Pecan praline Preheat the oven to 350°F. Line a baking sheet with parchment paper. Arrange pecans in a single layer on the baking sheet and bake for 8 minutes, until lightly toasted. Scoop the pecans into a bowl and set aside, reserving the lined baking sheet.

In a medium pot, combine sugar, brown sugar, cream, butter and salt over low heat, stirring constantly until sugars and salt have dissolved. When the mixture starts to simmer, stop stirring, increase the heat to high and bring to a rapid boil. Cook until a candy thermometer registers 236°F.

Carefully pour the mixture into the bowl of a stand mixer fitted with the whisk attachment. Add maple extract. Start the mixer at low speed and gradually increase to high; mix for 3 minutes.

Mix in toasted pecans at low speed, just to combine. Scrape the praline onto the lined baking sheet and let cool fully at room temperature.

To assemble Using a serrated knife and slicing horizontally, cut the cake into 3 equal layers and trim off the top to make an even surface. Set one of the cake layers on a 10-inch plate or cake stand and the others side-by-side on a clean work surface.

Using a spatula, gently stir the mousse to smooth it out. Spread one-third of the mousse over the cake layer on the plate, ensuring the mousse reaches the edge but does not fall off the side. Place a second layer of cake on top and, using your hands, gently press it down. Spread with another third of the mousse. Repeat this process with the last cake layer and remaining mousse.

Using your hands, crumble the pecan praline into large pieces and sprinkle them over the top layer of mousse. Garnish with ground cherries, if desired. (The assembled cake can be refrigerated, lightly wrapped, for 24 hours.) Let the cake sit at room temperature for half an hour before serving.

Chef says: I'm not a vegetarian, nor do I have any particular fondness for tofu, but I do find this recipe elegant and delicious. It's great as a main course but can also be cut and served in smaller portions as an appetizer. The butternut squash is perfect for the terrine layers, but feel free to change up the vegetables to blend with the tofu. Don't be afraid to try something new!

Pickled red onions
1 medium red onion, sliced into thin rounds (about ½ cup)
½ tsp salt
½ cup white or white wine vinegar
1 bay leaf
1 whole star anise
1 tsp white sugar

Serves 4 to 6

Butternut Squash and Tofu Terrine

Pickled red onions Place onions in a medium bowl and sprinkle with salt. To a small saucepan, add vinegar, bay leaf, star anise and sugar and warm over medium heat until you see the first bubble. Pour vinegar over onions and let stand for at least 1 hour. (Will keep refrigerated in an airtight container for 6 to 8 months.)

Vegetable stock Place all of the ingredients in a medium saucepan and bring to a strong simmer over medium-high heat. Turn down the heat to medium-low and continue to cook at a low simmer for another 45 minutes. Strain the liquid through a fine-mesh sieve into a small bowl; discard solids. Reserve stock until ready to use.

Squash and tofu terrine Preheat the oven to 375°F. Line 2 baking sheets with parchment paper. Lightly grease a 9-inch × 5-inch loaf pan with butter. Cut a rectangle of parchment paper large enough to fit the top of the loaf pan.

Peel the first squash and remove the stem and flower ends. Separate the neck from the bulb. Using a mandolin or a sharp knife, slice the neck of the squash lengthwise into 6 to 8 slices, no more than ¼ inch thick. Place slices onto one of the lined baking sheets, sprinkle with salt and cover with aluminum foil. Cut squash bulb in half and remove and discard the seeds. Cut into 1-inch pieces to make a total of 8 cups of cubed squash (if necessary, use the second squash). Arrange cubed squash in a single layer on the second lined baking sheet, add garlic, drizzle with 2 Tbsp of olive oil and a pinch of salt. Bake the slices for 12 to 15 minutes or until softened and just cooked through. Bake the cubes for 25 to 30 minutes or until both the squash and garlic have started to take on some colour and are cooked through. Remove from the oven and set aside. Leave the oven on.

Heat remaining 1 Tbsp of olive oil in a small frying pan over medium-low heat. Add onions and cook until soft and translucent, 7 to 10 minutes. Remove from the heat and set aside.

Place the diced squash and garlic, onions, tofu, honey and salt and pepper to taste in a food processor fitted with the metal blade and process until smooth (the mixture should be fairly stiff but smooth; if it is difficult to blend, add up to ¼ cup of the vegetable stock, as needed, to help process everything).

Vegetable stock

1 medium yellow onion, cut into
  1-inch pieces
2 carrots, cut into 1-inch pieces
2 stalks celery, cut into 1-inch pieces
2 to 3 sprigs fresh thyme
3 to 4 sprigs fresh parsley (curly
  or flat-leaf)
15 black peppercorns
3 bay leaves
4 cups cold water

Squash and tofu terrine

Butter, for greasing pan
1 to 2 medium butternut squash
Salt and freshly ground black
  pepper
6 to 8 cloves garlic
3 Tbsp olive oil, divided
1 cup diced yellow onions
1 lb (2 cups) firm tofu, cut into
  ½-inch pieces
1½ Tbsp liquid honey
10 to 12 fresh sage leaves +
  more, fried, for garnish

Squash emulsion

1½ cups diced peeled butternut squash
¾ cup Vegetable Stock (see here)
1 Tbsp butter
1 tsp liquid honey
Salt and freshly ground black pepper

Grilled oyster mushrooms

12 to 16 medium oyster mushrooms,
  cleaned
1 Tbsp olive oil
½ cup Vegetable Stock (see here)
1 Tbsp butter
Salt and freshly ground black pepper

Build terrine Arrange 2 to 3 slices of cooked squash in the bottom of the lined loaf pan. Place 5 to 6 sage leaves on the squash. Smooth half of the squash-tofu mixture on top. Repeat layers with 2 to 3 slices of cooked squash, remaining sage leaves, and remaining squash-tofu mixture. Finish with a final layer of cooked squash slices. Place the parchment paper, cut to fit, on top of the terrine and cover with foil. Bake for 35 to 40 minutes, then remove the pan from the oven. Remove foil and parchment and let cool for 10 to 15 minutes. Carefully turn terrine out of pan, and slice.

Squash emulsion Place squash and vegetable stock in a small saucepan and bring to a boil. Turn down the heat to medium-low and simmer until squash is cooked through, 8 to 10 minutes. Stir in butter and honey. With an immersion blender (or transfer to a food processor fitted with the metal blade), blend until smooth. Season with salt and pepper to taste. Set aside.

Grilled oyster mushrooms Heat a grill to high. Place mushrooms into a medium bowl, add olive oil and a pinch of salt and toss to coat. Place mushrooms directly on the grill and cook until lightly marked.

Transfer mushrooms to a skillet, add vegetable stock, butter and a pinch of salt and pepper and cook over medium heat until all the liquid is gone. Remove from the heat.

To serve Ladle about ⅓ cup of the emulsion into the centre of each plate, using the ladle to swirl it into a larger circle. Cut the terrine into 4 to 6 slices and place a slice into the centre of the emulsion. Arrange 3 to 4 oyster mushrooms beside the terrine and top with a few pickled red onions. Garnish with fried sage leaves (or your favourite fresh herbs).

town.
Marc Doiron
Lori Wojcik

FEELING AS THOUGH a restaurant has opened with the sole purpose of making you happy is rare, but I feel that way at town. The husband-and-wife team who run the place wanted two things: to be part of a downtown neighbourhood and to have a wood-burning pizza oven. Marc Doiron and Lori Wojcik found the right space, in the heart of Elgin Street, but it lacked space for a pizza oven. So they switched gears and opened a wine bar that served "inauthentic" Italian food. That's how chef Doiron describes it in self-effacing fashion. I'd call it inventive Italian, comfort Italian, generous Italian, but the sort of "Italian" not averse to putting ramen on the menu. (Though ramen with an Italian spin.) It's abundantly clear on plates that Doiron is a pastry chef by training; there's a delicacy in even the gutsiest dish. And a scrupulous attention to balance: "Where's the sweet, where's the sour, where's the fragrance, where's the colour?" You can hear his mind at work on the plate. His wife's background is in art restoration. Lori Wojcik ran an art gallery for a dozen years, and she brings to this narrow space sizeable style. And the couple hires well. The team at town are keepers. The day it opened, six years ago, was the day Elgin Street became a much more interesting place to eat.

296 ELGIN STREET, 613-695-8696

facing: **Wild Boar Bolognese with Ricotta Cavatelli and Marinated Curds**

Chef says: At its base, this recipe is Italian, which is what we love to cook at town, but it also includes traditional Quebec flavours, which honour my roots. It is a mix of a traditional bolognese and a French Canadian tourtière with a hint of Quebec poutine. If you have the time, make it the day before so the flavours can develop further. Tourtière spice can be found in some specialty stores or butcher shops. If you can't find it readily, combine three bay leaves, a tablespoon each of ground cinnamon, ground cloves, ground allspice and ground savory and a half tablespoon of ground mace in a spice mill or clean coffee grinder. You will need a cavatelli maker, which is a readily available and inexpensive tool, and a great addition to any kitchen. Otherwise, skip this step and purchase good-quality fresh pasta instead.

Serves 4 to 6

Wild Boar Bolognese with Ricotta Cavatelli and Marinated Curds

Marinated curds Place all of the ingredients in a 1-pint Mason jar (or similar container with a tight-fitting lid) and stir or shake well to coat. Seal tightly and refrigerate for at least 4 hours or, best, overnight. (Will keep refrigerated for up to 5 days if well sealed.)

Pâte brisée crumble In a food processor fitted with the metal blade, combine flour, butter and salt and pulse until crumbly. Add eggs and pulse until dough naturally starts to form into a ball. Remove from the food processor, gently shape into a ball and wrap tightly in plastic wrap. Refrigerate for at least 4 hours or, best, overnight.

Preheat the oven to 350°F and line a baking sheet with parchment paper. Lightly dust a clean work surface with flour. With a rolling pin, roll the dough into a rectangle about ⅛ inch thick and the dimensions of the baking sheet. Transfer to the baking sheet and bake until golden brown, 15 to 20 minutes. Remove pan from the oven and set aside to cool. Once cool, break into rough pieces, each ¼ to ½ inch, and set aside.

Bolognese sauce Heat olive oil in a medium pot over medium-high heat. Add ground boar, pork, beef and pancetta and cook until well browned. Turn the browned meat into a bowl and set aside.

Return the pot to the stove, turn down the heat to medium and add more oil, if necessary. Stir in onions, garlic, celery and carrots, seasoning with a pinch of kosher salt and pepper, and cook until soft. Return the browned meat to the pot, add red wine and cook until the liquid is reduced by half. Add milk, tomatoes and tourtière spice and stir to combine. Turn down the heat and simmer for about 1 ½ hours, stirring occasionally. The mixture should be well concentrated and meaty.

Remove the sauce from the heat, cover and refrigerate overnight to cool and let the flavours meld. Gently reheat the sauce while you cook the pasta.

Marinated curds

4 oz cheese curds

¼ cup extra-virgin olive oil

1 Tbsp finely chopped fresh basil leaves

1 Tbsp white balsamic vinegar

1 tsp salt

A pinch of dried Calabrian chili pepper or any dried red chili pepper

Pâte brisée crumble

2 cups + 6 Tbsp all-purpose flour

¾ cup cold unsalted butter, cut into ¼-inch cubes

¼ tsp salt

2 large eggs, room temperature

Bolognese sauce

¼ cup extra-virgin olive oil

½ lb ground wild boar

1½ lb medium ground pork

1½ lb medium ground beef

½ lb finely ground pancetta (or bacon)

2 medium white onions, finely diced

4 cloves garlic, minced

4 stalks celery, finely diced

6 carrots, finely diced

Pinch of kosher salt

Pinch of black pepper

2 cups red wine

4 cups 2% milk

¾ cup milled or puréed canned tomatoes

¼ cup tourtière spice (see headnote)

Finely minced fresh flat-leaf (Italian) parsley, for garnish

Ricotta cavatelli

1½ cups ricotta cheese (fresh—see recipe p.196—or good-quality store-bought)

1 large egg, beaten

2 egg yolks, beaten

4 cups all-purpose flour

Ricotta cavatelli In the bowl of a stand mixer fitted with the dough hook, combine all of the ingredients and mix at medium speed for about 5 minutes or until incorporated and the dough starts to cling to the hook. If it seems a little dry, add a touch of water; if too wet, add a touch of flour (humidity can be a factor when making dough). Transfer the dough to a clean work surface and knead for 2 to 3 minutes to develop the gluten. Shape into a ball and wrap in plastic wrap. Let rest at room temperature for 1 hour or, better, refrigerate overnight and let come to room temperature before rolling.

Have ready a cavatelli maker. Lightly dust a baking sheet and clean work surface with flour. Clamp the cavatelli maker onto the edge of a sturdy surface. Cut the dough into 3 equal portions. Roll each portion into a long rope about ¾ inch in diameter. Process the ropes through the rollers of the cavatelli machine, according to its instructions. Arrange the cavatelli in a single layer on the baking sheet. (If you are not using them right away, refrigerate the baking sheet wrapped in plastic wrap.)

To cook the cavatelli, bring a large pot of salted water (it should taste like sea water) to a boil. Add pasta and cook for about 1 minute or until it floats to the surface; drain well.

To serve Add cooked cavatelli to the warm bolognese sauce and toss to combine. Divide the pasta and sauce among six deep bowls or serve family-style on a platter. Top with marinated cheese curds, drizzling a little of the marinating oil on top. Sprinkle the pâte brisée crumble and parsley over the curds for a little colour.

Chef says: Bread was a big part of my past, as I spent a good portion of my early career as a baker. I know people generally stay away from bread making due to its difficulty and the time involved, but this recipe is unusual. It's extremely easy and almost impossible to screw up. Time and being left alone are how it develops flavour, rather than kneading, watching and coaxing. Sometimes it will be light and fluffy, sometimes a bit more dense, depending on the day, but it will always taste great! You can just eat it as is, or add other stuff to make it extra special. It's good as a snack or appetizer, or if you add any thinly sliced cured meat you can make a really kick-ass sandwich. Basically, this is my recipe for a really fancy grilled cheese. Start the bread the day before you plan to serve it. Make the ricotta the day before and refrigerate it, well wrapped, then bring it to room temperature before using. Or make it the morning of.

Serves 8 to 10

Stuffed Focaccia with Ricotta, Thyme and Truffle

Focaccia In a large bowl, whisk yeast quickly into warm water and let sit for 5 to 10 minutes to activate (it will bubble on the surface when ready). Using a wooden spoon, add flour and salt and stir until a sticky dough forms.

Pour olive oil into a second large bowl or a large plastic container with a tight-fitting lid. Transfer the dough into the olive oil, turning it to coat completely in oil, and seal the bowl tightly with plastic wrap or the lid. Refrigerate overnight to rise.

When ready to bake, grease an 18-inch × 13-inch baking sheet with olive oil. Set the dough on the baking sheet and use your hands to gently spread it out to fill the corners. Loosely wrap the baking sheet in plastic wrap and let sit at room temperature for 20 minutes in summer or up to 1 hour in cooler weather, or until the dough has risen again and is light and fluffy.

Preheat the oven to 400°F. Remove the plastic wrap. Dimple the surface of the dough by pressing down with your fingers. Drizzle dough lightly with a touch of olive oil and sprinkle with Parmesan and salt. Bake for 20 minutes or until golden brown. Set aside to cool but use the same day.

Ricotta In a large pot, whisk together milk, buttermilk, lemon zest and salt. Place the mixture over medium-low heat and, without stirring, heat the mixture to 180°F, about 15 minutes (use an instant-read thermometer). Once this temperature is reached, curds will form on the surface. Once the curds start to sink, remove the pot from the heat and let sit for 10 minutes.

Focaccia

1 tsp active dry yeast
3½ cups warm water
6 cups all-purpose flour
2½ Tbsp kosher salt
¼ cup extra-virgin olive oil
  + more for greasing
¼ cup finely grated Parmesan cheese
Maldon sea salt, for garnish

Ricotta

1 gallon (16 cups) 2% milk
4 cups buttermilk
Zest of 2 lemons
2 Tbsp salt
¾ cup whipping (35%) cream

Ricotta-thyme filling

2 cups ricotta cheese (fresh, or
  good-quality store-bought)
¼ cup freshly grated Parmesan cheese
2 Tbsp fresh thyme leaves
1 Tbsp white truffle oil
1 Tbsp kosher salt
2 tsp freshly ground black pepper

Using a fine-mesh sieve, scoop out and drain the curds; set aside to cool to room temperature. (Discard the liquid whey or refrigerate it in an airtight container for up to 1 week and use it as a brine for pork or as a replacement for water in soups and stocks.) Transfer the curds to a food processor fitted with the metal blade. With the motor running at low speed, slowly pour in cream and process until smooth.

Ricotta-thyme filling Combine ricotta, Parmesan, thyme, truffle oil, salt and pepper in a medium bowl and, using a rubber spatula, stir until well incorporated. (Leftovers can be refrigerated in an airtight container for up to 1 week.)

To assemble Preheat the broiler. Grease a large baking sheet with olive oil.

Place the cooled focaccia on a clean work surface. Using a serrated knife, slice through the bread horizontally, removing the top ¼ inch of bread. Repeat with the bottom ¼ inch. (Reserve the centre of the bread for croutons or bread crumbs.) Set the bottom section of focaccia on the baking sheet, cut side up, and spread with a generous layer of the filling. (Add some thinly sliced cured meat, too, if you have it.) Place the top section of bread on top, cut side down, and brush the outside liberally with olive oil. Broil for 5 to 6 minutes or until the cheese has melted.

To serve Cut the stuffed focaccia into eight to ten portions and serve hot!

Union Local 613
Darren Flowers

WITH CHARM and cheek ("Our fried chicken has been found to cure political BS"), Union Local 613 has been dishing up "inauthentic Southern cuisine" and a full measure of bonhomie since 2012. After spending some time south of the Mason-Dixon line, the UL team found three things they wanted to bring back home: "scratch" cocktails, communal dining ("Rolex next to Timex, Bentley next to bike") and a rich, gooey-good, rib-sticking cuisine. The food and drink and laid-back vibe became an instant hit, particularly with industry cookers who'd flop into Union post-shift. Conceptual artists were given free rein in the old brick house. Julian Garner murals cover the walls. The basement speakeasy (*shh…*) has its own unique charm. Co-owner Ivan Gedz would wince if I called the craft drinks served in Mason jars a "cocktail program" or its pourers "mixologists." (This is, after all, the guy who said "thanks, but no thanks" to *enRoute* magazine's attempt to include Union on a "Canada's top bar" contest sponsored by Rickard's beer.) So just say the drinks are treated with the same intense focus on quality and fancy that chef Darren Flowers brings to the Southern-inspired food. Smoked lamb ribs, seared duck hearts with pickled celery so bright it tingles, fried chicken with equal crunch and juice, and cheddar garlic grits with guts. The house cast-iron cornbread laced with bourbon brown butter has been known to cure just about anything. So too the chocolate pie. 315 SOMERSET STREET WEST, 613-231-1010

Old Bay mayo

1 large egg yolk
1 Tbsp freshly squeezed
   lemon juice
1 Tbsp water
¾ cup canola oil
Salt and freshly ground
   black pepper
1 Tbsp Old Bay seasoning

Pickled and fried green tomatoes

5 large green tomatoes
4 cups white vinegar
¾ cup white sugar
1½ cups water
⅓ cup yellow mustard seeds
¼ cup dill seeds
1 tsp red chili flakes
5 cloves garlic, sliced
¼ cup kosher salt
1 cup all-purpose flour
1 tsp salt
1 tsp freshly ground black
   pepper
1 cup buttermilk
1 cup fine cornmeal
Peanut oil (or other neutral
   oil), for frying

Serves 4 to 6 as an appetizer

Pickled and Fried Green Tomatoes with Old Bay Mayo

Chef says: Why eat green tomatoes? When I was a kid I wondered this. An early frost, coupled with a cool summer in Fredericton, New Brunswick, one year meant an abundance of unripened tomatoes in my grandmother's garden and, well, they weren't going to waste. We ate them either cooked in a pan with onions or, my favourite, preserved with some vinegar and sugar in a chow chow. There's something about the way the sugar and acid brought out the best of these tomatoes that I couldn't forget. This is where I got the idea for pickling the tomatoes for this Southern classic.

Old Bay mayo In a food processor fitted with the metal blade, combine yolk, lemon juice and water and process until fully incorporated. With the motor running, slowly pour in canola oil in a thin, steady stream and process until smooth (if the mayonnaise comes out a little thick, add a bit more water to reach desired consistency). Season with salt, pepper and Old Bay.

Pickled and fried green tomatoes Slice tomatoes ¼ inch thick and place them in a large glass or food-safe plastic container big enough to hold them. (The tomatoes can be stacked so long as the liquid covers them completely.) In a large saucepan, bring vinegar, sugar, water, mustard, dill, chili flakes, garlic and kosher salt to a boil. Set aside and let cool to room temperature.

Pour the pickling liquid over the tomatoes, cover and refrigerate overnight.

Line a plate with paper towels. Preheat a deep fryer or heat 1 inch of peanut oil in a large cast-iron skillet over medium-high heat to 350°F. In a shallow bowl, combine flour with salt and pepper. Pour buttermilk into a second shallow bowl and place cornmeal in a third bowl.

Using a slotted spoon, transfer the tomatoes to a plate or baking sheet. (You can discard the pickling liquid or refrigerate it in an airtight container for up to a week for use in a tartar sauce or salad dressing.) Working in small batches so as not to crowd them in the pan, coat tomatoes in the flour, tapping to remove any excess, then dip in buttermilk and coat in cornmeal, again tapping to remove any excess. Carefully place breaded tomato directly into the hot oil; it should start to sizzle right away (if it doesn't, the oil is not yet hot enough). Cook breaded tomatoes, turning once, until golden brown, about 4 minutes total. Using a slotted spoon, transfer the tomatoes to the lined plate to drain. Repeat with remaining tomatoes.

To serve While the tomatoes are hot, season them with salt and pepper and serve with a dollop of Old Bay mayo.

Chef says: Shrimp and grits are a culinary staple in the American South. From Louisiana to North Carolina, they are found in high-end restaurants and home kitchens alike. The dish quickly became an established favourite at Union as well. Our shrimp and grits combine tasso (Cajun ham) with trinity (onions-peppers-celery), tomatoes, white prawns and hot sauce, and are served over hominy grits. Hominy is dried field corn (not the sweet stuff we're used to) that has been softened in an alkaline solution (lye or wood ash).

You will need a smoker or outdoor grill plus one cup of mesquite wood chips soaked in water for half an hour to make the tasso. Start this dish the day before you plan to serve it so the ham has time to cure. If you do not have access to a smoker or grill, use Andouille sausage instead. And you can start to prepare the shrimp mixture while the grits are cooking.

Serves 4 to 6

Shrimp and Grits

Tasso In a small bowl, combine paprika, thyme, mustard powder, cayenne, salt, onion and garlic powders, black pepper and sugar. Use your hands to rub this spice mixture into the pork. Wrap pork and refrigerate overnight.

Preheat a smoker to 300°F or heat one side of your outdoor grill to medium and the other side to low. If you are using your grill, cut a piece of aluminum foil 1 foot square, place the drained wood chips in the centre and fold over the sides to form a pouch. Pierce the top of the pouch to allow any smoke to escape. Set the pouch on the medium side of the grill. Set the pork in the smoker (or on the low side of the grill, close the lid) and smoke for 1 hour. Remove from smoker (or grill), let rest on a cooling rack for 30 minutes, then wrap and refrigerate. (Leftovers can be packaged in smaller portions and frozen. You can never have too much extra tasso kicking around.)

Grits In a large saucepan, heat stock and milk over medium heat until it reaches a simmer. Add grits, skimming off and discarding any of the corn chaff and hulls that float to the top. Turn down the heat to low and cook for 2 to 3 hours, stirring every 10 minutes (the grits are cooked when the kernels are soft and the liquid is creamy). Remove from the heat, stir in butter, cream and cheese and season with salt and pepper to taste. Cover with a lid and set aside for plating.

Tasso

½ cup sweet paprika

2 Tbsp dried thyme

2 Tbsp mustard powder (we use Keen's)

2 Tbsp cayenne pepper

2 Tbsp kosher salt

1 Tbsp onion powder

1 Tbsp garlic powder

1 Tbsp freshly ground black pepper

1 Tbsp brown sugar

2 lb boneless pork butt

Grits

2 cups chicken, vegetable or shrimp stock

2 cups 2% milk

1 cup dried white hominy, well rinsed and drained

2 Tbsp unsalted butter

1 cup whipping (35%) cream

½ cup freshly grated old (sharp) cheddar cheese

Salt and freshly ground black pepper

Shrimp

2 Tbsp canola oil

1½ cups diced tasso

⅔ cup diced red onions

⅔ cup diced red bell peppers

⅔ cup diced celery

1 cup grape tomatoes, cut in half

2 cups chicken, vegetable or shrimp stock

½ cup hot sauce (we use Frank's)

24 Ocean Wise white shrimp, peeled and deveined (about 2 lb)

¼ cup unsalted butter

Salt and freshly ground black pepper

1 bunch green onions, white and green parts, thinly sliced

Shrimp Heat canola oil in a large skillet over medium-high heat. Add tasso and fry until crispy. Stir in trinity (onions, peppers, celery) and cook until onions turn translucent. Add grape tomatoes and cook for 2 minutes. Deglaze the pan with the stock and turn down the heat to medium. (For a thicker sauce, reduce the stock before adding shrimp.) Stir in hot sauce, shrimp and butter and cook for 2 minutes. Season with salt and pepper to taste.

To serve Place about a cup of grits into the bottom of four to six serving bowls. Divide the shrimp mixture evenly among the bowls. Top with sliced green onions and serve.

The Village House
Mike Houle
Sarah Swan

"I TRIED TO TAKE these ribs off the menu, but folks had a fit." I couldn't help my response: "Well, duh." Mike Houle figured if I'd come to his village house in Wakefield for a chat about recipes, he'd better feed me. And so he did, bless him, to excellent effect. Including some of the best short ribs I can remember, the mahogany meat crusty, fragrant and fork-tender, nestled on a bed of Le Coprin mushrooms, braised root vegetables and Houle's knockout gnocchi (recipe provided, thank you), with a pooled jus enhanced with foie butter, so dark and polished and vibrant I (almost) asked for a straw. "You were going to take these off the menu?" 'Nuff said. Houle comes to The Village House by way of Murray Street, and he credits chef Steve Mitton for his ability to really "get meat," to mine its flavour. The gnocchi know-how comes from his Italian neighbours in Sault Ste. Marie, where he grew up. And the tart from his French Canadian *mémère,* from whom he learned to bake and to love all things apple. He credits everything else to his wife, Sarah Swan, who runs the front of house with such warmth and charm, pouring well-chosen wines to match her husband's vigorously flavoured, happy-making food. If you come on a Sunday, it's small plates only. More to love. 759 CHEMIN RIVERSIDE, WAKEFIELD, QC, 819-459-1445

facing: **Apple-Walnut Butter Tarts with Caramel Ice Cream**

Chef says: This is a combination of my two favourite childhood desserts: homemade apple pie and butter tarts. The ice cream is super creamy yet not overly sweet and the perfect accompaniment to the tarts. At The Village House we serve it with our house-made bacon lardon and Maldon salt—it just works. The salty component really adds punch to the bitter-sweetness of the ice cream. So if you're game, give it a try. This tart is a staple at our restaurant, the number-one seller and a sure crowd-pleaser!

Makes 12 large muffin-size tarts

Apple-Walnut Butter Tarts with Caramel Ice Cream

Caramel ice cream Place egg yolks in a large stainless steel bowl and set aside.

In a medium, heavy-bottomed pot, combine sugar and water and cook over high heat, swirling gently to dissolve the sugar (do not leave unattended!). The sugar will start to darken, and once it has turned a deep straw colour, 5 to 6 minutes, immediately remove from the heat and slowly drizzle in all the cream (it's going to bubble aggressively at first so be very careful). Turn down the heat to low and return the pot to the stove to re-melt the caramel (it hardens when you add the cream).

Whisking continuously, slowly drizzle the liquid caramel into the egg yolks (this process, called tempering, warms the eggs gradually so you do not scramble them).

Fill the pot with ½ inch of water and place it over medium-low heat. Set the bowl with the egg mixture over the pot and cook, whisking often, for about 10 minutes. The custard will thicken, and it is ready when a wooden spoon dipped in the custard can draw a line that holds.

Pour into an ice-cream maker or another suitable container and let cool at room temperature, uncovered, for 1 hour. Freeze, uncovered, for 4 hours to make sure it's cold before you put a lid on it. Freeze for at least 12 hours before serving.

Butter tarts To prepare the dough, place the 2 cups of flour into a medium stainless steel bowl. Dip cold butter in the flour and, using the large holes of a box grater, shred it over the flour. Gently toss the grated butter in flour to distribute it evenly. Add water and knead in the bowl until the dough comes together, 1 minute. Shape the dough into a ball and wrap in plastic wrap; refrigerate for at least 10 minutes.

Caramel ice cream

8 egg yolks

1 cup white sugar

¼ cup water

4 cups whipping (35%) cream

Butter tarts

2 cups + 2 Tbsp all-purpose flour

1 cup cold unsalted butter

½ cup cold water

¾ cup corn syrup

1 cup packed brown sugar

2 eggs

½ cup melted butter + more for greasing the muffin pan

3 McIntosh apples, peeled, cored and diced

1 tsp ground cinnamon

½ tsp freshly ground black pepper

½ cup walnuts

To prepare the filling, place corn syrup, brown sugar, eggs and melted butter into a medium stainless steel bowl and whisk together until smooth. Add the 2 Tbsp of flour and stir just to combine. Set aside.

In a medium non-stick pan, sauté apples over high heat for about 1 minute. Stir in cinnamon and pepper and sauté for 1 more minute. Set aside.

Position the rack in the middle of the oven and preheat to 325°F. Lightly grease a 12-cup muffin pan with butter. Lightly dust a clean work surface with flour. Using a rolling pin, roll out the pastry until it is ⅛ inch thick. Using a 4-inch to 5-inch round cutter or a tea cup saucer, cut 12 discs. Place these rounds in the muffin cups, gently pressing them into the moulds. Divide the apples evenly among the tart shells, then pour the filling almost to very top. Garnish each tart with a few walnuts. Bake until the filling is set and the pastry is golden, about 40 minutes. Remove from the oven and let rest in pan for 5 minutes. With a small spatula, gently loosen and remove tarts from the muffin pan.

To serve Serve tarts warm, topped with ice cream and bacon lardons if you wish.

Chef says: This simple gnocchi recipe reminds me of my youth, growing up in Sault Ste. Marie. A predominately Italian community, The Soo is where my love of fresh pasta began. At our Wakefield restaurant we serve this gnocchi with a maple-and-herb-braised beef short rib, Le Coprin mushrooms, local veggies and a braising jus. But a simple sauté with mushrooms, spinach and Italian cheese is hard to beat! Fresh pasta is always a great way to impress guests and please the family, and for my two-year-old son, this recipe is a sure thing! A tip: If you have a ricer for the potatoes, it makes a fluffier end result. Also, if possible, measure ingredients by weight. The ratio is two parts potato to one part flour.

Serves 2 to 4, depending on the style of your dish

Traditional Potato Gnocchi with Mushrooms, Spinach and Pecorino

Bring 8 cups of the water and potatoes to a boil in a large pot and cook until soft, about 45 minutes. Turn off the heat, drain potatoes in a colander, then set the colander of potatoes over the empty pot on the stove for 5 minutes (the residual heat will steam and dry them).

Line a baking sheet with parchment paper. If you have a ricer, rice the cooked, dried potatoes directly onto the parchment paper, then fluff and spread them evenly with fork to cool. Otherwise, spread the potatoes over the parchment paper and begin to mash them with a fork. (Avoid stirring the potatoes, which will make them sticky and can cause a goopy result.) Set aside to cool completely, about 10 minutes.

Sprinkle flour and the 2 Tbsp of salt over the cooled potatoes, and using a fork, mash the flour into the potatoes, fluffing them as you go. Once the flour is cut into the potatoes, gently squeeze the dough with your hands until it comes together. Quickly, to avoid forming gluten, roll into logs ½ inch thick. Cut the logs into ½-inch chunks, about the size of a large piece of Chiclets chewing gum.

Dust a baking sheet with flour. Again, using a fork, gently roll each chunk, cut-side to cut-side, to dimple the dough. Arrange in a single layer on the baking sheet and freeze for at least 1 hour before cooking.

12 cups water, divided

2 cups russet potatoes, peeled and cut into ¾-inch cubes

1 cup all-purpose flour

2 Tbsp salt

½ cup olive oil

4 cups sliced mushrooms (use your favourites)

1 Tbsp minced garlic

1 Tbsp finely chopped fresh thyme leaves

1 Tbsp kosher salt

1 tsp freshly ground black pepper

½ cup cold unsalted butter, cut into 1-inch cubes

1 lb baby spinach leaves

1 Tbsp finely chopped fresh flat-leaf (Italian) parsley

1 cup freshly grated Pecorino cheese

In a large pot, bring about 4 cups of water to a boil. Set aside a lightly oiled baking sheet (for cooked gnocchi). Add frozen gnocchi to boiling water and stir gently to prevent sticking. When gnocchi float to the surface, after about 1½ minutes, they are done. Using a slotted spoon, transfer cooked gnocchi to the oiled tray, giving them a shake so they don't stick together.

In a large sauté pan, heat olive oil over medium-high heat. Add mushrooms and sauté until they are golden around the edges, about 5 minutes. Stir in garlic and thyme, and cook for 1 minute, then add the 1 Tbsp of kosher salt, pepper and butter, and cook for 1 minute more. Add blanched gnocchi and sauté for 1 minute. Add spinach and cook for about 1 minute or until it is just wilted.

To serve Spoon the gnocchi into a serving dish, garnish with the parsley and cheese and serve immediately.

The Wellington Gastropub

Chris Deraiche

MATURITY IS A fine state, and The Wellington Gastropub has reached it. Which isn't to suggest—not for a second—that it's stuffy up there in that upstairs room. Jeans and tees, beards and tats rule, but so does serious attention to what matters most: good food and drink, community, neighbours. And fun. That too. What other gourmet pub offers a beer school? Experiments with its own brews? Has a Record Club? (Every year, a dozen bands are explored. Radiohead this month, Nirvana next. Twenty-five bucks gets you in and fed, all proceeds to the Food Bank.) There is a relaxed sense of confidence at The Wellie, and chef Chris Deraiche, ten years running the show in his open kitchen, is at his peak. Ten years of the rigours of a daily menu too. Short menus, to be sure, but every day a new one. Ingredients might be entirely the same, but the plates on which they appear will be completely different. You might call it instinctive cooking, or cooking on the fly based on the food delivered by trusted purveyors, but none of the dishes seem tossed together. There is grand symmetry on these ode-to-the-season plates. The Wellie's co-owner (and Record Club spin-master) Shane Waldron will find you the perfect pour to match. The craft beer list is long and the wine list thoroughly well assembled. The surname "gastropub" is tossed around casually, as a marketing tool. Few deserve it more than this West Wellington gem. 1325 WELLINGTON STREET WEST, 613-729-1315

Duck meatballs

¾ lb ground duck meat (available at fine butcher shops)
¼ lb ground pork
1 egg
½ cup dried, unseasoned bread crumbs or panko
¼ cup finely grated Parmesan cheese
3 Tbsp chopped fresh flat-leaf (Italian) parsley leaves
Freshly ground black pepper
1 Tbsp canola oil

Cheddar beer sauce

1 Tbsp butter
1 shallot, sliced
2 cloves garlic, sliced
6 oz lager (drink the rest)
1 cup whipping (35%) cream
2 cups freshly grated cheddar cheese
Half-pinch of ground nutmeg

Cheesy polenta

4 cups chicken or vegetable stock
1 cup fine or medium cornmeal
¼ cup freshly grated cheddar cheese
¼ cup freshly grated Parmesan cheese
2 green onions, white and green parts, sliced
Salt and freshly ground black pepper

Sautéed broccoli

1 Tbsp canola oil
½ head broccoli, cut into florets

Serves 2

Duck Meatballs with Cheesy Polenta and Broccoli in a Cheddar Beer Sauce

Chef says: Meatballs, polenta and cheese are happy foods. Okay, broccoli too. We use beer in a variety of ways in the kitchen at the restaurant. A cheese and beer sauce never disappoints and is a great accompaniment to many foods.

Duck meatballs Preheat the oven to 350°F. Place the ground meats, egg, bread crumbs, Parmesan, parsley and pepper in a large bowl and mix by hand until well incorporated. Shape into 6 to 8 balls.

Heat a large, ovenproof sauté pan over medium-high heat. Add canola oil and the meatballs and gently brown on all sides. Transfer the pan to the oven and bake for 12 to 15 minutes or until meatballs are cooked through. Remove from the oven and cover loosely with foil to keep warm.

Cheddar beer sauce In a pot over medium heat, melt butter. Add shallots and garlic and cook for 2 to 3 minutes. Pour in beer and cook until reduced by half. Stir in cream and simmer for 5 or 6 minutes. Let cool slightly, then transfer the mixture to a blender. Add cheese and nutmeg and purée at medium-high speed until smooth. Strain the sauce through a fine-mesh sieve into a bowl; discard solids.

Cheesy polenta In a large saucepan, bring stock to a simmer over medium heat. Turn down the heat to low. Whisking continuously, slowly pour in cornmeal and cook until it no longer has a grainy texture, 15 to 20 minutes (if the polenta seems too thick, whisk in more stock or water). When the polenta is ready, stir in the cheeses and green onions. Season with salt and pepper to taste.

Sautéed broccoli In a sauté pan, heat canola oil over medium heat. Add broccoli and sauté until cooked, about 5 minutes. Some colour on the broccoli is stellar!

To serve Divide the polenta among a couple of bowls. Place three or four meatballs and half the broccoli on top of each serving and spoon generous amounts of the cheddar beer sauce over the meatballs.

Raisin-caper emulsion
⅓ cup capers
⅓ cup raisins
¾ cup water
1 Tbsp sherry vinegar

Cauliflower purée
1 small head cauliflower, cored and cut into bite-size pieces
1 small onion, sliced into thin strips
2 cloves garlic, sliced
Pinch of ground nutmeg
Whole milk, to cover
Vegetable stock or water, to cover
Salt and freshly ground black pepper

Apple, fennel and walnut salad
3 Tbsp apple cider vinegar
1 tsp liquid honey
1 tsp Dijon mustard
¼ cup canola oil
1 Honeycrisp or Gala apple, peeled, cored and cut into matchsticks or other thinly sliced shapes
1 fennel bulb, shaved on a mandolin or sliced very thinly
¼ cup walnut pieces

Scallops
1 Tbsp canola oil
8 scallops
Kosher salt
1 Tbsp butter

Serves 2

Sea Scallops with Cauliflower Purée, Apple Fennel Salad and Raisin-Caper Emulsion

Chef says: I'd guess people don't cook scallops too often at home, which is why they may be so popular at our restaurant. We don't fuss over them too much. Seared in a very hot pan, finished with butter and accompanied with these classic flavours, the scallops will be the very last thing you cook for this dish.

Raisin-caper emulsion With a fine-mesh sieve, rinse capers quickly under cold water and drain well. Combine all of the ingredients in a small pot over low to medium heat and simmer for 5 minutes. Let stand for 5 minutes, then transfer to a blender and purée at medium-high speed until smooth. Let cool. (Will keep refrigerated in an airtight container for up to 3 days.)

Cauliflower purée In a medium pot, combine cauliflower, onions, garlic and nutmeg. Top with half milk, half stock just to cover vegetables and simmer over low to medium heat for 20 minutes, until vegetables are soft. Strain the mixture through a fine-mesh sieve into a bowl, reserving the liquid in the bowl. Transfer cauliflower to a blender with just enough of the reserved liquid (add a tablespoon at a time) to make a thick purée. Season with salt and pepper to taste. (Will keep refrigerated in an airtight container for up to a day.)

Apple, fennel and walnut salad Place vinegar, honey, mustard and canola oil in a jar with a lid and shake vigorously for 10 seconds. In a bowl, combine apple, fennel and walnuts with enough vinaigrette to coat.

Scallops Line a plate with paper towels. Heat canola oil in a medium sauté pan over medium-high heat until slightly smoking. Season scallops with kosher salt to taste and place them flat side down in the pan; cook for 2 minutes or until golden. Carefully turn scallops over and add butter; cook for 1 minute. Spoon melted butter over the scallops, then transfer to the lined plate.

To serve Spoon a line of cauliflower purée down the middle of each plate. Gently place the scallops on the purée and arrange small mounds of salad in between the scallops. Spoon a small amount of raisin-caper emulsion on each scallop.

The Whalesbone

Michael Radford
Joshua Bishop

IT WOULD BE EASY to walk by The Whalesbone on Bank and barely see it. Or think it's just a boisterous little hillbilly pub with irreverent manners. But spend an hour in its company and you understand its charms. The space is narrow, usually packed, framed in excavated brick. With its beguiling flea market décor, it feels a deeply personal space. This could be Joshua Bishop's living room, decorated with whatever makes him smile: the old bike he first used to deliver cases of oysters, the lacquered mascot (Motley, the sperm whale) that hangs above the busy bar, the extensive vinyl collection. "I'm not a cook. I'm not a chef. I'm an oyster opener," he tells me when we talk about his roots. These include working at Rodney's Oyster House in Toronto and on fishing boats in Australia. Today Bishop's the biggest name in sustainably sourced fish in this town, his new Elgin Street fish shop (and soon to be 90-seat restaurant) is a destination for discerning cooks. Bishop might not be a chef, but this oyster opener knows how to hire them. Michael Radford's direct approach to fish and his deep understanding of their flavours and textures translate to pleasures on the plate. His short menu is mostly swimmers, but there's always a plate for the veggie and one for the fish hater. And often an ice-cream sundae bar for the kid in us all.

430 BANK STREET, 613-231-8569

Coconut sauce In a dry medium (6 to 8 qt) pot over medium heat, toast the star anise, cardamom, coriander seeds, cumin seeds and cinnamon sticks until the spices have released their aroma, about 3 minutes. Stir in coconut cream, coconut milk, palm sugar, ginger and lemon grass and bring the mixture to a boil. Remove from the heat, then add lime leaves, chili peppers and cilantro and let sauce steep for at least 1 hour. Strain through a fine-mesh sieve into a clean bowl; discard solids. Let cool completely.

Steamed mussels Wash and scrub mussels well. Discard any open mussels that do not close when gently tapped (these mussels are dead and should not be consumed).

Place a large, wide, shallow pot over medium-high heat. When the pot is hot, add canola oil, mussels, shallots and garlic and sauté, stirring mussels gently, for about 2 minutes. Add coconut sauce and butter, give the mussels a few good stirs and cover with a lid. Let mussels steam until all are cooked and open, about 3 minutes (do not overcook!).

Remove the pot from the heat, uncover, discard any mussels that do not open, and give everything a nice stir. Season with a few good splashes of fish sauce. Check the seasoning: there should be a nice balance of sweet and salty, with lots of umami flavour from the natural mussel liquor.

To serve Spoon the cooked mussels into a large serving bowl or a deep-dish platter. Pour the coconut cooking sauce from the pot over top. Garnish with wedges of lime. Sprinkle with crushed peanuts, lime leaves, Thai basil and chili peppers (if using).

Pickling brine

½ cup sherry vinegar
1 cup white vinegar
4 cups distilled water
½ cup kosher salt
½ cup cane sugar
1 white onion, sliced
12 cloves garlic cloves, smashed
4 to 6 Scotch bonnet peppers, halved and seeded (or left in for more kick)
3 Tbsp black peppercorns
3 Tbsp allspice berries
1 tsp whole cloves
8 bay leaves
1½ cinnamon sticks
½ bunch fresh thyme

Pickled vegetables

1½ cups cauliflower florets
1 cup sliced carrot rounds (each about the thickness of a loonie)
1 cup thinly sliced red onions
½ cup sliced celery
6 cloves garlic, thinly sliced
2 to 3 Scotch bonnet peppers, seeded and minced (or leave some seeds if you like it really hot and spicy)
1 recipe Pickling Brine (see here)

Cured mackerel

½ cup + 2 Tbsp packed brown sugar
¼ cup kosher salt
1 Tbsp freshly cracked black pepper
2½ lb fresh Atlantic mackerel fillets, skin on and pin bones removed

Garnish

½ pt grape tomatoes, sliced in half
½ bunch fresh cilantro, leaves picked
2 limes, cut into wedges
Saltine crackers, optional

Serves 6 to 8 as appetizer or part of a "Sunday lunch" buffet spread

Mackerel Escabeche

Chef says: As a teenager I lived in Barbados, a beautiful Caribbean island abundant in seafood. It is home to an incredible melting pot of cultures, each of which has an influence on the cuisine. In this instance, Spain plays its role. This dish is an ode to my memories of "Sunday lunch" at my friends' homes. In among the spread of food, there would be a plate of "soused" (lightly pickled) fish and soda crackers. Mackerel's strong flavours marry especially well with all the warm spices and vinegar, though the recipe works with many types of fish. Start the pickled vegetables up to two days before you plan to serve the escabeche and be sure to give the mackerel at least a day to cure. Serve escabeche with Saltine crackers.

Pickling brine In a medium pot, bring all of the ingredients, except the thyme, to a boil over medium heat. Remove the mixture from the heat, add thyme and let steep for 4 to 6 hours. Strain the brine through a fine-mesh sieve into a bowl; discard solids.

Pickled vegetables In a medium bowl, combine all of the ingredients. Cover and refrigerate for at least 2 days.

Cured mackerel In a small bowl, combine sugar, salt and pepper. Using your hands, lightly rub mackerel fillets with the cure mixture. Place in a shallow casserole dish and refrigerate for 8 to 12 hours.

Once cured, gently rinse the fish under cold running water and pat dry. Using a very sharp knife, cut fillets in half lengthwise down the bloodline. (The bloodline is the streak of strong-tasting red meat that runs down the centre of the mackerel fillets.) Heat a medium cast-iron pan over medium heat, add the mackerel fillets, skin side down, and sear until lightly charred, 2 to 3 minutes (the flesh of the fish should still be rare, as it will continue to cook in the marinade).

Place the fish, flesh side up, in a shallow casserole dish and pour the pickled vegetables and brine on top. Refrigerate for at least 6 to 12 hours. (Can be kept refrigerated for up to 5 days.)

To serve Let escabeche come to room temperature. Garnish with grape tomatoes, cilantro and lime, and serve with saltines, if you wish.

Wilf & Ada's

Dominic Paul
Jessie Duffy

I'M A BIG FAN of the modern chef-run diner, and this one tops the charts. Formerly Ada's Diner ("Good Food, Fast Service"), run for some twenty-one years by Ada and Wilf Laham, when the couple retired, the enterprising trio of restaurateur Ion Aimers, chef Dominic Paul and front-of-house star Jessie Duffy picked up the reins. The plan was to retain the diner's heart and the community soul while sandblasting off twelve coats of pink paint, chucking out the monster Coke machine and taming the long menu. They brought in an espresso machine, stocked sparkling wine for the brunch mimosas, started cooking from scratch in the newly opened kitchen. And charmingly rechristened the place in honour of the retired team that had entrusted it to them. It still draws in folks from all walks to its tables and it still serves bacon 'n' eggs, triple-decker Dagwoods and hot chicken sandwiches (with fries, yes, and now with an arugula salad too). The chicken's been brined, the marmalade's homemade, the bacon's house smoked, the gravy's from scratch and the house hot pepper vinegar lifts up everything it's shaken over. Paul's been playing with the Louisiana-style sauce since Day One. A local farm grows six different peppers for the diner, and the chef's now so confident the recipe's right, he's sharing it with us. As for the sugar pie, that reaches deep and sweet into his Franco-Ontarian roots. In late 2015 the Aimers-Duffy-Paul team also opened Arlington Five, a cosy little coffee and sandwich shop in the space next door.

510 BANK STREET, 613-231-7959

Chef says: This recipe is everything I like most in a hot sauce: good flavour to balance the heat, vinegary and thin. It's based on Louisiana-style hot sauces, which are salt brined and left to ferment for quite some time. Although this recipe might sound a little challenging, I think you'll be surprised by its simplicity and flexibility.

At Wilf & Ada's, we use a mix of peppers—Red Long Hots, cayennes, Espelettes, paprikas and Thais—which we source through Day Brighteners, a local organic farm just south of Ottawa. Choose any pepper that you can tolerate. Red peppers are traditional but any colour will do. Feel free to char the green onions. It adds a pleasant smokiness to the sauce.

3 lb mixed hot peppers, roughly chopped (use gloves if you wish)
1 head garlic, crushed
6 bunches green onions, green and white parts, roughly chopped and charred (optional; see Note)
¼ cup kosher salt or 2 Tbsp table salt + extra salt for covering peppers
Cold water
White vinegar, as needed

Makes 6 to 9 cups of vinegar

Hot Pepper Vinegar

Fill a large, very clean container with a lid (a Mason jar is best; the size you need will depend on the peppers you choose) at least three-quarters full with peppers, garlic, onions and salt, leaving 1 to 2 inches of headspace free from the vegetables. Fill the container with enough water to cover the mixture by about 1 inch. With a wooden spoon, mash and stir the contents of the container for about 1 minute. Sprinkle a little extra salt on top, place the lid on loosely (to allow gas to escape) and set the container in a cool, dark place.

In a few days, the contents should start to bubble and ferment. Continue to let the sauce rest for at least a week or until the bubbling subsides. If you notice a thin white, powdery layer developing on the surface, scoop off as much as you can and then stir your peppers. It is not mould but kahm yeast, a harmless by-product of lacto fermentation from exposure to air. If there is anything that looks like mould but does *not* fit the description of kahm yeast (i.e., if the mould is fuzzy and/or colourful), then the whole batch should be discarded. Once primary fermentation is finished (when you tap or pick up the jar, there

are no longer bubbles), proceed to finishing the sauce or store in the fridge to age and further develop flavours.

When you are ready to finish the sauce, strain and press the pepper mixture through a fine-mesh sieve into a large bowl; reserve the jar. Discard the peppers and measure the volume of strained liquid (this volume can change dramatically depending on the type of peppers you used and the length of fermentation). Add half that volume in white vinegar (for example, if you have 4 cups of strained liquid, add 2 cups of vinegar). Pour the vinegar mixture into the reserved jar, seal the lid tightly and refrigerate. (Hot pepper vinegar will last indefinitely but will start to lose its vibrancy—flavour, heat and colour—due to oxidation after about 3 months.)

Note To char the green onions, rub them with a bit of vegetable oil and roast on a hot grill or in a cast-iron pan. Cook until blackened on one side, then flip and blacken the other side. Continue with recipe.

Pastry dough
2 cups all-purpose flour
¼ cup white sugar
A little less than ½ lb cold
    butter (about ⅞ cup)
1 egg
Tiny pinch of salt

Sugar filling
1¾ cups + 2 Tbsp packed
    golden brown sugar
2½ cups whipping (35%) cream
½ cup cornstarch
⅓ cup water

Serves 8 to 10 (Makes one 9-inch pie)

Sugar Pie

Chef says: I've heard that sugar pie used to be made by stirring brown sugar, cream and flour with your finger right in the pie shell. That's something I like about traditional desserts; they tend to be homey and unsophisticated. In our family, we would make a similar filling, *sucre à la crème,* to pour over whatever dessert happened to be on the table. This recipe makes more dough than you would typically need for a lidless pie, but I like to make a double-thick bottom crust. The cookie-like crust is the perfect pairing for the rich, creamy filling. Serve with a dollop of whipped cream.

Pastry dough Have ready a 9-inch pie plate. In a medium bowl, combine flour, sugar and pinch of salt. Add butter and, using your hands or a pastry blender, crumble it into the dry ingredients. Add egg and knead the dough (still in the bowl or on a clean work surface) until it forms a ball. Wrap the dough in plastic wrap and refrigerate for 10 to 15 minutes.

Lightly dust a clean work surface with flour. With a rolling pin, roll out the dough in a circle until it is ¼ inch thick. Carefully place the rolled dough into the pie plate (there will be an excess of dough, so just fold it back into the pie for a thicker crust). Set aside while you prepare the filling.

Sugar filling In a medium pot, combine brown sugar and cream and cook, stirring, over low heat until it reaches a simmer. Let bubble gently, without stirring, for 3 to 4 minutes to dissolve the sugar, reduce slightly and concentrate the flavour.

In a small bowl, make a slurry of cornstarch and water and add it to the pot. Increase the heat to medium-high and whisk continuously until the mixture starts to boil. Remove it from the heat, whisking for a few seconds more, then let cool for about 5 minutes (do not allow it to cool completely).

Finish pie Preheat the oven to 400°F. Pour the filling into the pie shell. Bake for about 20 minutes or until the crust is golden. Let cool completely at room temperature before slicing.

Metric Conversion Chart

Volume

Imperial	Metric
⅛ tsp	0.5 mL
¼ tsp	1 mL
½ tsp	2.5 mL
¾ tsp	4 mL
1 tsp	5 mL
½ Tbsp	8 mL
1 Tbsp	15 mL
1½ Tbsp	23 mL
2 Tbsp	30 mL
¼ cup	60 mL
⅓ cup	80 mL
½ cup	125 mL
⅔ cup	165 mL
¾ cup	185 mL
1 cup	250 mL
1¼ cups	310 mL
1⅓ cups	330 mL
1½ cups	375 mL
1⅔ cups	415 mL
1¾ cups	435 mL
2 cups	500 mL
2¼ cups	560 mL
2⅓ cups	580 mL
2½ cups	625 mL
2¾ cups	690 mL
3 cups	750 mL
4 cups / 1 qt	1 L
5 cups	1.25 L
6 cups	1.5 L
7 cups	1.75 L
8 cups	2 L

Weight

Imperial	Metric
½ oz	15 g
1 oz	30 g
2 oz	60 g
3 oz	85 g
4 oz (¼ lb)	115 g
5 oz	140 g
6 oz	170 g
7 oz	200 g
8 oz (½ lb)	225 g
9 oz	255 g
10 oz	285 g
11 oz	310 g
12 oz (¾ lb)	340 g
13 oz	370 g
14 oz	400 g
15 oz	425 g
16 oz (1 lb)	450 g
1¼ lb	570 g
1½ lb	670 g
2 lb	900 g
3 lb	1.4 kg
4 lb	1.8 kg
5 lb	2.3 kg
6 lb	2.7 kg

Liquid measures (for alcohol)

Imperial	Metric
1 fl oz	30 mL
2 fl oz	60 mL
3 fl oz	90 mL
4 fl oz	120 mL

Cans and Jars

Imperial	Metric	
6 oz	170 g	180 mL
7 oz	198 g	200 mL
14 oz	397 g	398 mL
28 oz	794 g	796 mL

Linear

Imperial	Metric
⅛ inch	3 mm
¼ inch	6 mm
½ inch	12 mm
¾ inch	2 cm
1 inch	2.5 cm
1¼ inches	3 cm
1½ inches	3.5 cm
1¾ inches	4.5 cm
2 inches	5 cm
2½ inches	6.5 cm
3 inches	7.5 cm
4 inches	10 cm
5 inches	12.5 cm
6 inches	15 cm
7 inches	18 cm
10 inches	25 cm
12 inches (1 foot)	30 cm
13 inches	33 cm
16 inches	41 cm
18 inches	46 cm
24 inches (2 feet)	60 cm

Oven temperature

Imperial	Metric
200°F	95°C
250°F	120°C
275°F	135°C
300°F	150°C
325°F	160°C
350°F	180°C
375°F	190°C
400°F	200°C
425°F	220°C
450°F	230°C

Acknowledgements

BOOKS, LIKE RESTAURANTS, are all about the team. My thanks, first and foremost, to the "cooks" in these pages and to their kitchen crews, who shared their knowledge, their recipes and their enthusiasm for this great group effort. I have learned from all of you, I have dined well at your tables and it's been a treat to get to know you all, beyond the plate.

We were all bowled over by the wonderful work of Christian Lalonde of Photolux Studio. Chris, *merci beaucoup* for the incredible attention to detail, for the care you took with every shot and for your unwavering enthusiasm. And thanks to brilliant food stylist Noah Witenoff, and props stylist Irene Garavelli and her many, many treasures. Weren't we a merry band!

To everyone at Figure 1 Publishing, my thanks for the confidence you placed in me to assemble this dream team of chefs. To Chris Labonté, for that first meeting and firm handshake and your constant support and good humour throughout the project. To creative director Jessica Sullivan, for your brilliant eye, and to Lara Smith for the day-to-day details that mean everything.

To editor Lucy Kenward, copy editor Tracy Bordian and proofreader Renate Preuss, thank you for taking such meticulous care with my words and these recipes, plying me with all the right questions and making sure it all made splendid sense.

To my magnificent sisters, Jeanne and Henrietta, for testing recipes all summer long and reporting back with all those detailed questions that drove me mad. And to my fabulous sons—Peter, Sam, Erik and Thom—for eating every bite.

Thanks, finally, to my husband, Ken Nyhuus, there at the end of the day to open the wine, offer wise words, hold my hand, talk me down and be my dearest friend.

Index

About the Author

ANNE DESBRISAY is an award-winning food writer and restaurant critic. She is the author of *Capital Dining*, a trio of guidebooks to the city's best places to eat, the restaurant critic for *Ottawa Magazine* and a senior editor for *Taste & Travel Magazine*. For twenty years, Anne was the restaurant critic for the *Ottawa Citizen*, and for a decade has been senior judge at the Ottawa Gold Medal Plates culinary competition and a member of the judging panel at the Canadian Culinary Championships. She lives in Ottawa with her husband, Ken, and their four sons, now mostly making their own meatloaf in basement apartments across Canada and missing desperately the restaurant leftovers from their mother's fridge.